D0765289

THE
FEBRUARY
MAN

Evolving Consciousness and Identity in Hypnotherapy

Milton H. Erickson, M.D.

&

Ernest Lawrence Rossi, Ph.D.

BRUNNER/MAZEL *Publishers* • New York

Library of Congress Cataloging-in-Publication Data

Erickson, Milton H.
    The February man : evolving consciousness and identity in
hypnotherapy / Milton H. Erickson & Ernest Lawrence Rossi.
        p.   cm.
    Bibliography: p.
    Includes index.
    ISBN 0-87630-545-1
    1. Hypnotism—Therapeutic use—Case studies.   I. Rossi, Ernest
Lawrence.   II. Title.
    [DNLM: 1. Hypnosis.   2. Psychotherapy.   WM 415 E68f]
RC495.E718   1989
616.89'162—dc19
DNLM/DLC
for Library of Congress   88-38964
                                                                CIP

Copyright © 1989 by Brunner/Mazel, Inc.
Published by
BRUNNER/MAZEL, INC.
19 Union Square
New York, New York 10003

All rights reserved. No part of this book may
be reproduced by any process whatsoever without
the written permission of the copyright owner.

MANUFACTURED IN THE UNITED STATES OF AMERICA

10 9 8 7 6 5 4 3 2

Contents

Overview of Participants in Sessions and Commentaries

Session I, Part 1
Present in 1945: Dr. Milton H. Erickson, Dr. Jerome Fink, Mrs. Fink, the subject ("Miss S" or "Jane"), and the subject's friend, "Ann Dey."
Present for 1979 *Commentaries*: Dr. Milton H. Erickson, Dr. Ernest L. Rossi, and Dr. Marion Moore.

Session I, Part 2
Present in 1945: Dr. Milton H. Erickson, Dr. Jerome Fink, the subject ("Miss S" or "Jane"), and the subject's friend, "Ann Dey."
Present for 1979 *Commentaries*: Dr. Milton H. Erickson, Dr. Ernest L. Rossi, Dr. Marion Moore, Dr. Robert Pearson, and an unidentified visitor.

Session II
Present in 1945: Dr. Milton H. Erickson, Dr. Jerome Fink, the subject ("Miss S" or "Jane"), and Mr. Beatty.
Present for 1979 *Commentaries*: Dr. Milton H. Erickson, Dr. Ernest L. Rossi, and Dr. Marion Moore.

Session III
Present in 1945: Dr. Milton H. Erickson, Dr. Jerome Fink, the subject ("Miss S" or "Jane"), and the subject's friend, "Ann Dey."
Present for 1979 *Commentaries*: Dr. Milton H. Erickson, and Dr. Ernest L. Rossi.

Session IV
Present in 1945: Dr. Milton H. Erickson, Dr. Jerome Fink, the subject ("Miss S" or "Jane"), and the subject's friend, "Ann Dey."
Present for 1979 *Commentaries*: Dr. Milton H. Erickson, Dr. Ernest L. Rossi, Dr. Sandra Sylvester.

Foreword

Sidney Rosen, M.D.

How good it is to hear Erickson's voice again! And our reliable and steady guide, Ernest Rossi, after more than 15 years of studying and practicing Erickson's approaches, brings us his mature understanding, while allowing us to witness the process by which he came to this understanding. As in his previous books with Erickson, Rossi does not intrude himself between Erickson and the reader. He presents a transcript which allows us to actually witness Erickson at work, in 1945. Then, in his typically modest fashion, he acts as an inquiring student, encouraging Erickson to explain the thinking behind his therapeutic approaches. He and Erickson also discuss many other interesting subjects, including the nature of therapy, human nature, the development of consciousness, and even the evolution and function of slang and obscenity.

Perhaps because Erickson, one year before his death, was ready to explain himself more than he had previously, Rossi was able to get almost direct answers to some of his questions, rather than the colorful and metaphorical responses which Erickson seemed to prefer. Certainly those metaphorical and "guru-like" answers have stimulated the thinking and growth of hundreds of his students, but we appreciate some simpler, more easily grasped formulations as well. Even Margaret Mead (1977) wrote about the pleas which she and other students of Erickson made "for simpler, more repetitious, more boring demonstrations . . . ." Rossi, with his patience and persistence, was able to evoke some simpler, clearer explanations to help us understand the essence of Erickson's work.

In this book we can see the amount of work which Erickson put into preparing his patient for changing. Even though it was done in a playful, and sometimes offhand manner—playing games with words, having her write upside down and with both hands at the same time, and getting her to agree "absolutely," in advance, that she would be cured—it is apparent that he felt that this preparation was essential. At the same time he was fine-tuning the therapeutic relationship, maintaining a challenging and yet trusting tone. As Rossi points out, he was mostly concerned with encouraging and stimulating the *processes* which will enable the patient to change. Insight seeking was only one of these processes, perhaps one of the least important. When we observe Erickson guiding his patient towards insights and connections with the past, we may, indeed, speculate that this was done largely in response to *her* conviction that understanding of the past would be necessary before she could be cured.

Erickson would say to us, "It is the patient who does the work. All that the therapist does is provide conditions in which this work can be done." Erickson worked thoroughly and carefully to provide the necessary conditions. He explored and utilized all conceivable elements in communication and education in order to do so. He emphasized, for example, the importance of utilizing the evocative powers and the multiple meanings of words—the patient's and his own. A beautiful example of his respect for words is seen when he notices, in the patient's automatic writing, that she has written a word which can be read as either "living," "giving" or "diving." He uses this observation as a basis for organizing the therapy around the patient's swimming phobia ("diving"), with the belief that, when this phobia is overcome, she will also be freer in "living" and "giving" and will be relieved of her depression. Some readers may feel that he was arbitrary about the interpretation of this one word or of others. In fact, Rossi, himself, accuses him at one point of making "inferences." But we cannot help but be impressed by his painstaking attention to every expression of the patient, as well as to each of his own communications.

We witness, in addition to his deft and careful use of words, many forms of indirect suggestion—phrasing suggestions as questions, for example. While doing this "manipulating," he was constantly asking the patient for *permission* to intervene and was always ready to change his interventions in response to the patient's reactions. Thus, he demonstrated the respect which was a hallmark of his way of dealing with patients. In fact, we must comment at this point that, although much of the writing about "Ericksonian techniques" emphasizes the brilliance and ingenuity of the therapist, when we observe Erickson, himself, at work, we are impressed more by the presence and the unique creativity of his patients.

What is the value of utilizing regression as the dominant feature in this therapy? While I was reading this book, it became clear to me why Erickson tended to treat almost everyone like a child! I suddenly understood why, at least in his later years, he seemed to be so enamored of corny jokes, childish puzzles and games. I now feel that he understood, probably from having learned it from working with adult patients in the hypnotically regressed state, that it is precisely in this "child state" that we are most open to learning, most curious, and most able to change. In order to intensify the patient's experience of regression, Erickson worked consistently to create a remarkably convincing illusion that he really was an older person talking to a young child. He had the "child" reenact and abreact to traumatic experiences and, through discussions, guided her through a reeducation process. As a result, the "child" had new experiences to add to her memories—positive experiences with a caring and understanding adult. These "corrective regression experiences," as I have called them, exerted a long-lasting effect on the patient, even after she returned to her "adult self."

Among the reeducation experiences which the "child" underwent in her discussions with "The February Man" (Erickson "visited" her, in hypnotic age regression, for "several years" in February), were some which have become known as "reframing." There are some beautiful examples of reframing in this book. For example, the patient had been feeling guilty over death wishes towards her younger sister and had blamed herself for the sister's near drowning experience. Erickson's "reframe" of this led to his saying to her, "All of these years you have been condemning yourself, have you not? . . . Why? Perhaps so that you could reach a still better and larger understanding of yourself." (Self-condemnation is reframed as a step toward self-understanding.) Sibling rivalry is reframed as follows: "Being jealous of Helen when you were a little baby had one meaning. Now, when you are grown up, it has another meaning entirely. Wouldn't you want a little baby to appreciate its own worth, its own personality and its own needs enough to defend them in any way it understood?"

At one point, Rossi suggests to Erickson that the basis of his hypnotic therapy is "abreaction and a restructuring of the patient's mental processes." Erickson corrects him, saying, "It is not restructuring. You give them a more complete view." Rossi is then able to sum up his understanding with the comment, "It (hypnotic therapy) simply facilitates a more complete, comprehensive point of view and frees one from the limitations and literalism of childhood." This is a far cry from the belief of many therapists that hypnosis involves some kind of reprogramming.

In the treatment of this case we see the beginning of an approach which Jay Haley was to call, "prescribing the symptom." When the patient was apparently ready to try to swim, Erickson forbade her from doing so. He explains, "I place *my* inhibition on her swimming." After doing this, he points out, "I can change mine!" And, of course, he withdrew *his* inhibition at the time of his next session with her.

Erickson also gives an interesting rationale for having other people present during therapy. "... This fear, this anxiety about swimming, is observed in relation to other people.... You need to get over some of these fears and anxieties . . . that are manifested in relationship to other people and concealed from other people . . . by bringing them out so that it can be realized that one can live even if others do know. We like people best when we know that they are real in a lot of little things." Group therapists have known this for a long time, but we must remember that group therapy was not much used in 1945.

I admit that, like many others, when I first read the "February Man" case as it is presented in the books, *Hypnotherapy* (Erickson & Rossi, 1979) and *Uncommon Therapy* (Haley, 1973), I was excited by the idea that this appeared to be the first instance in which a therapist had actually changed the history of a patient. I now understand that this change, like many other changes in therapy, actually consists of "widening the frame," or expanding awareness, in the present, not in the past. In fact, I remember Erickson's frequent comment that "understanding the past will not change the past." The "reality" of age regression has been, justifiably, questioned. I believe that, in addition to an "opening up" to actual memories, a large element of fantasy is frequently involved. But regression does not need to be "real" in order to be helpful. Simply the subjective feeling of being young may make it possible for a patient to view matters from different perspectives. It may also intensify the therapist-patient contact and lead to therapeutic abreactions.

Before terminating the therapy, Erickson helped the patient to ventilate hostility towards him. He reasons that this is important because patients often are angry at the therapist for taking away their symptoms and may express their anger by destroying their therapeutic work. Here, again, he shows exquisite concern for maintaining all therapeutic gains.

The time is approaching when we will see more critical reviews of Erickson and his work. Even those of us who were "hypnotized" by him will evaluate our experiences differently with the passage of time. At this point, however, when I think of him, it is with love—even though he was not a particularly "loving" person, in the usual sense of the word. He conveyed his love and his respect, for me and for countless others, by "telling it like it is." For example, once, when I told him that I wanted to be able to experience rather than to intellectualize, he responded, "Your behavior indicates otherwise. You prefer to understand rather than to experience." Typically, he followed this incisive comment with the suggestion, "but you can intellectualize in different ways." Finally, he led me, in trance, into an experience which combined thinking *and* feeling. He began with a hypnotic induction which started with "In my way of living I often like to climb a mountain—and I always wonder what's on the other side." Thus he role-modelled a different way of intellectualizing—by *wondering*. And it is only now, eight years later, while writing this foreword, that I realized that he had done that!

For those of us who have worked with Erickson, there is always much more to learn from him as we peruse and study his work—especially the verbatim accounts of his work and thinking as presented here. For the vast majority of readers, for whom this may be the first or second book they have read about Erickson, it will prove well worth-

while to read it either quickly or slowly. If read quickly, it will lead
to an appreciation of why so much interest has been devoted recently
to Erickson. If studied slowly, it will stimulate ideas which will en-
rich the work of any therapist. Thank you, Ernest Rossi, for bringing
us this gift.

Sidney Rosen, M.D., President,
New York Milton H. Erickson Society
for Psychotherapy and Hypnosis.
Author, *My Voice Will Go With You:*
The Teaching Tales of Milton H. *Erickson.*

Introduction

Ernest Lawrence Rossi, Ph.D.

This volume on the "February Man" transcends the typical case report one finds in the literature of psychotherapy. It goes beyond the usual forms of analysis and psychotherapy to focus on the possibility of facilitating the evolution of new developments in consciousness and identity. The late Milton H. Erickson, M. D., who is widely regarded as the most creative hypnotherapist of his generation, originated the unique approaches documented in this book. What is most noteworthy and valuable about this material is that it is the only complete, verbatim record of an entire hypnotherapeutic case dating from the middle of Erickson's career when his innovative genius was in full flower.

In addition, we are fortunate in being able to add Erickson's own detailed commentaries on this case, recorded in 15 hours of discussion that provide an unparalleled understanding of his thinking and methods.

The February Man is a fascinating case study illustrating the use of profound age regression in the treatment of a depressed young woman. In addition to chronic depression, the young woman had a severe and dysfunctional water phobia stemming from a deeply repressed and traumatic memory of being responsible for the near drowning of her infant sister. In treating her case, Erickson assumes the supportive role of the "February Man" who "visits" the woman many times during the course of four lengthy psychotherapeutic sessions. During these sessions, he utilizes classical hypnotic phenomena such as age regression, time distortion, automatic writing, amnesia and others, to explore the patient's entire childhood and youth. As the "February Man," he provides her with the seeds for new developments in her adult personality.

It is unlikely that any more complete verbatim records of Erickson's work from this time period will ever surface. Even if such records were somehow found, still we would not have Erickson's own detailed commentaries on what he did—and without his commentaries, it is almost impossible to understand his work. This volume is thus the last of vintage Erickson: There can be no more of his most enlightening commentaries on human nature, the evolution of consciousness, the essence of psychotherapeutic work, and the essence of his own innovative hypnotherapeutic approaches.

The History of This Volume

This volume has a long history; it has slowly evolved over more than 40 years. It began back in 1945 when Erickson informally demonstrated his unique approach to hypnotherapy, using a nurse as a subject for a small group of professional colleagues and students.* There were only four hypnotherapeutic sessions with this nurse, whom we call "Miss S" and "Jane." The sessions were recorded verbatim in stenographic notation by Miss Cameron and typed up with only a few unimportant omissions. Many years later in 1986, I was able to contact Miss Cameron and ask her for her recollections about Erickson during that time period. She responded with the following letter.

Miss Cameron: A Secretary's Recollection

While taking a meeting one must concentrate almost exclusively on one's work, but I do recall a feeling of almost unbearable tension in Dr. Erickson's office at Eloise when the subject faced up to her feelings of extreme hostility toward her family. I thought at the time it was emotional surgery. The last session at which I was present was definitely lighthearted, with the subject laughing frequently and looking relaxed and happy.

---

*Jerome Fink, M.D., Mrs. Mary Fink, Mr. Beatty, and the subject's friend, Miss Ann Dey.

Dr. Erickson was a really great boss. He understood other people's limitations better than they themselves did, which naturally translated to consideration. My first few days in the office were memorable. Apparently he had had no secretary for a time. In one corner there was a table loaded with books, papers, and paraphernalia. The stenographer's desk was covered with reprints, letters, and all manner of items waiting to be filed or answered. I began to read and sort.

During the first two days Dr. Erickson dictated only one letter. I read, stacked, and tried to keep questions to a minimum. One thought kept recurring: This may be a case of biting off more than one can chew. But as Dr. Erickson left the office at the end of the second day, he remarked that he was going to enjoy having me work in his office. It was a moment to stand tall—all five feet of me.

A few days later he asked if I could draw. I was frank: not even a straight line with a ruler. So he set me to copying an illustration he used in lecturing to his medical students. The result was an abomination but he said it was "adequate" and proceeded to use it. My ears grew red every time he took it from the office.

Frequently Dr. Erickson would send me to take verbal productions of a patient. He used these later in teaching his medical students to distinguish different types of mental problems. One woman who had been a patient at Eloise for many years spoke constantly in single words or brief phrases which appeared to be totally unrelated. She was a dear little lady and talked to me for several minutes. During that time she spoke only one complete sentence: "Chase and son is the name." It would have been easy to believe that she had been listening to radio ads for Chase and Sanborn coffee, a highly advertised brand name at that time. Dr. Erickson went to the heart of the matter. A social service worker learned that many years earlier the patient, never married, had given birth to a child—a dire event when she was young. This was typical of his understanding of the crises in the lives of people he worked with and treated.

The people who came to study and work with Dr. Erickson made the job especially rewarding. The visiting doctors and the medical students at that time appeared to be tremendously interested in hypnosis and in Dr. Erickson's methods of treating patients, especially those who had recently developed problems. Any time that he was scheduled to speak, the designated area became filled to capacity. Whenever he told his students he would meet with them at a specified time in the afternoon or evening, word seemed to spread around Eloise with a speed that completely outclassed smoke signals or jungle drums. It was amazing. At the appointed time the room would be filled not only with students and people from Eloise, but with a fair quota of strangers. Always, Dr. Erickson's control of a crowd was unbelievable. As a long-time theater buff and one-time theater employee, I marvel whenever I recall it. Most performers watching him would have turned completely green.

One of Dr. Erickson's hobbies appeared to interest many people who came to his office. The windowsill behind his desk held containers of various shapes and sizes which he had made, and each one held different varieties of cacti. He explained that children didn't bother them so they made excellent houseplants.

An occasional dinner with the Ericksons was always an enjoyable event. Mrs. Erickson was a charming hostess; each of the children had a distinctly individual style. You may have heard this—if so, bear with me. The children were encouraged to work and save money. When I was at Eloise, Bert and Lance gardened and the family bought their produce, and each youngster was paid for work which was done around the home. At the end of the year they received a bonus equal to whatever had gone into the savings accounts. This idea has always seemed like such a winner to me that I keep relating it to young people I know who have children.

Working as Dr. Erickson's secretary was a privileged opportunity to observe and learn. It was, in fact, the high point of my experience in offices. I am happy to know that his work is being so widely recognized—obviously much of this is due to your efforts—and will become an important part of the world of tomorrow.

Miss Cameron's typescript of the case study of Miss S rested quietly in Erickson's files for about 30 years, until he gave it to me for private study when I began working with him in the early 1970s. During these early years, however, I simply was not able to understand the significance of this case and why Erickson kept referring to it in order to illustrate this or that unique feature of his work. My puzzlement about this case is easy to understand in the light of the views of Jerome Fink, M.D., who was actually responsible for Erickson's original meeting with the patient.

Dr. Jerome Fink's View of Erickson's Work

The other member of the original small group who witnessed this therapeutic case was Dr. Fink, who was a medical intern at the time. Following is an account of the development of the therapeutic situation:*

Fink: The patient, Miss S, was an unusually talented and intelligent 19-year-old student nurse who was invited to my home originally because of her interest in psychiatry. The purpose of the evening visit was that she see and participate in hypnotic behavior, with an eye toward a better understanding of elementary psychodynamics.

In the preliminary discussion of hypnosis, at which time the "average" behavior patterns of the trance state were discussed, it was noticed that Miss S was paying extremely close attention. I immediately recognized both the development of an intense transference and her keen desire to be put into a trance. She therefore was told that she would have the honor of being the first subject.

A profound trance was easily induced by the hand levitation method and, because of the limited time available, she was rapidly introduced to the various hypnotic phenomena. Less capable subjects often refuse to cooperate when adequate time is not allotted. It was my practice with naive subjects to allow them to write something during their first trance experience. Most subjects refrain from writing anything which might betray an old conflict—for example, they usually write their name. In this case, however, Miss S wrote: "This damn war." To avoid any premature psychodynamic confrontation, the paper was removed and she was awakened with the suggestion that she have an amnesia for events of that trance. It was also demonstrated, to her amazement, that she was capable of automatic writing. This latter fact was soon to be of further value to the patient.

---

*These remarks by Dr. Fink are summarized from several conversations with Ernest Rossi and Margaret Ryan.

Several days later, upon meeting Miss S on a hospital ward, I was questioned about events which had occurred during her period of amnesia. I gave her only indefinite and evasive answers. She persisted in her questions, adding an apparently unconscious statement of her "fear of water." I suspected this was an indirect plea on the part of her unconscious for psychotherapy. Her answers to my questions, worded so as to be understood only by her unconscious personality, confirmed my suspicion. Not long thereafter, I was approached by Miss S's friend, "Ann Dey," and a second evening of hypnotic experience was requested. Arrangements were made accordingly.

Dr. Erickson was brought into the situation because I was not a staff doctor; I was an intern, and all of a sudden this young woman had come to me with a phobia. I had worked with Milton every year since my sophomore year in medical school. Under his auspices I had given the senior medical students lectures in hypnosis when I was only a junior. Milton and I were very, very close.

I always had a need to be accepted, and I became exceptionally proficient in hypnosis—probably because it was so dramatic. Then people began referring to me as Svengali and became very much afraid of me because they thought Erickson's intuition was rubbing off on me and that I could "see through them." There was a big movement in our psychoanalytic group, and the message was, if you want to be a psychoanalyst, you had better reject Erickson. I don't have time for all those details, but the conflict ultimately resulted in the dissolution of the Detroit psychoanalytic society.

Ryan: Were they against his personality or the type of work he did?

Fink: I think it was the way he worked. He was *so* intuitive. I went out to the Menninger Clinic to talk to a group of medical students, and I remember the Chief of Staff telling me that Erickson was damnably intuitive. He'd been studying a case for three months (the patient was a female catatonic schizophrenic). Erickson was out visiting, saw the patient for 30 seconds, and said, "Well, this girl's a catatonic schizophrenic." I asked him how Erickson had come to this conclusion. He recounted that Erickson had said, "Well, if you noticed, this girl was moving her thumb from the palm of her hand to the end of her fingers, just unconsciously. She didn't know where her ego boundaries were. She didn't know whether she ended up at her elbows or outside of her body."

I worked with Erickson on the psychiatric examination staff at the army induction station during World War II, and I saw so many things like that. He was brilliantly intuitive. But I don't honestly believe that he was sufficiently organized at this stage in his professional life that he was conscious of all the things that are discussed in the case presentation as it was discussed with Rossi in this book.

Ryan: You believe that Erickson was doing something that he knew how to do on an intuitive level. Later on, after the fact, you can discuss it from any theoretical point of view, but it doesn't mean that is what Erickson saw at the time.

Fink: Exactly. That's exactly what happened.

Ryan: What this comes down to is that Erickson did much of what he said he did, just not for the reasons everyone is figuring out *post hoc*.

Fink: Exactly! Everyone seems to have 20/20 vision in retrospect. The difficulty I felt was that in many, many instances in the transcript of this book Dr. Rossi would say, "Did you do such-and-such?" And Erickson would say, "Uh-huh." In my way of thinking, it's barely possible that Erickson probably never thought of a particular viewpoint until Rossi asked him, and then he answered yes.

It was between July 1st of 1945 and the first of May of 1946 that Erickson gave me this stack of transcripts (the originals on which this book was based).

Ryan: Do the transcriptions strike you as representative of what transpired in the sessions? Or do they feel falsified to you?

Fink: I'm not quite sure yet. There is a point early on in the transcript when Dr. Rossi asks: "Are you actually doing such things with planned intent? Why?! I cannot believe you actually did this! I've been studying with you for seven years now and I still find it hard to believe you're not pulling my leg with all sorts of involved *post hoc* intellectualizations about a case like this. Yet this evidence from over 30 years ago is right here before us. Why do I find it so hard to believe?"

I believe Dr. Rossi was correct in that he almost dares to question the Master. I think Erickson always had this need to be right at all times, and Rossi, in my opinion, was "right on" in his feeling of doubt; many of the psychodynamics discussed were *post hoc* intellectualizations. Erickson was an exceptionally intuitive fellow, and that he cured this girl there is no doubt. What I'm questioning is whether Erickson actually thought everything out ahead of time.

I knew Erickson very well in his younger days. Any number of times he and Betty came up to our home for social visits. I was Erickson's protégé for about four years. Sometime during 1942, when I was a sophomore in medical school, Erickson began his lectures to us on hypnosis. We became very well acquainted, and he took me under his wing, so to speak.

Through the years I've had this absolute block about going into hypnosis myself. Erickson made several very serious attempts, including one or two with my consent—and for some reason, I was never able to go into a trance with him. I don't know why I didn't. I suppose I had enough resistance and enough disbelief. I became a good operator despite the fact that I could not go into a trance for anyone.

I think this book is very worthwhile, but some of the concepts developed herein need to be taken "with a grain of salt." As I said, Erickson was exceptionally intuitive, but he couldn't have consciously figured out all the psychodynamics at the time. He had never met the subject before the first long session.

Ryan: Is it possible that some of the concepts developed in this book might still have validity? Whether or not Erickson planned them consciously, he may still have been executing them on an intuitive level.

Fink: Oh, there's no doubt about that! He operated in that way, but I think he was the only man in the country who *could* operate that way!

This engaging, frank interview with Dr. Fink points out the limitations of this or any other *post hoc* case analysis. We simply don't know to what degree the highly intuitive therapeutic engagement of a brilliant clinician can be understood in the light of a later cognitive analysis. There is much recent research, in fact, that strongly suggests that the later rationalizations of the "left hemisphere" are simply stories to make any kind of comfortable sense of the "right hemisphere's" nonconscious processes (Gazzaniga, 1985). Even with these limitations in mind, I still persisted in my efforts to understand Erickson's approach.

The February Man Approach

Between 1973 and 1981 I coauthored a number of papers (Erickson & Rossi, 1974, 1975, 1976, 1977, 1980) and three books on hypnotherapy with Erickson (Erickson, Rossi & Rossi, 1976; Erickson & Rossi, 1979, 1981). I also edited four volumes of his collected papers (Erickson, 1980). Throughout this period, I gained more and more insight into his ways of thinking and gradually was able to comprehend something of the vast scope of what he called the "February Man approach." In 1979 we published a short version of the February Man as the final chapter of our book, Hypnotherapy: An Exploratory Casebook. In that example, I emphasized how Erickson had used the February Man to facilitate the creation of new identity and consciousness in patients who had experienced several levels of deprivation in their early life experience. This approach was a significant step beyond all previous forms of therapy that focused on the analysis and working through of psychological problems from the past.

With this preparatory background, I was finally ready to explore in greater detail the four sessions presented in this volume. Erickson and I recorded about 15 hours of commentaries on these four sessions,* going over each word, phrase, and sentence in repetitive and tedious detail to ensure that we were reaching an adequate comprehension of the fine points of his ways of working. A number of other professionals trained by Erickson (Marion Moore, Robert Pearson,

---

*These audiotapes are available for research and study at the Milton H. Erickson Foundation, 3606 N. 24th St., Phoenix, Arizona, 85016.

Sandy Sylvester) informally wandered in and out of one or another of these commentary sessions, asking questions and adding their perspectives to our developing understanding. I edited these commentaries and read most of them back to Erickson in a second set of commentary sessions for his final points of clarification and approval.

This state of the manuscript was completed between the Spring and Fall of 1979, the year before Erickson's death. The volume was to have been our fourth, co-authored project. It required only an introduction to make it suitable for publication. But with Erickson's passing in the Spring of 1980, I fell into a state of mourning and was not able to look at the manuscript for another eight years. During these years I distracted myself outwardly by quietly coediting a series of volumes on Erickson's seminars, workshops, and lectures (Rossi & Ryan, 1985, 1986; Rossi, Ryan, & Sharp, 1984), and by making a few independent forays into the psychobiology of what Erickson called the psychoneurophysiological basis of therapeutic hypnosis (Rossi, 1986b; Rossi & Cheek, 1988).

Inwardly, I had a series of dreams in which Erickson always appeared to me as a teacher about 40 or 50 years old. This was surprising since I did not know him until he was in his seventies. However, Erickson was in his 40s and 50s when he was creating the February Man approach, and giving the lectures, seminars, and workshops I was editing. Apparently, my inner mind was assimilating Erickson's teaching from that earlier phase of his career before I knew him.

I was finally able to return to this manuscript in 1987 with a fresh perspective, eager to learn if it still made sense and had anything of value for a new generation of students who were being overwhelmed by the sheer volume of books and papers that have been published about Erickson recently. As I reviewed the evidence of his carefully detailed thought, I realized that this volume could be an important corrective to those who describe Erickson's work as entirely intuitive and idiosyncratic. Erickson certainly was intuitive in the sense that he frequently relied on his spontaneous unconscious associations to initiate the psychodynamic exploration of a new case. He might even appear to have been idiosyncratic in some of his unorthodox ways of setting up "field experiments" to assess the phenomenological reality of hypnotic experience. Erickson always insisted, however, that his carefully prepared verbal and nonverbal procedures for facilitating hypnotic experiences were essentially rational in utilizing the patient's unique individuality and potentials. His commentaries in this volume are a testament to the depth and innovativeness of his thinking and therapeutic work with this utilization approach to widening consciousness and facilitating the development of new identity in hypnotherapy.

Approaches to Therapeutic Hypnosis

The first few sections of this presentation are very difficult to appreciate 40 years after they were recorded by a stenographer. Without the vocal tones and body gestures that gave important nuances of meaning to the jokes, puzzles, and games contained in these sections, the transcribed word alone is very confusing. The general thrust of this initial conversation between Erickson, Dr. Fink, and the subject is to indirectly attract, motivate and engage her attention (stage one of the microdynamics of trance induction, Erickson & Rossi, 1976/1980), and then to depotentiate her habitual conscious sets via confusion, shifting frames of reference, distraction, cognitive overloading, and non sequiturs (stage two of the microdynamics of trance induction). If the reader feels confused and overloaded trying to make sense of these first few sections, there can only be the consolation and wonder of how much more bewildered the subject must have felt—even though she tries to keep up a brave front in the face of the associative verbal onslaught going on about her.†

1.0   Confusion: Associative Games and Puzzles to Initiate Response Readiness and the Hypnotic Process

Erickson: . . . Getting away from the cockle shells, how do you like Gene Autry?

Fink: I certainly ought to be able to ride a horse like he can. Or

---

*Present in 1945 for this portion of Session I: Dr. Milton H. Erickson, Dr. Jerome Fink, Mrs. Fink, the subject (who is also referred to as "Miss S" and "Jane"), and the subject's friend, "Miss Dey." Present for 1979 commentaries: Dr. Milton H. Erickson, Dr. Ernest L. Rossi, and Dr. Marion Moore.

†Words or sentences printed in bold type are referred to in the commentaries that follow.

doesn't that make horse sense? I'm off on the wrong foot! How do I like Gene Autry?

Erickson: **What's that got to do with a garden?**

Fink: Well, it contributes fertilizer to a garden.

Erickson: **How do you get from tumbled to garden to Gene Autry?**

Fink: Purely schizoid.

Erickson: Can you hum it? [Dr. Fink hums Drifting Along with the Tumbling Tumbleweed.]

Fink: Tumble ... tumbling tumbleweed ... Gene Autry.

Erickson: Yes, that's it. He's not tumbling. I inquired about his garden—Gene Autry sings, The Tumbling Tumbleweed.

Fink: It's a song to remember.

Erickson: It's not a song—just a horse of another color!

Subject: **Here I was trying to connect it up with. . . !?** [Subject blocks in confusion.]

Fink: And yet I missed it.

Erickson: I'm very certain he doesn't remember it. And your remark should have refreshed his memory. But his memory wasn't refreshed. Therefore he didn't hear you. [Subject moves closer to Miss Dey.]

Fink: Well, that's one on me.

Subject: What's she doing?

Fink: She's writing a letter. To a friend.

Rossi: [In 1987]* The session begins with an apparently irrelevant conversation wherein Milton Erickson asks Dr. Fink if he likes Gene Autry (a popular singing cowboy in that time period).

Dr. Fink replies spiritedly but with poor puns about horse sense and getting off on the wrong foot. Erickson then introduces an associative game by asking the non sequiturs of, "What's that got to do with a garden?", and "How do you get from tumbled to garden to Gene Autry?"

---

*When commentaries were written by Rossi in 1987, they are indicated by the bracketed information [In 1987].

The outcome of this initial word play, however, is immediately evident in its effect on the subject's consciousness: she is obviously confused but does not realize that Erickson is doing it to her *indirectly*. It seems as if Erickson is not even addressing her; he knows she is listening but he acts as if he is engaging only Dr. Fink.

The subject soon shows evidence of trying to join the puzzling associative game going on around her when she says, "Here I was trying to connect it up with [she blocks in confusion]." She thereby indicates that she is confused—an ideal state for initiating hypnosis, because her attention is apparently focused within the ongoing dynamics Erickson is initiating, yet she needs a clarifying direction which she hopes to receive from either Erickson or Dr. Fink. This need for clarification indicates that she is now in a state of *response readiness*: she is ready to respond by accepting any clarifying suggestions. Erickson regards this state of response readiness as an ideal preparation for initiating a hypnotherapeutic experience.

1.1   Questions, Confusion, Not Knowing, and Non Sequiturs to Facilitate the Microdynamics of Trance Induction

Erickson:	What color is that brown?
Subject:	I haven't any idea. All I know is that it is brown.
Erickson:	What study was mentioned?
Fink:	Obviously a study in brown.
Subject:	I'm glad I know what that word is.
Erickson:	Who's in a brown study?
Fink:	I am—a billowy, dark brown.
Subject:	Does that mean anything?
Erickson:	No. He's just fascinated by the sound of words.
Mrs. Fink:	Dr. Erickson, how can you tell brown?
Erickson:	It was easy, after I was formally introduced to him.
Fink:	That was sort of a bilious green.
Erickson:	**Why did Jerry challenge you with automatic writing?**
Subject:	**I must think up an appropriate answer here.**

Erickson: Now let's give Jerry some excellent help. What was my question?

Subject: I don't think I can help him. **I was lost three or four blocks back.**

Rossi: It's difficult to follow these passages but one thing is abundantly clear. The subject, Miss S, is again admitting confusion when she says, "**I was lost three or four blocks back.**" In this we see the typical five stages of the microdynamics of trance and suggestion (Erickson & Rossi, 1976/1980, 1979) beginning to take place:

(1) her *attention has been focused* on the topics you[Erickson] are introducing;

(2) her own *habitual mental sets have been depotentiated* and she becomes *confused* as she desperately tries to follow the conversation;

(3) she is, without quite realizing it, being sent on *creative inner searches* within her own mind;

(4) the inner searches are *activating unconscious processes* which

(5) establish a *readiness for a creative hypnotic response*.

Indeed, it is in this context that you bring up the first hint of the hypnotic work to come by asking, "**Why did Jerry challenge you with automatic writing?**" The subject responds with perplexity ("**I must think up an appropriate answer here**"), whereupon you immediately compound her confusion by presenting yet another non-sequitur about giving Dr. Fink help and answering your question.

Erickson: Into each life some confusion should come—also some enlightenment!

Rossi: Confusion is necessary to break down her learned limitations so that the new can be received into consciousness. You continue this confusion approach in the next section with a series of questions and statements that evoke a further sense of *not knowing*. This not knowing sets in motion the unconscious processes of inner search which may evoke the hypnotic response of automatic writing.

1.2 Enigmas, Puzzles, and Cognitive Overloading; Activating the Subject's Potentials; The Ethics of "Mind Games"

Fink:	This isn't a warm brown, is it?
Erickson:	I'll give you the help you want. All you have to do is take it. Now here's the help. St. Peter ought to catch halibut. Why?
Miss Dey:	We'll let you figure it out. That will give you the clues.
Fink:	Will you fill in two missing letters for me?
Subject:	Now comes the dawn. It's so simple, isn't it?
Erickson:	My error, Jerry.
Fink:	Maybe it should be St. Andrew.
Erickson:	My error. I'll correct it. But that will be a dead giveaway if I correct it now.
Subject:	Are you going to let it go on like that?
Erickson:	Some poor lad over the canyon hollered, "Why?"
Subject:	Now I'm straightened out, too.
Erickson:	Mary, if you're suffering so much, I'll take you out to the kitchen and tell you about it.
Fink:	That's why he's a genius and I'm not.
Miss Dey:	It's really an enigma, isn't it?
Fink:	Would you answer one question?
Erickson:	Yes.
Fink:	Are you giving me the letters with which to spell the word?
Erickson:	I've already answered your question. You asked me if I would answer one question and I said, "Yes." Do you recognize that?
Fink:	I do, only too well. Let's see, how can I reword that? Is each word a clue to a letter?
Erickson:	Do you suppose he is trying to get me to answer a second question now that I have answered one?
Fink:	Uh-huh!
Erickson:	That's right. Now how late was that train?

Fink: About twenty minutes.

Erickson: I thought you never would get around to it.

Fink: It's so simple! Does that mean anything that is very important related to something that should be known now?

Subject: God! Wow! Now answer that one!

Fink: You answer it.

Erickson: [*Taking a clipboard*] But you're the one that was looking.

Fink: The word was *splotchy.*

Erickson: Well, what's that got to do with this page?

Fink: Oh, gee!

Erickson: How would you describe that page?

Fink: Do you mean to tell me that all the time I was trying to figure out that word—

Erickson: I was just describing to you by that sentence the appearance of the page, and you are still over there and not here.

Fink: No, I'm right over there now!

Erickson: All right. Now what's that got to do with Ella Fink?

Fink: I guess we're both dumb animals.

Erickson: That was simple.

Fink: Very simple.

Erickson: How did you like his process of figuring that out?

Subject: It was beautiful.

Miss Dey: Why did you take *s-t* from *saint* and leave the rest?

Fink: *Saint* is abbreviated to be *St.*

Erickson: I used St. Peter to remind him of the enigma, and I **began with the reminder and ended with the reminder to mess him up in his thinking.**

Fink: I was following the pattern you had followed there.

Erickson: There were four things there. That's why he couldn't figure it out. If I had only thought of: "St. Peter's lady ought to catch halibut," you might have caught on.

Fink: St. Peter didn't have a lady. Oh, me! Because if he had, he would be ruler of the other domain!

Miss Dey: Do you have proof of that?

Fink: No, and I don't care to pursue that statement any further, either.

Subject: I still want to get that four-letter detail.

Erickson: Constantinople is a long word. Can you spell it? Does "that" mean something? There are four letters, aren't there?

Subject: It's so simple—once somebody else works it out for you.

Fink: That was very good.

Erickson: You have been a very willing worker tonight, Jerry.

Subject: You're joking, of course.

Erickson: I'll bet it doesn't look that way.

Subject: No, it doesn't. **It's so complicated, though.**

Rossi: [In 1987] The degree of confusion and non sequitur is so great in this section that one gets the feeling of a rather chaotic mental ping-pong game. A sense of play can be detected as we watch Erickson go back and forth merrily between Dr. Fink and Miss S. Indeed it was no small part of Erickson's charm that he would tell people at carefully selected times just what approach he was using to play mind games even as he was doing it. There usually was a rather sweet yet hyperalert and questioning expression on his face as he offered these explanations. As usual, there were many levels of meaning in his behavior, and he would carefully observe which levels were being picked up by the subject.

On one level he was genuinely having fun playing mind games that shifted people's associative processes about in ways that they usually could not discern. On another level these games were an important form of *field experimentation** wherein he was doing exploratory research on the nature of consciousness and the hypnotic process. On still another level his seeming ingen-

---

*See "The 'Surprise' and 'My-Friend-John' Techniques of Hypnosis: Minimal Cues and Natural Field Experimentation," in Erickson, 1964/1980.

ious explanations of how he was manipulating one's associative processes were a clear demonstration of his skill in an openhanded manner: if the subject wished to continue the game, the subject's own expectancy and belief in Erickson could then further potentiate the next steps in the hypnotic process.

This is an interesting illustration of our developing conceptions about what could be called *the ethics of mind games*. A basic principle of this new ethic is that the subject is aware of some of the approaches being used, and has agreed to submit to the process for previously established purposes.

When Erickson describes how he "**began with the reminder and ended with the reminder to mess him up in his thinking,**" he is illustrating what we later termed *structured amnesias:** all the associations that come between the beginning and ending reminder tend to be lost in an *amnesic gap* such that the listener's conscious thinking becomes confused and depotentiated.

When the subject ends this confusing but fascinating section with the statement, "**It's so complicated, though,**" she is admitting her state of cognitive overload. Indeed this section illustrates the seemingly irascible and tedious lengths to which Erickson would go in his use of enigmas, puzzles, and arcane associative games. He went to such lengths because he recognized the importance of confounding the subject's conscious mental processes while activating those unconscious associative processes which would do the eventual hypnotic work. In fact, Erickson repeatedly stressed the point that it is this state of inner activation—a state wherein the subject's potentials were activated to a threshold of therapeutic work—which was the ideal of his hypno-

---

*See "Varieties of Hypnotic Amnesia" in Erickson and Rossi, 1974/1980.

therapeutic approach.* This viewpoint contrasts sharply with the still prevalent misconception of hypnosis as a quiet blank state in which the subject becomes a passive automaton, prey to the hypnotist's suggestions and programming.

1.3 Questions, Implication, and Wonder Indirectly Evoking an Early Learning Set to Facilitate Automatic Writing

Erickson: What's the matter with your hand? It raised right up off your lap—getting closer to the pencil already.

Subject: You can't even take a breath around here.

Erickson: Sure you can. Try it.

Subject: All right. So I picked up the pencil—so what? She made me get up and look at the alarm clock last night. I was so mad at her.

Rossi: What was actually taking place when you question what was happening to her hand? Was her hand just lifting in an apparently random movement, whereupon you seized the opportunity to comment that the movement might be an indication that the hand was going to move toward the pencil to do automatic writing?

Erickson: Yes.

Rossi: Simply by raising that question, by implying that she may be unwittingly making an unconscious movement toward the pencil, you are initiating a confusion that will tend to depotentiate her consciousness and facilitate the hypnotic mode wherein she must simply wait for automatic responses.

Marion Moore, M.D.: It always makes the patient wonder what Dr. Erickson is seeing that the patient isn't feeling yet.

---

*See Chapter One of Erickson and Rossi, 1979.

Rossi: Yes, questions that the patient's conscious mind cannot answer easily are useful for activating unconscious processes.

Erickson: As an infant you start learning the moment you hear something: you wonder what is being said, what does it mean, and so forth.

Moore: The infant goes on an inner search to make meaning out of what is said.

Rossi: With such questions, you are also *evoking an early set* that goes right back to infancy.

1.4   Questions Evoking Memories; Expectation Evoking Automatic Responsiveness

Erickson: **What happens next will be in reference to something out of this room.**

Subject: **What am I supposed to do?**

Erickson: **What did I say?**

Subject: [*Pause*] It's a very good pencil. [*Dead silence.*] It always amazes me. **Tedious process**, isn't it?

Erickson: **Good work has to be done slowly.**

Subject: I'll have to ask him over to talk to the supervisors. I know what it's going to say. It's going to say yes. It's so complicated. All that work to get yes out of it. [It *is referring to her automatic handwriting.*]

Erickson: **What do you suppose it means?**

Subject: I refuse to answer that. I don't think it means anything.

Erickson: You refuse to answer that. **You want to know, don't you?**

Subject: **Sure.**

Erickson: When I say, "**What happens next will be in reference to something out of this room,**" I am evoking memories which she didn't get in this room.

Rossi: Was that your actual purpose in making that statement—to indirectly evoke memories not related to this room?

Erickson: Yes.

Rossi: She then asks, **"What am I supposed to do?"** You answer with another question, **"What did I say?"**, which activates another inner search. This compounds the confusion so she must now question herself about what you originally said. Does it also insinuate doubt about herself and thus further depotentiate her conscious sets?

Erickson: Um-hum.

Rossi: You are very patiently watching her hand with an attitude of interested expectancy, waiting for it to make some further automatic movements. She comments that it is a **"tedious process,"** but you positively reinforce the process with the truism that **"Good work has to be done slowly."** She cannot argue with that, and so must also accept the implication that she is doing **"good work"**— which will presumably culminate with automatic writing. She then comments with some impatience that she knows all that work is going to end with her hand answering yes. You ask her what that means but she throws up a defense by refusing to answer and denying that it means anything. You acknowledge this truth of her experience and yet seek to motivate her via her natural curiosity with your question, **"You want to know, don't you?"** With her response of, **"Sure,"** she is actually reversing her previous attitude that it (automatic writing) doesn't mean anything, and is probably wide open at this point to receive new meaning.

Erickson: Yes.

1.5   *Questioning to Further Facilitate Automatic Writing*

[*Subject writes yes in the slow, hesitant manner characteristic of automatic writing.*]

Erickson: I'll ask you a question and you give the first answer that comes to your mind. Is that **yes** a contradiction of something you have said?

Rossi: You really don't know that this **yes** is a contradiction of something she's already said. You are simply beginning another inner search process to further facilitate the automatic writing.

Erickson: Yes.

1.6 Contradiction and Confusion on the Conscious Level to Deepen Inner Search and Trance Depth Automatically

Subject: I'll say no.

Erickson: This time reply with one word. Is it a contradiction of something?

Subject: No.

Erickson: Does it relate to something you have said?

Subject: Yes. That doesn't make sense.

Erickson: Was it said elsewhere than here?

Subject: No.

Erickson: Was it said only here?

Subject: **Yes.**

Erickson: Only here?

Subject: **No.**

Erickson: Her last **yes** and **no** contradict each other.

Rossi: So her conscious mind is genuinely confused at this point.

Erickson: That's right!

Moore: This confusion deepens her inner search, which deepens her trance automatically.

Rossi: Practically all of your questions and statements in this and the following section cannot be answered easily by her conscious mind. The hypnotic mode is therefore being evoked: her conscious mind and intentionality are shunted a bit aside as she waits for answers to come from unconscious searches and processes that are being activated within her.

Erickson: Yes.

1.7 *Further Contradictions, Confusions, and the Conscious-Unconscious Double-Bind Deepening Trance; Two-Level Responses of Yes and No; The Hypnotic Mode*

Erickson: Is what you have just been saying the truth, or does that reply indicate the truth more accurately?

Subject: Yes. But you can't think of anything. I just have the choice of saying yes or no.

Erickson: Is that in any way connected with pain from here down [*points to subject's shoulder*]?

Subject: No.

Erickson: Is it in any way connected with pain from here up?

Subject: No.

Erickson: **Have you forgotten something?**

Subject: Yes. Don't ask me what. I don't know.

Erickson: **Is it connected with something you have forgotten?**

Subject: Yes.

Erickson: **Do you believe you have forgotten it?**

Subject: No.

Erickson: **Have you forgotten it?**

Subject: **Yes. It doesn't make sense.**

Erickson: Doesn't it? Would you like to dispute with yourself?

Subject: Not particularly.

Erickson: Wouldn't it be fun?

Subject: Yes.

Erickson: Let's see your answer to this. Does it make sense?

Subject: No.

Erickson: See what your hand writes.

Subject: It will probably say yes.

Erickson: It always says what you don't say.

Subject: Most of the time. I know what it's going to say.

> Erickson: Notice the contradictory series of yes and no responses she gives to my questions which begin with, "**Have you forgotten something?**" First she answers yes; then she answers yes in response to my question, "**Is it connected with something you have forgotten?**"; but

when I continue with, "**Do you believe you have forgot-ten it?**", she says no. I then persist with "**Have you forgotten it?**", and she says, "**Yes, it doesn't make sense.**" She herself is recognizing the contradiction.

Rossi: She is contradicting herself because she is confused?

Erickson: Yes.

Rossi: Actually, as I study this in greater detail it appears as if her confusion may be related to her being caught in the conscious-unconscious double bind. Here she is responding yes and no alternatively to the same question from two different response systems or levels: namely, the conscious and the unconscious. Her yes response may be her conscious response: she knows her conscious mind has forgotten something. Her no answer in response to the question, "**Do you believe you have forgotten it?**" may be her unconscious response, which recognizes that it hasn't forgotten anything.

All in all, her confusion, inner searching, and automatic writing indicate that she is entering the hypnotic mode of responding without conscious intentionality—even though you have not induced trance with any kind of formalized ritual.

1.8   The Use of Surprise to Facilitate Inner Focus and Search; The Essence of Ericksonian Hypnosis Is to Evoke Potentials and Bypass Learned Limitations

Erickson: We might interrupt there. **Are you going to be surprised tonight?**

Subject: Yes.

Erickson: Who is going to do it?

Subject: You are.

Erickson: I am.

Subject: Yes.

Erickson: **You will help?**

Subject: Yes.
Erickson: Anyone else?
Subject: Dr. Fink.
Erickson: What does your hand say? Anybody else going to help?
Subject: It will probably say yes.

Rossi: Again you are focusing on inner processes with the phenomenon of surprise. She thinks the surprise will come from the outside—from you or Dr. Fink. Most patients look outwardly for solutions, but you imply that it will come from within her by gently questioning her with what is really a declarative statement ("**You will help**"). You try to further facilitate an inner focus by asking what her hand will say, because the automatic writing focuses her attention on responses from within her—which is where the symptom resolution will take place.

Erickson: Yes. There is something I want to get out of her. She doesn't know what it is and I don't know what it is. Therefore I get her to contradict herself and admit that somebody else might be of help. This implies that whichever way it comes—from me or from her—she will get the information. In other words, I'm trying to prevent her from getting the information in relation to a consciously chosen point of view. I don't want her to get the information on the assumption that it is Dr. Fink or I who is giving it.

Rossi: You're facilitating a general search process within her that will remain unbiased by her conscious frames of reference. The essense of Ericksonian hypnotherapy is not to put something into patients but rather to evoke something without the bias of their own conscious frames of reference and learned limitations. This is an important issue because the general public as well as many professionals still believe that hypnosis is used to control or program people as if they were mindless automatons.

Moore: That's the wrong idea.

Rossi: The essence of hypnotherapy is to evoke unbiased answers and potentials from within the patient. Would you agree?

Erickson: Yes! [Erickson now tells of a criminal investigator who gave up using polygraph equipment for lie detecting because his work could be done better with hypnosis by asking questions that (1) covered all possibilities of response, (2) evoked confusion, and (3) made allowance for both negative and affirmative answers.]

1.9   Initiating an Indirect Search for a Traumatic Memory: "Be Unwilling to Answer," Erickson's Intuition as an Unconscious Response to Minimal Cues

Erickson: We can interrupt there. I would like to have you be unwilling to answer this question: Is there something about those flowers you don't like?
Subject: Yes.
Erickson: Will you write it?
Subject: No.
Erickson: So you won't write that?
Subject: No.
Erickson: Are you positive?
Subject: I shouldn't say yes, but I will.
Erickson: I want a promise.
Subject: All right, I promise.
Erickson: If you promised not to take a bus home, what would you do?
Subject: I'd take a bus home.
Erickson: But if you really promised, what would you do?
Subject: I'd probably walk.
Erickson: If you had to go downtown, what would you do?
Subject: Take a taxi—or a streetcar.
Erickson: Why would you prefer to take a taxi?
Subject: I don't like streetcars very much.
Erickson: Anything else in favor of taxis?
Subject: They're faster.

Erickson: They're faster, aren't they? They get you there much more quickly. And so by promising not to take a bus, you would actually speed up getting downtown, wouldn't you? Good.

Subject: Something's going to happen here.

Erickson: I'm going to let Dr. Fink take over now. I have been taking everything over so far. Now for a while let's see what he does. What do you think he is going to do?

Subject: That's hard to say.

Erickson: Can it be said?

Subject: Yes. Oh, brother!

Rossi: What on earth is the purpose of this curious request for her to be **unwilling to answer this question** about flowers?

Erickson: Flowers is the important word if there is something in her mind that she has repressed. Flowers, in general, are likable. But often there are some things about something which is likable that you don't like!

Rossi: I don't follow.

Erickson: I suppose Betty [Erickson's wife] has forgotten that her favorite dog, Roger, has died. Now she liked Roger very much, but she didn't like him dead. And so she forgot about Roger completely.

Rossi: So things we don't like are very often associated with things that we do like.

Moore: Such as the thorns on the rose.

Rossi: So you're evoking a set to look for something she does not like—some kind of traumatic memory—which is important and precious to her?

Erickson: Yes, it's a way of looking for a traumatic memory without letting her conscious mind know that I'm doing so.

Rossi: This is an indirect way of searching for a traumatic memory?!

Moore: By getting the patient to do all the work.

Rossi: So the phrase, "**be unwilling to answer**," is actually an indirect suggestion to search for "the repressed." It tends to evoke Stage 3 of our paradigm of the micro-dynamics of trance induction and suggestion—that of the unconscious inner search.

[In 1987] Erickson's full statement, "**I would like to have you be unwilling to answer this question: Is there something about those flowers you don't like?**" may be an illustration of his incredible intuition. For as we shall see at the very end of this case, the subject has a fear of flowers she was unaware of; flowers were associated with her main presenting problem of a fear of water.

What exactly is intuition? Erickson has described it as an unconscious response to minimal cues. In this situation, for example, we could assume that Erickson unconsciously picked up a very minimal negative behavioral response from the subject in relation to some flowers in the office. He might have noticed that she made a slight frown, avoided looking at the flowers, or possibly flared her nostrils to block out their scent. Erickson's unconscious, "intuitive" and associative process then brought this minimal negative response of the subject to a conscious level with his statement/question—and without either of them yet grasping the deeper significance of flowers.*

[In 1979] Milton, did you really think all this out ahead of time? Did you plan this ahead of time as an approach toward uncovering a traumatic memory? Did you know at this point that the basis of her problem was in fact a repressed traumatic memory?

Erickson: No, I was just searching.

Rossi: But how did you know at this point to begin searching for a traumatic memory? Did Dr. Fink tell you something about it ahead of time?

---

*See Section II in Volume I of Erickson, 1980, for many illustrations of Erickson's use of minimal cues in trance induction.

Erickson: No. Dr. Fink did not know what the problem was. He just sensed there was something wrong with her. She was a nurse on his staff who seemed depressed every now and then. She was not a regular patient.

1.10 Allowing the Patient's Conscious Mind to Win Minor Battles; Multiple Levels of Response and Meaning

Fink: Are you all set for everything that is to be said and done for Dr. Erickson now?
Subject: No, I'll keep him puzzled.
Fink: Do you want to keep him puzzled?
Subject: Yes.
Fink: Do you want to keep me puzzled?
Subject: Yes.
Fink: Do you want to keep yourself puzzled?
Subject: No.
Fink: **Are you taking taxis now?**
Subject: Yes. **I don't know what kind of sense that makes.**

Rossi: The subject seems to have caught on to the game style, and now tries to turn the tables by playing at keeping *you* puzzled.

Erickson: Oh, yes, you always let the patient win at these games, and get the best of you in every possible *minor* battle.

Rossi: What's important is that Dr. Fink got her to state clearly her desire *not* to be puzzled about herself. In other words, she wants to know—whatever it is we have all been puzzling over. She is then asked the question, "Are you taking taxis now?" which would be a completely meaningless question on the conscious level. On an unconscious level, however, the question about taxis is probably associated with the indirect search for a traumatic memory initiated in the last section. Her unconscious, therefore, responds with an immediate and clear yes—meaning yes, she is now in the process of moving quickly toward unraveling the puzzle of a traumatic memory. Her conscious mind then adds the befuddled afterthought, "I don't know what kind of sense that makes."

This is a wonderful demonstration of the multiple levels of meaning by which you achieve your therapeutic purposes. On one level, the above transaction appears to be a superficial and somewhat repetitive interchange, ending with the apparently oblique and meaningless taxi question. On another level, however, the literal content of the dialogue functions as a kind of code for the deeper meanings actually being dealt with. The subject beautifully confirms this multiple-level phenomenon with her final statement, which well represents the conflict she is experiencing between her conscious and unconscious understandings of what is taking place in her therapy.

1.11   *Confusion Facilitating a Traditional Hypnotic Sleep Induction;*
       Metaphor and Indirect Associative Focusing to Initiate Talk About
       Depression

  Fink: Are you thinking of anything in relation to Ichabod Crane?
  Subject: No.
  Fink: **And that was a taxi also?**
  Subject: Yes.
  Fink: Go ahead with that.
  Subject: **I have even forgotten the original issue.**
  Fink: Go sound asleep. Deep down, sound asleep. Continue to sleep. You may even close your eyes and go deeper, deeper. Continue sleeping deeply. And sleep soundly, very soundly, very deeply and very soundly. To enable you to go even much deeper asleep, you may block out everything except the voices of Dr. Erickson and myself and you. Go deeper, progressively deeper asleep. Continue sleeping deeply, soundly. Easily, deeply, soundly asleep. Go even deeper, deeper, deeper, and protect that sleep. Just sleep in your own way so that you can

accomplish everything that you want to accomplish. And sleep restfully, sleep confidently, very relaxed. Deeply, soundly asleep. Establish that sleep. Continue to sleep, deeper and deeper.

Erickson: And keep sleeping very deeply. Very deeply, soundly asleep. We will take this pencil away so you can sleep even more deeply and feel more comfortable. And we will take this chart away so you can sleep still more soundly. And you do have a purpose in going to sleep. And you are going to accomplish that purpose in a comfortable way. And you will really sleep deeply so that you can hear only Dr. Fink and me. With just a vague understanding that all is well and will continue to be well. Is that agreeable?

Subject: Yes.

Erickson: If I talk to Dr. Fink, that won't disturb you, will it?

Subject: No.

Rossi: What is the meaning of the question about Ichabod Crane?

Erickson: He was a fearsome and depressing figure in dark clothes. We are introducing a possible gambit for her to open up about her depression.

Rossi: That is an example of indirect associative focusing. Ichabod Crane is then associated with the taxi metaphor by asking, "And that was a taxi also?" When she answers yes, she confirms, in effect, that she is rapidly approaching her problem area.

Erickson: Yes, and it is also a way of confusing her, so she ends up admitting, "I have even forgotten the original issue."

Rossi: She is obviously in a bewildered yet response attentive state when she admits to having forgotten the original issue. It seems Dr. Fink cannot resist the opportunity and suddenly jumps in with a tyro's enthusiasm to begin a vigorous and directly traditional hypnotic induction by telling her to go to sleep. It seems paradoxical to

have gone through such elaborate preparations to activate her associative processes in all the preceding sections, only now to do the exact opposite by blatantly
asking her to sleep. The paradox is resolved, however, if
we recognize that you regard sleep as simply another
metaphor (and indirect suggestion) that leads consciousness to give up its intentionality to direct itself and give
the unconscious more latitude in expressing the associative processes you have been activating.

1.12   *The Implied Directive and an Involuntary Behavioral Signal of Trance
Depth: Depotentiating Resistance with* "You Will, Will You Not?"

Erickson: I think you ought to just continue to sleep by yourself for
a few minutes, until you really feel within yourself that
you are sleeping satisfactorily to you and to Dr. Fink and
to me. **And you will, will you not?** Just keep on sleeping
deeply, soundly. And when you feel you are really sound
asleep, your right hand will lift up to let me know. And
your hand is lifting, is it not?

Subject: Yes.

Rossi: Here you use an implied directive to signal that her
right hand will lift when she is "sound asleep." You
regularly use some involuntary signal of this sort to
prove to yourself that the patient is responding to your
suggestions and is ready for the next step. When the
patient acknowledges that she is "really sound asleep,"
she is actually indicating her cooperation with you and
is presumably ready for the next suggestion.

Erickson: Yes. there is a use here of that very careful
wording I worked out: **"And you will, will you not?"**

Rossi: Why did you work that out so carefully?

Erickson: I don't want her saying *not*. If she has a feeling
the word *not* should be said, she cannot say it because
I've already said it. I've taken it away from her.

Rossi: You have depotentiated any *not*—any negativity or
resistance—she may have been experiencing in relation

to you and what you were presenting to her. Did you feel she was a resistant subject at this point?

Erickson: No, but she was hesitant.

1.13   Facilitating a Doing Mental Set and a New Learning Set by Writing Backwards and Upside Down: The Action Metaphor

Erickson: Would you like to learn how to move your hand rapidly? I would like to have you practice moving your hand freely and easily and comfortably. It's very easy, isn't it? Now suppose you show me how to make other movements of the hand with ease and comfort. Now finger movements. Do you ever take off your ring? Now keep sleeping but take it off and slip it right back. Don't take it off—just half way off. Now slide it back. Now you can move both hands freely and easily and comfortably. Now another thing—you can take this pencil and write your own birthday. Not the year, just the day. All right. Now write it backwards. That's a rather difficult task to accomplish so quickly. Do you often do that? Would you like to try something else?

Subject: Yes.

Erickson: See if you can write that upside down. That was beautifully done, wasn't it? Is that the first time you have tried that? You didn't know you could do that, did you? Now I'm going to change the pencil into your other hand, and now write your birthday backwards. All right. Do you think you could actually write it more rapidly? I am going to give you a little assistance here. Put this pencil there, and put that one there; and now start writing with both hands. That's really very nicely done. Would you like to see this after you are awakened? All right, we will take out this sheet. And incidentally, you don't know which one it is, since your eyes weren't open. Is that right?

Subject: Yes.

Rossi: Why do you engage her in these peculiar tasks like writing backwards and upside down?

Erickson: I am introducing a certain *do* mental set.

Rossi: A mental set to do something unusual: an exploratory new learning set?

Erickson: Yes. You try it right now. [*Erickson directs Rossi to write backwards and forwards at the same time with a pencil in each hand. Rossi ends up laughing in the realization that he feels peculiar and curious about the whole thing, is wondering what will come next, and is feeling a need for further direction from Erickson.*]

Rossi: You are depotentiating her habitual *mental frameworks* by giving her the *physical experience* of writing in a way totally different from her habitual writing skills. Writing backwards and upside down is really a kind of *action metaphor* for learning to think in new ways. That's why patients come to therapy—to break out of their learned limitations and develop new patterns of living. But wherever did you get the idea to develop an exploratory new learning set in patients?

Erickson: In grade school.

Rossi: Because of the questions you had about how your own sensations and perceptions worked?

Erickson: Partly. But I also just noticed that there were righthanded kids and lefthanded kids—and I wondered about that.

1.14 *Two-Level Communication: Posthypnotic Suggestion for Fascination, Responsibility, and Comfort in Dealing with Distress; Reframing a Trauma via Structured Tasks*

Erickson: Do you think it would be a fascinating thing for you after awakening to puzzle upon this and discover which hand wrote which? We will slip it in back of this pad here and it will be a task for you just to bear in mind that you won't let me forget to bring that up for you later. You can take that responsibility. **If I should forget, you will see to it that I am reminded, will you not?** Now are you sleeping deeply?

Subject: Yes.

Erickson: **Is it beginning to seem to you that you might accom-**

plish your purpose, just as you wrote *January* backwards and upside down? It's really a task, is it not? And
you actually can understand a lot more in your sleep
than you do when you are awake, isn't that right? And
you will be comfortable about it, will you not? **Isn't it
pleasing to be comfortable about it? To be comfortable about things that might distress you when you
are awake?**

Erickson: Now I orient her to taking responsibility for her
own productions, which she will be fascinated to puzzle
over after awakening.

Rossi: You are using two-level communication: on one
level you're talking about her handwriting exercise, while
on another level you're talking about the fascinating
recovery of her traumatic memory—for which she can
now take responsibility. And if any forgetting occurs, it
will be in your camp, not hers (**"If I should forget, you
will see to it that I am reminded"**).

Erickson: Yes. In my final remarks in the section—**"Is it
beginning to seem to you that you might accomplish
your purpose,"** and **"Isn't it pleasing to be comfortable
about it? To be comfortable about things that might
distress you"**—I'm telling her she can be comfortable
about that traumatic memory.

Rossi: You are *reframing* the trauma from something which
must be kept buried and forgotten, to something which
can be comfortably remembered —just as a new way of
writing was comfortably learned.

1.15 *Confusion Converting a Negative to Positive: Depotentiating Learned
       Limitations and the Microdynamics of Trance; Process Versus Content
       as the Essence of Erickson's Approach*

Erickson: Now, you remember that *yes* that was written when you
         were awake? Do you know what it related to?
Subject: No.
Erickson: Would you like to guess?

Subject:	No.
Erickson:	**Did you say no?**
Subject:	Yes.
Erickson:	All right. Shall I tell you what I had in mind?
Subject:	Yes.

Erickson: Notice this series of responses in which two negatives are converted into a yes when I say, "**Did you say no?**"

Rossi: Are you actually doing such things with planned intent? Why?! I cannot believe you actually did this! I've been studying with you for seven years now and I still find it hard to believe you're not pulling my leg with all sorts of involved *post hoc* intellectualizations about a case like this. Yet this evidence from over 30 years ago is right here before us. Why do I find it so hard to believe? [*Much laughter between Erickson and Moore over Rossi's incredulity.*] It may be so difficult to believe because most therapists are still focused on the content of what is said rather than on utilizing the processes of mental dynamics, as you do here. It seems almost like concrete thinking to believe that two negatives converted to a positive by a shift of meaning can have the kinds of significances you imply here. What is the purpose of converting these negatives to a positive? Are you again depotentiating some negative resistance, or what?

Erickson: By the end of the next section, you will see how she is acknowledging that she does not understand consciously but that *she does understand unconsciously.*

Rossi: By converting these negatives to a positive, you are actually predisposing her to accept that?! This is highly typical of your approach. The patient comes to acknowledge that the unconscious knows more—that *the unconscious is the locus of symptom resolution and change* (Erickson & Rossi, 1979). *The patient's conscious sets and learned limitations are thus depotentiated, and the microdynamics of inner search and unconscious processes come into play to facilitate a hypnotic response.*

1.16 *Trance Induction by Association Without Awareness: Unconscious Understanding; Subtle, Multilevel Trances and Transference Phenomena*

Erickson: When you were awake, did you believe you had never been hypnotized? Have you ever entertained that belief? I tried to word my question so that you would understand unconsciously. Did you ever have that feeling?

Subject: Yes.

Erickson: And that is paining from here up?

Subject: Yes.

Erickson: Did you understand consciously?

Subject: No.

Erickson: Did you understand unconsciously?

Subject: Yes.

Erickson: Did you mind my knowing that?

Subject: No.

Erickson: Now I'm going to ask Dr. Fink to work with you a bit more. Will it be all right in your presence to talk to him?

Subject: Yes.

Erickson: And for him to talk to me?

Subject: Yes.

Erickson: Will you listen?

Subject: Yes.

Erickson: Could you not listen?

Subject: Yes.

Erickson: Suppose you listen, and if it proves to be uninteresting, don't pay attention. You don't have to pay attention, do you? But you can if you wish. All right. [To Dr. Fink:] Now, what ideas do you have in mind on reorientation?

Fink: I thought of reorientation with the establishment of proper attitudes.

Erickson: [To subject] Do you know what we talked about?

Subject: Yes.

Erickson: How did you feel about that? Is it all right?

Subject: Yes.

Rossi: When you ask her, "When you were awake, did you believe you had never been hypnotized?", was there another trance induction here that I missed?

Erickson: Well, if she's been in a trance, she's going to be in a trance.

Rossi: Huh?

Moore: When patients have been in a trance with you either formally or informally, whenever they work with you again they will be partially in a trance. When they give these kinds of answers, it indicates that they are in a second- or third-level trance—however you want to describe it. Just presenting these confusing questions reinduces trance after it has once been induced between Milton and her.

Rossi: I get it—you just have to keep banging me over the head with it! [*Much laughter*] Once a therapist has been associated with a patient's trance behavior, there is forever after some association between that therapist and the patient's previous altered state of trance. The therapist can indirectly reinduce trance simply by using the same tone of voice, manner, line of questioning, or whatever, to reevoke that earlier trance by association. The patient may or may not be aware of these later trances. Often these later trances are so subtle or momentary that both therapist and patient may be completely unaware of them unless they are looking carefully for microtrance indicators. These subtle and intermittent second- and third-level trance experiences may be the basis of all sorts of misunderstood transference and countertransference reactions between therapist and patient—precisely because of the unawareness involved.*

1.17   *Affect Bridge, Dissociation, Enigmas, and Mind Games to Initiate an Age Regression Set*

Erickson: I would like to have you remember just how you *felt* when you were writing January the first time for me. I want you

---

*For a detailed overview of the many behavioral signs of these subtle momentary trances that most of us are unaware of, see Rossi. 1986a.

to remember so vividly that it seems as if you were writing it right now. Remember it until you can feel your hands writing—until you do feel your hands writing. Continue to *feel* it so plainly you know just where you are, and know that there are a lot of things you can do like that. [*Subject writes.*] That was a pleasant experience, was it not?

Subject: Yes.

Erickson: And doing it righthandedly and lefthandedly and upside down, it didn't seem like just writing your birthday, did it?

Subject: No.

Erickson: It seemed like a task you were doing. And there are a lot of things that have taken place in your experience where you can go over them and do it as a task, isn't that right? As a task that has to be accomplished, and looked at, and understood, and read later. Isn't that right? Now tonight I played a game with Dr. Fink on that sentence I composed. The enigmas were a nice game, were they not? There are a lot of enigmas in one's own experience, are there not? And I would like to suggest that you view them as enigmas to be puzzled over for **amusement and with satisfaction**, and then discover how simple the puzzle is and how satisfying it is to solve it. **Now the other night you forgot a lot of things.** You forgot about March 1945, about February 1945, about January 1945, and even about December 1944, did you not?

Subject: Yes.

Erickson: You could do that again, could you not?

Subject: Yes.

Erickson: And you could do it very, very completely, could you not? **And even thinking about it you are a bit hazy about it**, are you not? **It makes you wonder who I am.** Isn't that right?

Subject: Yes.

Rossi: You begin this section asking her to remember how she *felt* when writing January the first time for you. You are thus using an *affect bridge* (Watkins, 1949) to reach a recent memory in order to initiate a *set for age regression*. You facilitate this age regression by initiating a *dissociative process* by writing with both hands and upside down so that "**it didn't seem like just writing your birthday, did it?**" You associate this with the enigmas and puzzles of the beginning of this session to introduce further depotentiating confusion into the situation along with "**amusement and with satisfaction**" for solving a puzzle (that will be an understanding of her own psychodynamics).

When you say, "**Now the other night you forgot a lot of things,**" you're implying you've had a previous session with her?

Erickson: Yes. I'm sorry I did not keep that [entire record] chronologically.

Rossi: That's okay. The important thing is to get an accurate record of what occurred so that our readers understand that there was a previous meeting between you and the subject that was not recorded. Since this subject was not a regular patient, you probably had no idea when you first met her that you would be doing such significant hypnotherapeutic work with her. We are really thankful that you had a stenographer with you by this second meeting.

You then continue with, "**And even thinking about it you are a bit hazy about it,**" which further depotentiates her limiting conscious sets and propels her into inner search. You end by giving her a rather enigmatic hint, "**It makes you wonder who I am,**" which deepens the inner search while giving it a specific direction and expectancy. In effect, you have laid all the groundwork for the first age regression and the introduction of the February Man that occurs in the next section.

SESSION I: PART 2*
Identity Creation of the February Man

1.18 *Introducing the February Man: Stage One: The Dynamics of Age Regression*

Erickson: But somehow or other you will realize that you are safe, that you are secure, that there is somebody you know and can trust, and whom you can recognize who will be with you, with whom you can talk, with whom you can shake hands. And you learned to shake hands when you were very young. You saw big people shake hands, did you not? It's awfully hard to remember the first time you saw that [handshake] and understood what it was. It's awfully hard to remember the first time you ever shook hands. It is very hard to remember that—the day after having shaken hands for the first time. And if you forget a number of things that have happened to you since the first time you first shook hands, you will really get closer and closer to that memory, will you not? Now I would like to have you make a guess. Do you suppose you know what month it is right now?

Subject: February. [It is actually March. Miss S has regressed to a point in early childhood, as the following sections will indicate.]

---

*Present in 1945 for this portion of Session 1: Dr. Milton H. Erickson, Dr. Jerome Fink, the subject (who is also referred to as "Miss S" and "Jane"), and the subject's friend, "Miss Dey." Present for the 1979 commentaries: Dr. Milton H. Erickson, Dr. Ernest L. Rossi, Dr. Marion Moore, Dr. Robert Pearson, and an unidentified visitor.

31

Erickson: Simply talking about the first time she shook hands initiates an unconscious search for that memory even if it does not reach consciousness. This inner search itself facilitates the age regression process I am structuring.

Rossi: You then acknowledge how hard it is "**to remember the first time you ever shook hands.**" To this she probably made an internal affirmative response. She must also acknowledge that "**it is very hard to remember . . . the day after having shaken hands for the first time.**" She is thus in a strong yes set by this time.

Erickson: I'm setting her up for age regression with that search for early memories.

Rossi: Then you add the critical suggestion for age regression: "**And if you forget a number of things that have happened to you since the first time you shook hands, you will really get closer and closer to that memory, will you not?**" This critical suggestion flows naturally from those preceding it and continues the yes set phenomenon. Further, its inherent logic cannot be disputed: she does actually get "closer and closer" to that memory because all the amnesias she has had since the first time she shook hands become, in effect, blank spots in her memory. Time is actually contracted back to an earlier age level and she finds herself in an age-regressed state (as we shall see in the next section).

The dynamics of age regression as demonstrated in this section, then, are something more than merely putting the subject in trance and telling her she will be a younger age. Your complex sequence runs somewhat as follows:

(1) The first and second stages of the microdynamics of trance are activated when you secure her attention and depotentiate her habitual mental sets. You know that this has taken place when she evidences extreme response attentiveness by following your suggestions so completely that she falls into contradictions without even realizing it.

(2) You engage an *affect bridge* to early memories via puzzling tasks that open an early learning set.

(3) You ask questions that (a) cannot be answered by her conscious mind and (b) further orient her to earliest childhood learnings and memories (like remembering the first time she shook hands).

(4) Then there is the critical suggestion wherein you carefully balance opponent processes—what we have previously called the *apposition of opposites* (see Erickson & Rossi, 1979): you emphasize all the things she has *forgotten* since she first shook hands, which paradoxically brings her closer and closer to an early *memory.* In her precariously balanced mental state, you *utilize all of her forgetting* to suddenly trip off an *early memory and age regression.*

If we assume there is a mental set that controls remembering and forgetting, we can say that you have found a means of activating it. The remembering-forgetting process mechanism is brought to a nascent state of response readiness and is suddenly discharged along the channel of your suggestion. In this is the essence of hypnotic suggestion: A *subject's habitual mental sets (or learned limitations) are depotentiated so that certain mental mechanisms can be activated (a nascent state of response readiness) and discharged along a channel of suggestion.* This is a much more complex matter than the simple direct suggestion that has been used in the past. Such direct suggestion was notoriously unreliable, however, so many psychologists have doubted the validity of age regression as a genuine hypnotic phenomenon. Although your approach places vastly greater demands upon the operator, it may lead to more reliable results once other therapists learn how to use it.

I wonder if there is any neurological model that can help us with this work? Do you believe Karl Pribram's holographic approach (Pribram, 1971) may hold some possibilities?

Erickson: Yes, but I don't know enough about it.

1.19   *Stage Two in the Creation of the February Man Identity: Therapist's Search for Orientation in Patient's Age Regression*

Erickson: What year is it? February, 1929—is that right?
Subject: I don't know [*spoken in a childlike voice in this and the following responses*].
Erickson: You don't know.
Subject: No.
Erickson: Do you care?
Subject: No.
Erickson: Would you like to find out what year it is? Can you write?
Subject: No.
Erickson: You can't write?
Subject: No.
Erickson: But you can talk, can you not?
Subject: Yes.
Erickson: But it is February?
Subject: Yes.
Erickson: And do you know how you know it is February?
Subject: No.
Erickson: I know. I know how you know that it is February. Shall I tell you? Shall I tell you right away, or shall I wait? Would you like to know?
Subject: Yes.
Erickson: We are talking, aren't we? Do you know who I am? Do you know my voice?
Subject: No.
Erickson: Would you know me if you opened your eyes and looked at me?
Subject: I don't think so.

Rossi: On the basis of previous work you guessed that she had age regressed to February of 1929, but she is not able to confirm this because she's regressed to an age when she cannot yet write and does not even know how she knows it is February. Thus, while you had something to do with providing cues for her age regression, you had no control over just what time period she chose to regress to. Is that right?

Erickson: Yes.

Rossi: The reality of her age regression is then further confirmed when she denies knowing you or recognizing your voice. You have extended the first hint of an identity change in yourself (Section 1.17: "**It makes you wonder who I am**") into the first critical stage of wiping out your real identity. This newly established anonymity, fragile though it is at this point, gives you ample space to begin exploring and reinforcing her age regression.

1.20 *Stage Three in the Creation of the February Man Identity: Establishing a Likable Relationship; Vocal Dynamics and Exploring Age Regression with Real Objects and Games*

Erickson: Well, that's all right, isn't it? You can tell by the tone of my voice you will probably like me a lot. Now I'm going to put your hands on your lap, just like this. And I'm going to put two things there—one between the little finger and this finger, and one between this finger and this finger. Now I want you to tell me what the yellow things are you see on your hand. You will have to open your eyes, won't you?

Subject: Yes.

Erickson: Open your eyes and tell me the yellow things you see there.

Subject: [*Opens eyes*] It looks like gold.

Erickson: Point to it with your left hand. And you see something there? What is that?

Subject: Ring.

Erickson: Is there anything more yellow there?

Subject: No.

Erickson: Is there any silver there?

Subject: I can't tell silver from gold.

Erickson: Is this silver?

Subject: I think it's gold.

Erickson: And this?

Subject: It's gold.

Erickson: What are those things?

Subject: Pencils.
Erickson: How do you know?
Subject: 'Cause [more obviously childlike voice].
Erickson: Do you know now how you know it is February?
Subject: No.
Erickson: Do you want me to tell you? What happened last month?
Subject: Grandma went home.
Erickson: What happened to you last month?
Subject: I just stayed here.
Erickson: But what about your birthday?
Subject: I had a birthday.
Erickson: That was last month, wasn't it? And what's the month you
             have a birthday?
Subject: January.
Erickson: You can figure things out quickly, can't you?
Subject: Sometimes.

Rossi: You're using a soft, agreeable manner of speech here, as people do when they are being nice to a child. This naturally tends to reinforce the age regressed state she has assumed. You then explore her age regression further by playing a simple game of placing two objects between her fingers: one is apparently a ring, and the other a pencil(s). Her childlike answers to your simple questions about the objects ratify the reality of her age regressed state and establish a simple question-answer set that allows you to begin to ask more pointed questions about the age period she is in, her birthday, and what's happening in her life. You're now exploring the age regressed state, searching for those childhood situations that may require therapeutic intervention.

Erickson: Yes.

1.21   First "Visit" of the February Man: Posthypnotic Suggestions
       Establishing Security and Lightheartedness as Basis of the
       "New" Relationship

Erickson: Shall I take this? Would you like to guess who I am?
Subject: I don't know.

Erickson: Can't you even guess? **Shall I give you a little help?**
Subject: You look as though I have seen you before.
Erickson: **You are going to see me again some time. Again and again. That's just a promise. Someday you will tell me a joke and you will enjoy doing it.** Do you like to tell jokes?
Subject: I don't know any jokes.
Erickson: You like to laugh, don't you?
Subject: Uh-huh.
Erickson: I promise you that some time, a long time from now, you will see me and have some good laughs. Do you believe that?
Subject: Uh-huh.

Rossi: Here we see the culmination of your careful work in creating a new trance identity for yourself in relation to Miss S. In stage one (Section 1.18) you established an expectancy for "**somebody who will be with you**"; in stage two (Section 1.19) you established an anonymity for yourself which wiped out the subject's identification of you as Dr. Erickson; in stage three (Section 1.20) you assure her that it's all right if she doesn't recognize you because "**you can tell by the tone of my voice you will probably like me a lot.**" In this section you clearly establish your new therapeutic role via the questions, "**Would you like to guess who I am?**", and "**Shall I give you a little help?**" and via the statements: "**You are going to see me again some time. Again and again. That's just a promise. Someday you will tell me a joke and you will enjoy doing it.**"

Thus while still maintaining a certain anonymity in that you don't tell her your name or specific relationship, you do provide her with a clear sketch of the nature of your relationship to her. In effect, you are giving her posthypnotic suggestions setting up your continual appearance throughout her to-be-relived childhood in age regression. This promise of continual reappearance has therapeutic value in itself for the subject because her childhood was a lonely one in which a father disappeared through death. Your casual mention of jokes also implies that your appearance in the future will be fun and lighthearted, which again contrasts markedly with the emotional set from her childhood. You are very careful not to overwhelm her childlike mind, and you say just enough—and in the kind of language she can understand—to establish your presence as reliable and pleasant. When she concludes this section by answering that she does believe what you have said to her, your new therapeutic trance role is ratified and the groundwork for further relating is clearly in position.

1.22 Dealing with First Reported Childhood Trauma: Utilizing the Implication That "Things Are Going to Change" via Therapeutic Analogy and the Relativity of Age

Erickson: **What do you think you will be when you grow up?**
Subject: Not anything. Just marry a rich man. That's what mother says.
Erickson: Do you think it would be fun if you could look ahead and see what you will be like?
Subject: Yes.
Erickson: Do you think you will have to work hard?
Subject: Yes.
Erickson: Why do you think you will have to work hard?
Subject: Don't everybody?
Erickson: Even if you marry a rich man. Yes. Is there anything you don't like or understand?
Subject: Oh, there's lots of things.
Erickson: What are those things?
Subject: Oh, just lots of them.
Erickson: Tell me one—the most troublesome.
Subject: **Where did Daddy go when he died?**
Erickson: Don't you really know?
Subject: I'm not sure.
Erickson: Would you like to be sure?

Subject: Yes.

Erickson: Now a little girl like you has to have that explained so that you can understand it, isn't that right?

Subject: Uh-huh.

Erickson: When you grow older and bigger, **that explanation has to be changed**, doesn't it, because you will understand different things. Now your daddy, when he died, went to heaven. That's the explanation, isn't it?

Subject: That's what they say.

Erickson: And when you were a very little girl, you were told God was a great big, kind old man. Is that right? Do you think Mother thinks about God that way?

Subject: No.

Erickson: She is older, isn't she? And she understands lots of things. Little children go to school and learn one plus one is two, and they think that is hard. And when they learn two plus two equals four, that is really hard. Do you think that's hard for Mother?

Subject: No.

Erickson: It's very easy because she knows a lot more. Do you think a child is wrong in saying it's hard to learn to add one plus one?

Subject: Yes.

Erickson: It isn't wrong. It's hard for a child. Do you think Mother is wrong when she says it's easy?

Subject: No.

Erickson: It's easy for Mother and hard for the child. Now. So an explanation has to be given you that Daddy went to heaven, and when you grow older and bigger you will have the same kind of understanding, but a bigger and better understanding. But really it will be the same thing. Does that answer your question?

Subject: Yes [*hesitantly*].

Rossi: In beginning this section with the orienting question, **"What do you think you will be when you grow up?"**, you are again reinforcing her age-regressed state by implication. You then begin fishing for the kinds of hypnotherapeutic intervention that will be required, since the whole object of her case is to help her feel good about having children. Do you have anything to say about the child's concept of language and the rationale that applies to your approach in this section?

Erickson: For a child, one plus one is hard. Two plus two is still harder to learn. But it isn't hard for Mother. And so it was once hard for Mother when she was a little girl like you. And so *things are going to change for you when you grow up.*

Rossi: Things are going to be easier. So you are careful to answer her poignant question, **"Where did Daddy go when he died?"**, with a therapeutic analogy that her childlike frame of reference could understand. At the same time you have given her an indirect therapeutic suggestion with the statement that **"that explanation has to be changed"** when she grows up.

1.23 *Hypnotherapy as the Facilitation of Each Individual's Unique Learning Pattern; Burt's Self-Weaning; The Unanswerable Questions of Childhood; Emotional Security with the Metaphor of Unconscious Body Knowledge: The Utilization Approach*

Erickson: Is there some other question you would like to ask, or something else you want to say that troubles you a lot?

Subject: There's a lot of things.

Erickson: Tell me another one.

Subject: I don't really worry about it. How do birds know enough to come back?

Erickson: Because birds understand things for themselves. Now, how does a little baby understand why to swallow?

Subject: I don't know. They just do.

Erickson: And when you get thirsty, you don't have anybody explain to you that you should drink, do you? That is the way you grow. And when something comes toward your eyes, you shut them, don't you? Did anybody ever tell you to do that? You just learn that. And how did your hair learn to grow just on top of your head? It's just the way we grow. That's the nice thing about it. Sometimes you get hungry for meat and potatoes, and sometimes you don't want meat and potatoes. Did your stomach ever explain that to you?

Subject: I don't know.

Erickson: And when you play too long, what does your body tell you? To go to sleep, doesn't it? Did anybody ever teach you to sleep?

Subject: No.

Erickson: That's the way we all are. And that's the way the birds know when to come back and when to go away, and the leaves know when to fall off the trees and when to blossom. And that's why the flowers know when to bloom. Isn't it a nice world?

Subject: Yes.

Erickson: Here I'm answering the unanswerable questions of childhood.

Rossi: Why are you doing that now?

Erickson: Children have an endless number of questions, so I point out that your body can tell you when to grow. Sometimes it tells you that you don't want meat or potatoes, but that you *are* hungry. And so you shift your inability to answer questions to the body's knowledge. Your hair knows how to grow.

Rossi: She can experience a great deal of emotional security knowing that the answer to her therapeutic problems can come from inside her, even though her conscious mind does not know.

Erickson: Yes, [an example of this was when] Burt [one of Erickson's sons] was on the bottle. One morning he woke up hungry. I prepared his formula, but when I turned to open the refrigerator door, I heard a crash! Burt had been sitting on a chair at the table watching me. The baby bottles had somehow all crashed down to the floor, and every one of them had broken! I got out a new set of bottles and made a second formula. This time I kept my eyes on Burt when I turned to open the refrigerator door, and I saw him carefully pulling the tank containing the bottles toward the edge of his chair. I interrupted that [so the bottles would not fall a second time]. Burt got down off the chair, went into the dining room, sat down at the table and said, "I'm hungry." He had weaned himself. No more bottles!! And he had weaned himself thoroughly!

Rossi: So crashing the bottles was his way!

Erickson: [*Continues with other stories of how each of his children had their own unique way of letting the adults know when they were weaned. Much laughter in the group, which has by now been joined by Dr. Robert Pearson.*]

Pearson: I big boy now!

Erickson: Each child has an individual pattern of behavior.

Rossi: Each person has a unique learning pattern. Your hypnotherapy seeks to evoke these patterns rather than superimposing foreign contents or ideas on the patient. Many therapists still use this traditional approach of imposing their own viewpoints.

Moore: If this were really understood as true, it would cause a revolution [in the field of hypnotherapy].

Rossi: Milton, would you comment on this viewpoint that *your hypnotherapeutic approach—and all the indirect forms of suggestion it utilizes—is intended to evoke the unique learning processes of each patient rather than to impose the therapist's ideas? This is the essence of your utilization approach.*

Erickson: Yes. How do I know if my ideas will have any effect?

Rossi: That's a nice way to summarize your approach: you

evoke processes that you're sure will have an effect because they belong to the patient; you do not impose your own ideas because you have no way of knowing how they would effect another person. You know, it's very hard to get this idea across to the professional because it's so much easier to say to the patient, "I want you to deal with such-and-such"—but that's not what you are doing. [An unidentified visitor now joins the group.]

Visitor: Aren't you really *redirecting* the processes? At least at times you want patients to use their processes in a way they have not previously used them. I usually assume that somewhere along the line, the patient developed a bad habit.

Rossi: A learned limitation.

Visitor: Do you redirect the processes, Dr. Erickson?

Erickson: *Once you [the hypnotherapist] evoke the processes, the patient can then use them. That leads to a spontaneous correction.*

Moore: Is that what I did when I played the role of Mr. August for one of my patients several years ago? Her father had died when she was eight, so I introduced myself [during age regression in hypnotherapy] as "Mr. August." Mr. August told her how she could dream about the two of them going to the zoo, going to the playground, going any number of places; how she could dream about Mr. August buying little things for her, doing little things for her, showing her the attention that she had craved as a child after her father was gone. But *it was all her own dreams and her own ideas of what Mr. August would have done with her and for her.*

Erickson: *Her own ideas!* When her father died, she must have done some thinking of that sort.

Moore: But she would have done some additional thinking, too, in her dreams that she no longer wanted to face the other way [consciously].

Erickson: Yes.

1.24   *Facilitating Naturalistic Ways of Ending Limitations, Excuses, and*
       Bad Habits; Surprise and Not Knowing as the Signature of
       Unconscious Work; Therapeutic Metaphors of Psychological Growth

Erickson: Have you got anything else that troubles you a lot?
            Anything you are afraid of?
Subject: **I don't want to go away.**
Erickson: Where do you think you are going to go?
Subject: I don't know.
Erickson: Does that scare you a lot? What do you think will happen?
Subject: I don't know.
Erickson: **I told you I would see you again and again.** And I keep
            my promises. And so I am going to come back. Do you
            know that?
Subject: Yes.
Erickson: **I have told you I would see you again and again.** And I
            always keep my promises. And so even if you do go away,
            you will come back.
Subject: Sure?
Erickson: Back to the things you like and want. It doesn't make a bit
            of difference whether we are here or over there, does it?
            Do you think you will ever like another house?
Subject: No.
Erickson: Do you like all the people you know?
Subject: No.
Erickson: **Do you think you will ever like some other people?**
Subject: Yes.
Erickson: Do you think as much of the people you know now?
Subject: Maybe.
Erickson: Don't you think you might like some of them better than
            some of the people you like a lot but not an awful lot?
Subject: Yes.
Erickson: I think that's very true. You like this house. Do you think
            you will ever learn to like another house?
Subject: I might. I don't want to.
Erickson: Don't you want to? **I think it's very nice to have a house**
            you like when you are a child; a house you like when

you are bigger; a house you like when you are all grown up. I think it's nice to have a house that you like when you are old. Isn't that nice?

Subject: I think so.

Erickson: I think that is what is going to happen to you. I hope it will. I hope every time you have something important and good happen to you, that you will have a lot of new things—things that you will like just as much as you like the things around you right now. So you will have a lot of things that you don't even know about now that you will like just as much as you like this house—in a different way, but you will like them. This house has its very special things that you like, and a lot of other things will have their special things that you like a lot. You can understand that, can't you?

Subject: Yes.

Erickson: "I don't want to go away": what does that mean?

Rossi: She enjoys being here?

Erickson: [Erickson tells a story about one of his daughters who was sad on her birthday because she realized she was leaving childhood.] "I don't want to go away" is often heard in this situation, and our subject doesn't want to go away from this little girlhood to big girlhood.

"I told you I would see you again and again" reassures her that even if she does go away [that is, even if she does grow up], she would still have me.

Then her yes response to my question, "Do you think you will ever like some other people?" reinforces her growth: when she grows up, she will like people.

Rossi: [In 1987] Erickson ends this section with a therapeutic metaphor of having an appropriate house (a world view) for each stage of life. As a compensation for having to grow up, she "will have a lot of things that you don't even know about now that you will like just as much as you like this house—in a different way, but you will like them." This is a form of open-ended, in-

direct suggestion that as she grows older she will become
enriched by many things she does not yet know about.
Not knowing is being used as an indirect suggestion for
the unconscious to do its creative work independently
of the limitations her conscious mind has acquired. She
will not be restricted in her later life to the limitations of
her childhood. She will outgrow her learned limitations!

1.25   *Reframing Fears and Pain via the Concepts of Age Relativity:*
       Evoking Learned Concepts of Change in Body, Mind, and Emotion;
       "Acting Out" as Behavioral Rigidity; Ethics of Mind Facilitation
       Versus Manipulation; First Hint of Swimming Fear

Erickson: Do you worry about anything? Are you afraid of anything?
Subject: Lots of things. I'm afraid of that **big dog down on the
            corner.** I don't like to go swimming so well.
Erickson: How old is that dog now?
Subject: I don't know. He's a great big one.
Erickson: What do you think you will think about that dog when
            you grow up? **And what will you do to that dog?**
Subject: **I'll laugh at him.**
Erickson: And yet you will remember that once you were scared of
            him. But you will just laugh at him then, won't you?
Subject: Yes.
Erickson: Is it bad to be scared of him?
Subject: I don't like to be scared.
Erickson: You don't like to stub your toe. But do you think you
            ought ever to grow up without stubbing your toe?
Subject: It would be nice.
Erickson: Weren't you glad when you got a tooth loose, even if it
            did hurt?
Subject: Yes.
Erickson: **Because that meant that you were growing up.** But
            don't you think that everybody should stub their toes,
            too, just so they will really know what it is like?
Subject: Yes.

Erickson: Maybe sometime you will talk to a little girl about her stubbing her toe. You will really want to know what a stubbed toe felt like. Isn't that right?

Subject: Yes.

Erickson: I don't think it's fun to stub your toe. But I'm glad I did because I know how much it hurts. And when somebody talks about it, I know what they are talking about. Don't you think that is so?

Subject: Yes.

Erickson: In reaching her present age she has learned that she cannot escape the future changes in her body. A child learns she is too short to reach the top of the table now, but will soon be tall enough. The child has already learned, "There was a time I couldn't creep—a time I could creep; there was a time I couldn't walk—a time I could walk." And *you are relating everything to that learned concept of change.*

Rossi: You are always evoking and reinforcing the learned concept of change that comes from our own natural life experience.

Erickson: And making it a continuous thing. [*Erickson now recounts examples of teenagers who need help in learning to accept the reality of the good changes that are continuing in their bodies, emotions, and understanding.**]

Rossi: Learning to appreciate our own changing nature is an essence of mental health.

Erickson: Yes. The child can learn to recognize the reality of body changes, but it is harder to learn about the reality of affective and cognitive changes—those are so abstract.

Rossi: Most adults do not understand their own affective and cognitive changes either. They are angry, so they act

---

*See Section 9 in Volume IV of Erickson, 1980, "Facilitating New Identity," for numerous examples of Erickson's approaches in this area.

out the anger; they are depressed, so they passively act out the depression. We might say that *acting out* is a form of *behavioral rigidity*: we do not understand that the state we are presently experiencing will change, and we do not understand how to facilitate and direct that change. What alternative is left but to act out the state as if it were an autonomous function?

[*In* 1987] In this section Erickson also begins the process of reframing the patient's fears in terms of the concept of age relativity he had introduced earlier (Section 1.22): just as learning to add one plus one is hard to the child but easy to the adult, so also is the "**big dog down on the corner**" terrifying to the child but laughable to the adult. Similarly he reframes the pain of a loose tooth in terms of its maturational significance of value ("**that meant that you were growing up**"), and he reframes the pain of a stubbed toe in terms of its relational and experiential significance or value ("**Maybe sometime you will talk to a little girl about her stubbing her toe. You will really want to know what a stubbed toe felt like.**").

This type of reframing could appear to be in contradiction to the previous section (1.23) in which Erickson was adamant about evoking psychological processes in a patient while *not* adding any new ideas or contents. We did not ask Erickson to clarify this possible contradiction at the time. As I reflect on this issue in 1987, however, I can guess at the important differentiation Erickson would probably have made to show that he was in fact evoking and not adding: he was evoking the patient's own latent knowledge by verbalizing ideas which were present but not active (unconscious). This is confirmed by the subject's responses to Erickson's "new" ideas. In the first reframing she herself provides the new idea ("**I'll laugh at him**") in response to Erickson's prompting question ("**And what will you do to the dog?**"). In response to the subsequent two reframings in which Erickson uses the typical childhood experiences of losing teeth and stubbing toes as analogies, the subject gives ready agreement. Her immediate and unqualified yeses suggest that Erickson indeed only turned on the light switch, so to speak—he did not insert the actual light bulbs.

This brings us to an important conceptual differentiation between unethical mind manipulation techniques such as brainwashing and approaches to ethical mind facilitation such as reframing. In unethical mind manipulation techniques, ideas that are foreign or even harmful to an individual are forced upon him through some means of pressure, deprivation, or negative stimulus. In ethical mind facilitations, however, *ideas which may be present but unconscious in the individual are brought into consciousness by therapeutic implications that may evoke the patient's own potentials for self-understanding and behavioral choice.*

1.26 *Posthypnotic Suggestion for Therapeutic Exploration in the Future: Recognition of the Swimming Phobia; Time Distortion Facilitating Multiple Visits by the February Man*

Erickson: And you don't like swimming?
Subject: No.
Erickson: Why?
Subject: I don't know.
Erickson: What about the swimming?
Subject: People get drowned.
Erickson: Do you know anybody who got drowned?
Subject: No, but they do.
Erickson: Did you ever get your mouth full of water and your nose full of water?
Subject: Lots of times.
Erickson: Did it scare you an awful lot?
Subject: Oh, not an awful lot.
Erickson: Sometime when I see you again I'm going to shake hands with you—sometime again. Would you like to see me again?
Subject: Yes.

Erickson: When shall I see you again? **After your next birthday?**
Would that be nice?
Subject: Yes.
Erickson: **The next time I see you, I want you to tell me a little bit**
more about swimming, and like it. Will you do that?
Subject: Yes.
Erickson: The next time I see you, it will be after your next birthday.
Subject: But I won't be here.
Erickson: No matter where you are I'll see you. That's a promise. Is
that all right? Do you think I can keep that promise?
Maybe you ought to close your eyes and rest a bit. Next
time I see you, I'll shake hands with you again.

Rossi: This is your first approach to her swimming phobia,
which will become a major therapeutic preoccupation
in future sessions. At this point you sense its importance
and so you carefully give her a posthypnotic suggestion
for a future meeting with the February Man in which she
will tell you more about it: "**The next time I see you, I**
want you to tell me a little bit more about swimming,
and like it." Is there anything else you want to say about
your preparation at this point? This is still your first
meeting with her as the February Man that began some
five sections back [1.21], and you're going to have many
February Man "visits" with her in this one hypnotherapeutic session.

Erickson: Shaking hands with her is the cue.

Rossi: Shaking hands becomes a cue for her to have
another visit with the February Man at a later age ("**After**
your next birthday?") in trance. Each time you shake
hands with her you are, in effect, having another February Man visit—another minitherapeutic encounter—so
that you can condense many therapeutic visits into one
single hypnotherapeutic session. In real time the visits
are separated only by a moment or two, but in her
subjective trance time there could be weeks, months or
years separating each of your visits.

Erickson: Yes.

Fink: [*This commentary came in* 1987 *when Dr. Fink reviewed this entire manuscript.*] The first point I want to make is that this was not just a phobia for swimming—that would not have been nearly as important. Actually, this was a phobia for *water in general.* At times, this girl was unable to take a shower or a bath and took only sponge baths for years! When she went over a span of water in a car on a bridge, she would sit paralyzed with fear!

1.27 *The Second "Visit" of the February Man: Ratification of the First "Visit" as a Past Trance Memory; Ratification of Successful Reframing; The Subject's Own Associative Processes as the Creator of the February Man Identity*

Erickson: [*Shaking hands with subject*] Hello. I wonder if you remember me?

Subject: Yes.

Erickson: **Do you remember me? When did I see you before?**

Subject: **Yes. A long time ago.**

Erickson: Can you remember when?

Subject: Yes.

Erickson: When was it?

Subject: In February—after my birthday.

Erickson: What time is it now?

Subject: February.

Erickson: Will I always come in February?

Subject: Maybe.

Erickson: I wouldn't be surprised. We had a nice little visit, and you remembered it, didn't you?

Subject: Yes.

Erickson: What do you think about our visit?

Subject: It was nice.

Erickson: Do you think we will have another nice one this time?

Subject: Yes.

Erickson: How's the dog?

Subject: I don't know.

Erickson: After all, I suppose he was a good dog. But you didn't like
            him, did you?
Subject: **I'll go back and kick him someday.**

Rossi: [In 1987] Erickson gives the handshake cue and
initiates the second February Man visit. He asks if she
remembers him as a means of reestablishing his rapport with her. Since she does remember seeing him "a
long time ago," she ratifies the fact that the first visit is
now established as a memory in her trance past. Notice
how smoothly, subtly, and indirectly Erickson has established this "past memory." He does not give any direct
hypnotic commands such as: "This is the second time
I'm meeting with you, little girl. It is now February, one
year after the first time I met you when I first established
my relationship with you as the February Man. You are
now having therapeutic memories established in you
that will function as real memories when you awaken."
    Quite to the contrary! Erickson never labeled himself
as the February Man. He only gave a posthypnotic suggestion and cue for a visit with her at a future time. The
subject's own associative processes then took over and
"decided" that the next visit would be again in February,
one year later, because that's apparently what was needed.
*It was the subject who decided the visits would be in February,
and thus it was the subject who gave Erickson the February
Man identity.*
    Was there any therapeutic value from the first visit?
Notice how Erickson subtly tests for this by simply asking
her about the frightening dog they had discussed in the
first session. She now says, **"I'll go back and kick him
someday."** This means that the reframing Erickson established two sections back (1.25), wherein he implied that
she would outgrow her fear of the dog in the future, is
beginning to take effect. She now makes spontaneous
remarks indicating that she is gaining enough ego strength
to realize that she indeed will be able to **"kick him
someday."** Having thus ratified the spontaneous and

appropriate process by which she utilizes suggestions via her memory of the "past," Erickson opens the next section with a question initiating further exploration—an exploration that again will be guided solely by her associative processes in determining what she and he will talk about next.

1.28 *Uncovering the Repressed Traumatic Memory of an Accidental Near Drowning: Separating Thinking, Feeling, and Doing in Initial Explorations of Traumatic Material Versus Traditional Catharsis*

Erickson: **What else shall we talk about?**
Subject: Do you like Kapac?
Erickson: What is Kapac?
Subject: A town. Don't you know what it is? It's no good.
Erickson: Why?
Subject: I don't like it.
Erickson: You have grown a lot, haven't you?
Subject: A little bit.
Erickson: Do you do anything different now than you did when I last saw you?
Subject: Yes.
Erickson: What things do you do now?
Subject: I can write. I can print, and that's almost writing.
Erickson: That's really a good way to learn how to write. Anything else? Can you tell me where we are?
Subject: Kapac. I don't like it. It's too little.
Erickson: Do you think you'll always stay here?
Subject: Huh-uh!
Erickson: Do you think we'll meet again?
Subject: Oh, I don't know.
Erickson: **Were we supposed to talk about something?**
Subject: Swimming.
Erickson: What about swimming?
Subject: You asked me why I didn't like to go swimming. I thought of something. Once my little sister Helen fell in a tub of water and she was all blue. I pushed her in—I was trying to carry her.

Erickson: How is Helen now?
Subject: She's all right.
Erickson: Did you ever find out what you really did to her? What
            was wrong about it?
Subject: Nothing.
Erickson: Did you get scolded?
Subject: No.
Erickson: Did you feel bad?
Subject: I cried.
Erickson: Cried an awful lot?
Subject: Yes.
Erickson: What are you going to do about it?
Subject: I wouldn't have thought about it if you hadn't asked me
            to.
Erickson: Now you are really glad you told me, aren't you? How old
            were you when you did that?
Subject: About three. I might have been four—I don't remember.
Erickson: Did you like Helen then?
Subject: I thought I did.
Erickson: What was done for her?
Subject: Mother just picked her up and hit her on the back.
Erickson: Did it hurt her?
Subject: No.
Erickson: Why did she hit her?
Subject: To make her breathe, I guess.
Erickson: Did Helen get some water in her throat?
Subject: Yes. She coughed. She coughed a lot.
Erickson: Did you ever swallow something that made you choke
            and cough?
Subject: Yes.
Erickson: That's awful, isn't it? It's unpleasant.
Subject: Dirty old water, too.

Rossi: [In 1987] Erickson begins this section with the
open-ended inquiry, "**What else shall we talk about?**"
He is rewarded with a train of associations that leads to
the uncovering of a repressed traumatic memory of how
the subject almost drowned her younger sister by accident at the age of three or four. Erickson casually uncov-

ered this memory by the subtle test question, "**Were we supposed to talk about something?**" It is a subtle test of how well his posthypnotic suggestion given two sections back had taken hold. In that section (1.26) Erickson said, "**The next time I see you I want you to tell me a little bit more about swimming, and like it.**"

In this section the subject responds to that earlier suggestion with this recall of the near drowning of her younger sister. Why doesn't the subject display a great show of emotion, tears, and anguish as is so often the case when patients recall a traumatic past memory? Note the last part of Erickson's suggestion: "**and like it.**" To **like it** means that she will not have to go through the painful affect usually associated with traumatic memories. She can simply recall the event in a matter-of-fact way without the distorting effects of emotionality.

This is a very different approach from the traditional psychotherapeutic methods of rushing right into emotional catharsis before the whole situation is understood. Throughout his career, Erickson was fascinated with what he called the separation or dissociation of thinking, feeling, and doing,* whereby a patient could calmly receive insights into the repressed traumatic situation (thinking) without the disturbing affects that accompanied it (feeling and doing). At a later time the patient could then undergo an appropriate catharsis from this safer foundation of understanding and perspective—as we shall see in later sections of this case.

1.29   *The Rose-Thorn Therapeutic Metaphor: Mistakes as a Natural Part of Growing Up and Learning; Questions, Juxtaposition of Positive and Negative, and the Apposition of Opposites to Evoke Patient's Own Reframing Correlates*

Erickson: Do you think that [*coughing*] will do anything to Helen that is bad?

---

*See "An Audio-Visual Demonstration of Ideomotor Movements and Catalepsy: The Reverse Set to Facilitate Hypnotic Induction" (Erickson & Rossi, 1981), for a detailed analysis of this type of dissociation.

Subject: No.
Erickson: It was really nice to hear her cough.
Subject: She cried, too.
Erickson: Do you think it's bad that it happened?
Subject: Yes.
Erickson: What would you say if I said it wasn't bad?
Subject: She got all blue.
Erickson: I think there's something about that you don't understand. Have you stubbed your toe again?
Subject: Yes.
Erickson: Did you mind it so much?
Subject: No.
Erickson: Do you think you'll make any mistakes as you grow up? What are you going to do about those mistakes? Learn from them?
Subject: Sort of—and forget about them.
Erickson: Did you ever pick a pretty purple flower and find stickers on it?
Subject: I have done that.
Erickson: What kind of a flower was it?
Subject: Roses.
Erickson: It's an awful way to learn that roses stick. But aren't you glad you learned from that? Some time you might have stuck yourself a lot worse. **You didn't try to hurt the rose, did you? You just liked it and picked it. Do you suppose you really learned something nice about it? And do you suppose you learned something nice about you and Helen when you pushed her in the water?**

Rossi: Your first therapeutic approach is to reframe the trauma with a simple metaphor: the subject bears no greater culpability for her "mistake" with her younger sister than she did for her natural mistake of picking a rose and getting hurt by the thorns. Instead of trying to directly persuade her that she didn't do a "bad" thing, you use a metaphor which communicates both freedom from culpability (**"You didn't try to hurt the rose, did you? You just liked it and picked it"**) and a positive learning experience ("Do you suppose you really learned something nice about it?").

The rose-thorn therapeutic metaphor initiates a yes set for positive learning through painful experience. It is a very typical, naturalistic way of learning—we all have had innumerable experiences of learning something important and good through a painful experience. The rose-thorn metaphor tends to evoke a set for *deutero-learning* (Bateson, 1979) that we have all learned "incidentally" from everyday life.

You then directly tie in the metaphor to her trauma with the question, "**And do you suppose you learned something nice about you and Helen when you pushed her in the water?**", *but in such a way that her own unconscious processes are activated to search for their own reframing correlates.* Part of this activation would occur through your skillful juxtaposition of the positive, pleasant experience of learning "something nice about you and Helen" with a blatant statement of the traumatic event, "when you pushed her in the water." This juxtaposition acts as a new associative bridge to depotentiate her lifetime interpretation of the accident as a wholly bad occurrence. As we shall see in the next section, however, there were additional dynamics operating in this accident which led to its becoming a psychological trauma.

Erickson: [Nods yes.]

Rossi: You often use these apparently simple metaphors that can be readily understood at the child's own level of experience. If the metaphors are not sufficient, you then know there is something more in the situation.

1.30 *Reframing Trauma via Therapeutic Analogies and Informal Syllogisms*

Subject: I shouldn't have picked her up.

Erickson: You learned something, didn't you? Suppose you had waited to try to pick her up until she was bigger and heavier, and then dropped her and hurt her a lot more. That would have been worse than pushing her in the tub.

Subject: She got all blue.
Erickson: What do you suppose that blueness was?
Subject: She was dying.
Erickson: Did you every stay in the water too long?
Subject: Yes.
Erickson: Until your teeth chattered? How did you look then?
Subject: Kind of blue.
Erickson: Did you think you were dying?
Subject: No.
Erickson: Do you think blueness just happened when Helen was dying?
Subject: But she coughed. And Mother was awful scared.
Erickson: Have you ever coughed?
Subject: Yes.
Erickson: Were you dying?
Subject: No.
Erickson: So blueness and coughing doesn't mean dying, does it? Do you think that's a good thing to know? Do you think you should remember that?
Subject: Yes.

Rossi: You now use therapeutic analogies in a further effort to reframe her understanding of the near drowning accident. But she is not satisfied. In the next section she reveals why the simple accident was elaborated into such a psychological trauma for her.

Fink: [In 1987] In my opinion, there were a number of factors in this phobia that were like an equation—and this may be a bit of a psychoanalytic interpretation. First, there was an intense sibling rivalry between the subject and her sister. And it was no accident that she pushed the sister into the large No. 3 washtub they used to bathe in. The subject pushed her in, the baby turned blue and coughed and almost drowned. This may not be accurate, but as my memory serves me, her mother had been quite severe with her about this.

Then, another incident occurred with the subject's

father, who was later to be discovered to have tuberculosis. He went in swimming (probably in Lake Michigan, which is horribly cold), and he coughed and turned blue. In the time sequence of perhaps six or eight months, he died, so that she developed an equation of water equals *coughing, turning blue,* and *dying.* So she developed a phobia for *all* water; as I said, she could neither shower nor bathe, and only took sponge baths.

1.31 *Reframing a Threatened Loss of Mother Love with Folk Language and Therapeutic Analogies; Does Hypnosis Reduce Conflict Between the Cerebral Hemispheres?*

Erickson: Is there something else we should talk about?
Subject: Yes. Do you think Mother loves us?
Erickson: Now suppose you tell me what you really think?
Subject: I don't know.
Erickson: Because you can talk to me easily, can't you, and very honestly. Do you know you have really told me the answer to the question—does your mother really love you? How did your mother feel when she was patting Helen on the back?
Subject: She was awful scared.
Erickson: Now, if you saw that nasty old dog shivering and choking and coughing, what would you do?
Subject: Just run away.
Erickson: Would you feel awful scared and bad?
Subject: No.
Erickson: But your mother felt scared and bad, didn't she?
Subject: Yes.
Erickson: She liked Helen, you are sure of that. Well, you know how you would feel about the dog. If you liked that dog, you wouldn't want him to cough. Were you glad Helen was cold and blue?
Subject: No.
Erickson: Were you scared, too?
Subject: Yes.

Erickson: Does your mother ever get scared about you?
Subject: I don't think so.
Erickson: You don't think so. Maybe you will remember something.
Subject: She makes us put rubbers on.
Erickson: Why does she make you put rubbers on? So you won't
            cough—so you won't catch cold. Why doesn't she want
            you to get sick?
Subject: We would miss school.
Erickson: Why go to school?
Subject: We got to know something.
Erickson: Do you care if the dog knows anything? Do you care if he
            ever knows any tricks?
Subject: No.
Erickson: You don't care because you don't like him. Why does your
            mother want you to go to school and learn something?
Subject: She likes us.
Erickson: You are sure of that?
Subject: Yes.
Erickson: Is there something else to talk about now?
Subject: I don't think so.
Erickson: I am going to come back and see you again. Would you
            like to have me? Do you think February would be a good
            time? Next February? Now, let's see. I talked to you last
            February, and now. I wonder if you will be able to tell me
            some more things next February. This time you told me
            you thought of something you had forgotten about. Will
            you remember some other things for next February?
            You never can tell until next February comes. Is that
            right? This is a very nice visit we have had. I'm glad to see
            you growing so much.
Subject: I'm growing out of all my clothes.
Erickson: I suppose you are tired. Suppose you rest. You can go to
            sleep for a bit now.

Erickson: Here we see the difference between adult behavior and a child's behavior.

Rossi: You're differentiating between them? Why?

Erickson: Because her mother did the right thing, and her [childish understanding is wrong].

Rossi: I would say that you're reframing a threatened loss of mother love. Would you say that's what you're doing?

Erickson: [*Nods yes*] I assume that threatened loss is a child's misunderstanding.

Rossi: From this section we can infer that her early perception of a loss of her mother's love may be the real source of the enduring psychological trauma that emerged from the near drowning incident. You are very careful to use therapeutic analogies within her child's frame of reference in your effort to reframe this early experience of a loss of mother love. Your emphasis in the end that she is growing concludes the session on a positive note, and her acknowledgment that she is outgrowing her clothes is an indication that she is following your suggestions—and hopefully accepting your therapeutic analogies. Is this, in your view, the basis of the therapeutic change that eventually will lead to a resolution of her trauma and a "cure" of her swimming phobia?

Erickson: You undergo enlightening. Folk language: things grow on you.

Rossi: I see. Are these therapeutic analogies, which you present in folk language, the basis of restructuring her frames of reference and curing her phobia?

Erickson: Yes!

Rossi: You use folk language as a way of cementing it in.

Erickson: Folk language is language you share in common even with children.

Pearson: That's why it's harder to teach children grammar and later formed English.

Rossi: I guess folk language is also an appeal to the right hemisphere.

Erickson: [*Erickson now tells stories about his children's concepts of growing up. One day when the family went swimming, one of his younger sons said to an older son, "Gee, Burt you're growing older." Burt replied, "Age is growing pubic hair."*]

Pearson: I'm intrigued that one of the main characteristics of hypnosis may be that it stops the "arguments" between the right and left hemispheres—which is an analogy in itself. In hypnosis one hemisphere cannot say no to the other. This reduces the anxiety that arises from the hemispheres fighting back and forth, saying to one another, "You are crazy for that point of view." Hypnosis helps communicate that each point of view has validity.

Rossi: Hypnosis permits each hemisphere to have its own proper sphere of action without interference from the other. Because the dissociative aspect of hypnosis reduces the arguing or conflict between the hemispheres, the insights of each can be appropriately utilized. This would be an interesting hypothesis to test experimentally.

1.32   The Third "Visit" of the February Man: Solidifying the Hypnotic Reality and Therapeutic Frame of Reference via Questions, Puns, Jokes, and Amnesia: Creating Hypnotic Realities

Erickson: [*After a short pause, Erickson administers the handshake cue for the third visit of the February Man in this session.*] Hello.

Subject: How are you?

Erickson: I'm fine. And you?

Subject: All right.

Erickson: What should I notice about you?

Subject: I have grown an awful lot.

Erickson: Are you sorry about it?

Subject: No.

Erickson: Growing up is really exciting fun, isn't it? Where are we?

Subject: At Uncle Quimby's.

Erickson: Who am I?

Subject: I don't know. But I have seen you.

Erickson: When have you seen me?

Subject: In February.

Erickson: Had you ever seen me before that?

Subject: Yes, months before.

Erickson: What are you going to call me? The February Man?

Subject: Sure.

Erickson: Does that remind you of something? Remember a long time ago I told you I would see you again?

Subject: I remember.

Erickson: What was it—you would see me again, shake hands with me—

Subject: I could talk to you.

Erickson: And even laugh with me. I'm the February Man!

Subject: That's not a real joke, though.

Erickson: But you laughed. And that was a real laugh. Have you got a good joke?

Subject: Do you know what Eddie calls his car? Puddle Jumper, 'cause it lands right in the middle of all the puddles!

Erickson: When it rains cats and dogs, does the car jump right into the middle of a poodle? Did you ever see a poodle?

Subject: Do you mean *puddle* or *poodle*?

Erickson: **What shall we talk about this time?** How you are growing, or something else?

Subject: Something else. Everybody grows.

Erickson: I don't grow.

Subject: But you are grown up.

Erickson: What shall we talk about?

Subject: What do you want to talk about?

Erickson: Anything that will give you happiness and understanding. What do you think about smoking? Do you think you will ever smoke?

Subject: No. Aunt Mary says it's terrible.

Erickson: I think smoking is terribly good. How old are you now?

Subject: Eight.

Erickson: What shall we talk about?

Subject: Well, school is pretty much the same. Do you know what? Uncle Quimby and Aunt Mary take care of everybody's kids. How come when they like kids so well they

don't have any of their own? They take care of everybody else's.

Erickson: Some people don't always get the things they want very
much in this world. People that are wise are the people
that try to do the things that help them to have the
happiness they would get from having the things they
would like. Your aunt and uncle like children, don't they,
and yet they haven't got any of their own. And yet how
many children are going to have many happy memories
of them?

Subject: I see.

Erickson: Isn't that good—and something everybody would like to
have—children that grow up with happy memories of
them? So are you sure they haven't got children? They
have children in a special way. Isn't that right? And the
memories those children have are all going to be happy
memories.

Erickson: Note the care with which I build up the meeting
I'm having with her as the February Man. She now sees
me at Uncle Quimby's, and time has elapsed so she has
grown up some. Then there is the childish joke about
Eddie's car, the Puddle Jumper, and my poodle-puddle
pun—a pun on a child's level.

Rossi: Why?

Erickson: To establish the reality of the February Man
talking to a little girl.

Rossi: Right. You are allowing the mental set—the hypnotic reality of her relation to the February Man—to be
built up. Any other reason for adding a pun here?

Erickson: [Gives the analogy of being distracted by a telephone
call and forgetting what we are doing before we answered it.]

Rossi: So you're distracting her to produce an amnesia?
Why?

Erickson: To clear her mind!

Rossi: Oh, so you can have a clear field to go on to

something else with your next question, "**What shall we talk about this time?**"

Erickson: Yes.

Rossi: In this third visit you begin as usual by getting oriented to her trance reality. You then tie it to the subject matter of her previous trances through questions which 1) affirm her continued "growing up"; 2) ratify and solidify your identity as the February Man; and 3) request the joke you told her she would tell you back in Section 1.1. In this way you produce a continuity between her February Man visits; *you build a stable "hypnotic reality," or all-embracing therapeutic frame of reference, between each trance-visit experience. You are creating a hypnotic reality that will become—*

Erickson: —a basic attitude toward life.

Rossi: Right! It will become a part of her unconscious memory system. And on another level you actually reinforce this idea of the importance of having happy memories by your reinterpretation of Uncle Quimby and Aunt Mary's childless situation. The happy memories you are giving the subject as the February Man will be warm and supportive of her, just as the memories of Uncle Quimby and Aunt Mary were warm and supportive to the kids they cared for. These memories will then become the basis of her future self-esteem and confidence in raising her own children.

Erickson: Uh-hum.

1.33 A Spontaneous Age Regression and Reexperiencing of a Traumatic Swimming Lesson: Acting Out and Ideodynamic Behavior as Right-Hemispheric Responses?

Erickson: Is there anything that worries you or troubles you?

Subject: I never see Mother.

Erickson: Does that trouble you?

Subject: No.

Erickson: Is there something about that you want to tell me?
Subject: She never comes out here. She's working.
Erickson: Who is she working for?
Subject: I don't know.
Erickson: Why is she working?
Subject: For money.
Erickson: For whom?
Subject: For us, I guess.
Erickson: Do you want to think about that a bit? You think about it and tell me for whom she wants that money.
Subject: Helen and me, and herself, too.
Erickson: She has to look after herself so she can look after all of you. Aren't you glad you have a mother who likes to work to look after her children?
Subject: I wish she didn't work.
Erickson: Don't some grown-ups like to work?
Subject: I guess they do.
Erickson: Is there anything else that troubles you?
Subject: No.
Erickson: What happened to that old dog?
Subject: Maybe he just up and died.
Erickson: What about swimming?
Subject: I haven't been swimming. Not for a long time. Nobody goes very often and I don't like to go. I don't like water so well.
Erickson: Can you tell me why? [Pause] Can you tell me why?
Subject: It doesn't feel very good.
Erickson: In what way doesn't it feel well?
Subject: And I always think about drowning.
Erickson: Can you remember the first time you thought about drowning?
Subject: When Helen got all blue.
Erickson: What are you going to do about that?
Subject: Stay out of the water.
Erickson: **Would you like to learn to swim?**
Subject: Ya.
Erickson: Do you think that some time you may learn to swim?
Subject: Uh-huh.

Erickson: Anything else you can talk to me about?

Subject: No. [Subject begins coughing and strangling.]

Erickson: Are you thinking? Are you thinking? [Subject coughs and strangles. At this point Erickson takes hold of her hand.] Why are you coughing?

Subject: [Choking] Mouth full of water. Mr. Smith—I'm not going to let him show me how, either.

Erickson: Soon you will be **nine years old**, won't you?

Subject: No.

Erickson: How old are you?

Subject: **I think I'm four.**

Erickson: Someday you will be **nine years old.**

Subject: No, I won't.

Erickson: Someday you will be **nine years old.**

Subject: I thought you said Sunday.

Erickson: Will you promise me something? Sometime, when you are **nine years old**, you tell me all about Mr. Smith, will you?

Subject: I'll probably forget him.

Erickson: When I'm talking to you, you will remember everything, won't you? Now just have a rest for a while and I'm going to see you again when you're **nine years old.**

Erickson: [She age regresses to] four years old, which means some [trauma] is coming through.

Rossi: You were undoubtedly perplexed by this sudden and initially inexplicable turn of events in which the subject spontaneously reexperiences an unfortunate swimming lesson she had with Mr. Smith. This was an ideodynamic response apparently brought about by your questions, **"Would you like to learn to swim?"** and **"Anything else you can talk to me about?"** She does not give you a rational and verbal answer from her left hemisphere, but rather reenacts a near drowning with choking and strangling. That is, she responds in right-hemispheric language.

It may be interesting to note here that many (if not all) forms of acting out behavior may be right-hemispheric responses to situations in which society might have hoped to get a left-hemispheric (verbal) response. This concept could be amplified in a hypothesis that many (if not all) forms of ideodynamic associations and behaviors are mediated by the right hemisphere in contrast to the logical and verbal associations which are mediated by the left hemisphere. What do you think of that? Is this a new insight into the dynamics of acting out behavior?

Erickson: They used to call it *catharsis*. Acting out is another way of expressing meaning.

Rossi: Next you try to orient yourself to the situation by asking her if she will soon be nine years old. She responds that she thinks she is four. Just a few minutes ago she said she was eight[Section 1.32]. Thus she spontaneously underwent a four-year age regression to act out the answer to your question about swimming. You are confused, so you wisely end the visit by telling her that she will be **nine years old** at your next visit, and able to tell you about Mr. Smith.

Erickson: Yes. [Then at the end] I think it was a pun she produced. She made an unintentional pun when she thought I said *Sunday* instead of *someday*. It took the action out of her right hemisphere and put it in her left.

Rossi: That's an interesting *post hoc* speculation, since it was a cognitive expression that brought it to her left-hemisphere. Certainly you didn't think in terms of left- and right-hemispheric interaction back in 1945—since that was well before Sperry introduced the concept in the 1950s.

1.34   *Fourth "Visit" of the February Man: Momentary Confusion of Age Regression Levels; A Healing Heuristic for Posttraumatic Stress via Subtle Changes in the Maps of Memory*

Erickson: Hello.
Subject: Hi.
Erickson: How old are you?

Subject: Nine.

Erickson: **Where did I see you before?**

Subject: I don't know [*shows much confusion*].

Erickson: You have seen me before.

Subject: I don't remember.

Erickson: **Do you remember when you see me?**

Subject: February. Now I remember. You're the February Man.

Erickson: I think you have to do something for me.

Subject: I got to do something for you. You're always doing things for me.

Erickson: But this time you're going to do something for me.

Subject: I know. I was going to tell you about Mr. Smith.

Erickson: Go ahead.

Subject: I don't know what to tell you about him. He lived next door and he had two little kids, Alicia and Barney. **They were real cute.** He was German—blonde hair—real tall.

Erickson: [*I ask her*], **Where did I see you before?"** [She answers, **"I don't know,"** because she had suddenly regressed in the previous section.] So she had to be confused.

Rossi: Even though she says she is at a nine-year-old level, she is confused because she is still under the influence of that powerful and spontaneous age regression to the age of four when she had not yet met the February Man. You clue in the age nine level by asking her, **"Do you remember when you see me?"** The question is sufficiently reinforcing to elicit her immediate recall of the February Man, as well as her compliance with your previous [Section 1.33] posthypnotic suggestion to tell you about Mr. Smith. She then responds to your question in that peculiarly perfunctory way that characterizes the child's effort to relate something unpleasant.

Erickson: Mr. Smith is a memory of a man who did a bad thing. But Alicia and Barney are little friends of hers. They were not bad like Mr. Smith.

Rossi: **"They were real cute."**

Erickson: She's now altering her memory!

Rossi: So this is an important part of the hypnotherapeutic process. Into the original traumatic memory of Mr. Smith she now introduces more pleasant memories of her cute playmates. She is altering or diluting the original traumatic memory. We could say she is already subtly changing the "map" of her past traumatic memory. Every time a traumatic memory is reviewed in hypnosis, there is an opportunity to dilute it by adding new, pleasant, non-traumatic contents until finally the trauma becomes only a small, insignificant part of the whole.

Since the trance state facilitates a more vivid ideo-dynamic recall or activation of the original traumatic memory, the new, more pleasant contents that are being added have an opportunity to get bonded or associated more adequately to the trauma. An effective dilution thus occurs. When the trauma is recalled in the less vivid manner characteristic of the ordinary waking state, however, the new contents that are added will not bond as well to the trauma—and a less significant dilution occurs. *This is a heuristic for conceptualizing how hypnosis facilitates the healing of posttraumatic stress by making therapeutic alterations in the maps of memory.*

1.35   *Childlike Language Validating Age Regression: Distraction and the Early Training of a Hypnotherapist*

Erickson: Tell me something more.

Subject: He used to come over and play cards sometimes. But I didn't like him. He was kind of crabby sometimes.

Erickson: Do you remember something more about him?

Subject: He was awful big.

Erickson: What else?

Subject: He was always going to show me how to swim, and I wouldn't let him. So one time he put me in the water, and I kicked him.

Erickson: How do you feel about that?

Subject: About learning how to swim? I was scared.

Erickson: Did you think you were being a bad girl?

Subject: No.

Erickson: What did your mother think about it?

Subject: Mother wanted me to learn how to swim. But I didn't care. I just kicked him.

Erickson: Why did you kick him?

Subject: I didn't want to learn how to swim.

Erickson: Why didn't you want to learn how to swim?

Subject: **I didn't want him to learn me how to swim.** I guess I was scared of him—kind of.

Erickson: Why?

Subject: I don't know.

Erickson: Did he do something you didn't like to you?

Subject: No. He just scowls at everybody.

Erickson: Did he put you in the water?

Subject: Yes. I didn't like that.

Erickson: You didn't tell me about that yet.

Subject: He was teaching me how to swim and when I told him no, he just picked me up and put me in the water. I got water in my eyes and ears and in my mouth, and I kicked him and started to cry.

Erickson: Why?

Subject: I didn't want to learn to swim.

Erickson: "**I didn't want him to learn me how to swim.**"

Rossi: Childlike language in her use of "**learn me**" tends to validate her age-regressed state.

Erickson: Yes. the best part [of this section] is how she shifts from being scared to kicking. I recall when I was a youngster selling books in the country. One summer there was a certain farmer with his dog. The farmer had trained the dog to attack anybody who came in the yard. When I came in the yard that dog came charging toward me. He was only a dog and didn't know any better. I took my handkerchief out and held it up like this. That fool dog snapped his jaws shut on it and I kicked him right here [*pointing at his throat*]! The dog really had to think that one over. The farmer was so startled he said, "That's the first time I've ever seen my dog get the worst of it!" He then invited me in to have dinner.

Rossi: That's how you displaced that dog's aggression. I'm going to publish this story to show how Milton learned hypnotherapy by kicking dogs in the throat!

Erickson: Well, that was so stupid of the dog! You always want to know what the other fellow is going to do, but don't let him know what you're going to do. The farmer and I got on so well he invited me stay for the night.

Rossi: This is a story for a future biographer: the early training of a hypnotherapist, learning techniques of distraction in everyday life!

1.36   *Dissociating a Traumatic Memory: Implication and Therapeutic Analogy; Separating Thinking and Feeling; A Posthypnotic Reframing of Emotions; A Time Double Bind*

Erickson: Can you tell more about that? Why? He picked you up and put you in the water, and you didn't want to go in the water and you started to choke and cough. What did that remind you of?

Subject: I guess I thought about Helen when I pushed her in the water, and I didn't want to be all blue like she was.

Erickson: See if you can remember just what those feelings were.

Subject: I was scared.

Erickson: You were awful scared. Just scared stiff. And you coughed. You coughed and Helen coughed. Helen was pretty scared, too.

Subject: She was too little to be scared.

Erickson: But she didn't like it either, did she?

Subject: She cried.

Erickson: **And you coughed and she coughed. She was unhappy and you were also unhappy. A lot of the same things happened.** What are you going to do about it? Are you going to remember it?

Subject: I don't want to remember it.

Erickson: You just don't want to remember. Do you think it might be a good thing to remember?

Subject: No. **Mother says you should just remember the nice things.**

Erickson: Did your tooth hurt when it came out?

Subject: Not bad.

Erickson: Did it hurt?

Subject: Sure.

Erickson: Are you glad you remembered?

Subject: Sure.

Erickson: Was it nice, or did it just have to be?

Subject: Both.

Erickson: Do you think it might be a good idea to remember about this swimming? And just to forget how to feel bad about it?

Subject: Scares me.

Erickson: Do you think you should be scared of what you can remember?

Subject: No.

Erickson: No, you really shouldn't be scared about things you can remember. **Maybe someday you can laugh about how scared you were. That would be a nice thing to do, wouldn't it?**

Subject: Yes.

Erickson: Maybe you will someday.

Subject: I don't think so.

Erickson: I think you will. **Shall I come to see you next year, or shall I skip a year?**

Subject: You can skip a year if you want to. **I'll be really grown-up then.**

Erickson: How tall will you be?

Subject: I'll bet I'll be as tall as Mother.

Erickson: I think it would be very nice to see you then.

Subject: Of course, she's pretty tall.

Erickson: We don't know how tall you will be. You'll just have to grow up and find out. How will it be if I come back to see you when you are 11 years old? You ought to have a joke for me then. What do you think?

Subject: I don't know. I'll try.

Erickson: Well, you've got a couple of years' time. And the next time I see you, what shall we talk about?

Subject: I'll be higher up in school. Maybe I won't live here anymore.

Erickson: I'll find you. What do you think?

Subject: You probably will.

Erickson: That's right. And everytime you see me, I come to visit you, and you rest, don't you? And you never see me in between times. That's what all February men do. Maybe someday I'll be a March Man. Do you know what a June bug is? And maybe I'll be shorter.

Subject: Uh-huh.

Erickson: I think you're getting tired.

Subject: [*Lapses into quiescence.*]

Erickson: "**And you coughed and she coughed. She was unhappy and you were also unhappy. A lot of the same things happened.**" But, "**Mother says you should just remember the nice things.**"

Rossi: In this section the subject is able to provide the facts about the crucial traumatic associations between her choking and coughing in her swimming lesson and that of her younger sister's near drowning. But she does not want to remember either trauma. This is a peculiar dissociation: she has a grasp of the connections between the two incidents, yet she does not want to remember them because her mother says she should only remember "nice things." Such is the hypnotic repressive power of a mother's suggestion on a child troubled by fears and guilts she does not know how to handle. You encourage her to remember or reexperience the emotional content of the incident, but she stays rigidly within her mother's frame of reference.

Because of this you introduce the therapeutic analogy about a tooth that hurts when it comes out, and you explore the possibility of separating thinking and feeling* in the hopes of freeing the cognitive aspects from its repressive emotional charge. She seems fairly resistant at this point, so you suggest that maybe she will someday be able to laugh at how scared she was. You are hereby actually giving her a casual posthypnotic suggestion to reframe her fears when you say: **"Maybe someday you can laugh about how scared you were. That would be a nice thing to do, wouldn't it?"** She still doubts she can do this, though.

You then present her with a time double bind when you say, **"Shall I come to see you next year, or shall I skip a year?"** Whichever alternative she chooses, she is committing herself to another visit with you. She wants to skip a year because **"I'll be really grown-up then."** This may be a subtle hint that by then she will be able to deal with her traumatic memories more effectively *because* she will "be really grown-up."

You end this visit with an emphasis on the themes of growth and humor: from a child's point of view, an adult does seem to get shorter as he or she gets taller! This also contains a subtle implication that she will be bigger, more mature, and more able to deal with difficult emotions. Do you agree with that analysis?

Erickson: Yes, I end with the possibility of becoming a March Man, and that's associated with the June bug, which is the foundation of a joke she might make up later. She will be taller and I will be shorter. I'm confirming her idea that she will be taller and older. I'm making that plain to her cognition. The ideas are all there.

Rossi: The ideas are all there by implication. You use

---

*See Part Two of Chapter 8 in Erickson and Rossi, 1979, for a more detailed discussion of dissociating thinking and feeling.

implication rather than a direct statement to bypass any possible criticism.

Erickson: That's right.

1.37 Fifth "Visit" of the February Man: A Successful Reframing of Emotions in Psychological Growth; Altering "Memory Maps" Rather Than Original Trauma

Erickson: [After a short pause, Erickson gives the subject another handshake to initiate the fifth visit.] Hello.
Subject: Hi. I remember who you are.
Erickson: You do?
Subject: How come you know me all the time?
Erickson: February men always remember. And I'm the February man.
Subject: Yes, I guess you are.
Erickson: You are getting pretty well grown-up.
Subject: Almost big enough to be a bride.
Erickson: Are you thinking about brides?
Subject: Oh, no. But Lisa is.
Erickson: How old is Lisa?
Subject: She's 14. You can get married when you're 16.
Erickson: Is Lisa thinking about it?
Subject: No, I don't think so.
Erickson: Let's see. Do you remember what we were talking about the last time I saw you?
Subject: Uh-huh.
Erickson: What?
Subject: Mr. Smith.
Erickson: You thought you might forget about that.
Subject: **I thought I would, but I guess I didn't.**
Erickson: Now that you think about it, how do you feel about it?
Subject: About Mr. Smith, **I shouldn't have been scared.**
Erickson: Why not?

Subject: He probably wouldn't have hurt me. He just wanted to teach me how to swim.

Erickson: What do you think about getting mad and kicking him?

Subject: I shouldn't have kicked him, but he shouldn't have tried to teach me if I didn't want to learn to swim.

Erickson: You really are getting grown-up ideas. They are better than those scared feelings, aren't they? Isn't it grand to grow up?

Subject: I can use powder now.

Erickson: Do you put on a lot?

Subject: No.

Erickson: You should be very dainty about it.

Subject: I'm not going to put on a lot.

Erickson: By the way, how do you feel about swimming? Still scared of water?

Subject: Not so much.

Erickson: Is there something else you are scared of?

Subject: No.

Erickson: In regard to forgetting Mr. Smith she says, "I **thought I would, but I guess I didn't.**" She then says, "**I shouldn't have been scared.**" She is *reperceiving* her emotional processes now.

Rossi: So this is a basic process of hypnotherapy: *reperceiving emotional processes as the essence of reframing them.*

Erickson: You don't alter the original experience; you alter the perception of it, and that becomes the memory of the perception.

Rossi: We cannot alter the original perception, but we can alter our experience of the memory or "map" of it.

Erickson: She says, "**He probably wouldn't have hurt me. He just wanted to teach me how to swim.**"

Rossi: So here is a total reevaluation or reframing of the early traumatic incident.

Erickson: She continues with, "**I shouldn't have kicked**

him, but he shouldn't have tried to teach me if I didn't want to learn to swim." That's a complete change in her total understanding. [*She has gone from being scared and angry to seeing both sides of the situation in a balanced way.*] So then I tell her, "**You really are getting grown-up ideas. They are better than those scared feelings, aren't they? Isn't it grand to grow up?**"

Rossi: So this exchange reinforces and solidifies her growing up with more mature understanding.

Erickson: And she proves it by saying, "**I can use powder now.**"

1.38   *Reinforcing Minimal Cues of Psychological Growth Toward Fun and Happiness; The Generation Gap: Debunking the Old for the New*

Erickson: How long have I been visiting you?

Subject: A long time.

Erickson: Do you remember one of the first things you asked me? What was it you asked—where Daddy went? Now that you are grown up, what do you think of that explanation?

Subject: Maybe you were kidding me. Were you kidding me?

Erickson: Do you think I'm kidding you?

Subject: Not everybody goes to heaven.

Erickson: Who do you think goes to heaven?

Subject: Oh, I don't know. Not very many.

Erickson: Why?

Subject: I guess everybody likes to have too much fun.

Erickson: And what does fun do for people?

Subject: It doesn't land them in heaven. **Anyway, that's what Grandma says.**

Erickson: I think fun makes people happy.

Subject: Do you think you can be happy and go to heaven too?

Erickson: I don't think you should be sad.

Subject: We got an old lady here and all she does is read the Bible. She will probably get to heaven, though. But she doesn't have any fun.

Erickson: **I think heaven is for happy people.**

Erickson: I'm trying to get across the idea that's it's OK to have fun. She makes a subtle remark, "**Anyway, that's what Grandma says.**" And Grandma is awfully old-fashioned—everyone knows that [*laughs*].

Rossi: Since Grandma is old-fashioned, that implies she is not up-to-date. This becomes the subject's subtle way of debunking her grandma's view that fun doesn't land people in heaven. Her psychological growth is evident in this adolescent's debunking of the past generation. She is now oriented to fun and happiness, which you strongly support with the statement, "**I think heaven is for happy people.**" You are not imposing this idea on her; you are simply reinforcing her own subtle debunking of the old-fashioned moralistic view that you can't have both fun and heaven.

The great significance you attach to her very "subtle remark" is an excellent example of how you have learned to pick up the growth implications contained in the "minimal cues" of psychological development. It is all too typical of parents, teachers, and authority figures to be blind to the subtle manifestations that signal jumps in a child's or adolescent's level of understanding. Because of this, a *generation gap* develops with all its *sturm und drang*: there is a tragic disruption of relationship wherein the older generation maintains that it doesn't understand where the younger is "coming from," and the younger generation gives up in despair in the face of older stupidity, ill will, and apparent lack of trust. The older generation does not know how to pick up the growth implications of the younger generation, hidden as they often are in youth's uncertainty and feeling of inferiority.

On the intrapersonal level we can infer that most young people likewise do not recognize the implications of psychological growth taking place within themselves. They do not know how to support their own new

phenomenological levels of awareness and understanding that develop within them in a spontaneous manner.*
Our educational system still teaches primarily by "rod
and rote": rather than teaching children to learn to
recognize and nurture the creative process within
themselves, the typical educational system teaches *contents* that the child is required to swallow whole (the rote)
and then regurgitate on *tests* (the rod) that are the so-called
criteria of learning. The students thus remain blind to
their own inner process of learning and discovery—a
process which is essential if they are to become capable
of any form of creativity. It is this inner blindness that
leads to (so-called) mental illness and psychological
maladjustment wherein the individual does not know
how to recognize, reinforce, and integrate the new psychological growth that is being spontaneously gener-
ated from within. From this perspective the essence of
psychotherapy is to facilitate this understanding of the
growth process so that people can solve their own
problems.†

1.39   *Utilizing a Moral Background to Reframe Feeling States; A
       Hypothesis Regarding Therapeutic Analogies (Right Hemisphere)
       and Reframing (Left Hemisphere): Erickson's Integrative View*

   Subject: Daddy was pretty happy. But he was kind of sick, so
              maybe he wasn't so happy. And maybe he would go to
              heaven. I don't know. I guess it doesn't matter.
   Erickson: It seems to me that heaven is for people who enjoy life,
              who are happy, and who do the best work they can.
   Subject: He worked hard all the time. I guess he was pretty happy,
              too. He coughed a lot. That couldn't have made him
              happy. [*Subject shakes head.*]

---

*See Part One of Rossi, 1972a/1985 for a discussion of the *breakout heuristic* in relation to
psychological growth.

†See also articles by Rossi (1967–1980) listed in the References.

Erickson: I think quite a lot of things happened to Jesus.

Subject: But He didn't have much fun.

Erickson: Do you think He didn't enjoy some of the things that happened to Him? It seems to me that He had happy things happen to Him.

Subject: He never laughed.

Erickson: Why do you say that?

Subject: Nobody ever talks about Him laughing. They talk about Him crying. They talk about Him praying. But He was never laughing. But He went to heaven.

Erickson: Did He ever do any good work?

Subject: Lots of it.

Erickson: What do you do when you do a good piece of work?

Subject: Pat myself on the back.

Erickson: Do you feel happy about it and enjoy it?

Subject: Sure.

Erickson: Do you have to laugh aloud, or can you laugh inside when you enjoy yourself?

Subject: Sure.

Erickson: What do you suppose Jesus did when he did a good piece of work? He laughed inside, too. Is there anything that troubles you or worries you?

Subject: No.

Erickson: Essentially I'm moralizing. I'm providing a moral framework for her understanding that working and doing the best you can is the essential background for happiness. That all fits in with her Catholic background. I made a comparison: Jesus suffered, so he went to heaven. Life is not a bowl of cherries, but being able to laugh and feel good on the inside when you do good work is a compensation.

Rossi: You're utilizing her moral background to rationalize a process of feeling good about herself on the inside. You're also suggesting that her father probably felt good "inside," even though he was sick a lot, just as Jesus felt good on the inside even though he suffered a lot. So you are really helping the subject to reassess and possibly reframe some of her early ideas about her father's death, as well as some of her fairly conventional religious ideas.

Erickson: Yes.

Rossi: You provide stimuli and cues, usually in the form of questions and situations, that allow the subject's unconscious dynamics to manifest themselves. You must then follow her associative processes, which will indicate what therapeutic work must be done. The essence of the therapeutic work in these visits of the February Man seems to be a simple answering of the age-regressed subject's childhood questions about the world. These questions are usually answered with *therapeutic analogies and metaphors*, or by *reframing* her overly rigid and limited orientations and frames of reference. The therapeutic analogies often seem to be right-hemispheric language, while the reframing may be oriented to her left-hemispheric patterns of understanding.

Erickson: [*Hands Rossi a note which was apparently written after one of our discussions of the dynamics of left-right hemispheric interaction in hypnosis.*]

Rossi: You say here: "Experiencing, remembering, and perceiving are entirely different things, and left and right functioning are different combinations of those three things."

Erickson: I don't think there are any "pure" right- or left-sided functions. Something may be on the right side before it's completely perceived, however. [*Erickson now gives many examples of the learning process in humans and animals that suggest to him that we cannot separate psychological functions into the left and right hemispheres, as Rossi hypothesized above.*]

Rossi: Some people have speculated that right-hemispheric contents are more unconscious such that *insight* would require a shift from the right hemisphere to the more conscious left hemisphere. If that were true, your therapy would be more right-hemispheric. Or would you say it always involves an integration of both hemispheres?

Erickson: It always involves an integration.

1.40   A Double Bind Utilizing Moral Attitudes; Dealing with Habit Problems in Age Regression; Caution and "Leaving Well Enough Alone" in Exploratory Hypnosis; Illusory Choice

Erickson: Is there something about you I should notice now?
Subject: I got long hair. But I bite my fingernails. I just bite them.
Erickson: Why do you bite them?
Subject: They taste good, I guess.
Erickson: But really, do they taste good?
Subject: No, but it's fun to chew them.
Erickson: What do you think about when you are biting your nails?
Subject: Sometimes I get mad and then I chew them right down.
Erickson: Is it as good to chew them down as to kick people?
Subject: You can't go around kicking people. Grandma doesn't like it.
Erickson: Does she like you to chew your fingernails?
Subject: No, but I just tell her.
Erickson: Are you going to change your mind about that sometime?
Subject: Oh, yes. I don't want to bite my fingernails when I'm grown up.
Erickson: Have I changed any?
Subject: No.
Erickson: I thought I was going to be shorter.
Subject: I guess maybe you are. You don't measure people like that, though. You stand them up against the wall. I can't remember how tall I am. I'm growing up, though. Grandma says she can tell by how short my dresses are getting.
Erickson: That's a good way of measuring. What shall we talk about next time I see you?
Subject: I don't know.
Erickson: Do you think you'll tell me about anything unhappy or unpleasant?
Subject: I don't think I'll be unhappy.

Erickson: But if anything unpleasant or unhappy did occur, do you think you could tell me—any time, any place, anywhere?

Subject: Sure.

Erickson: No matter what it was?

Subject: Sure.

Erickson: No matter how old you were?

Subject: Sure.

Erickson: When shall I see you again?

Subject: Better come back in February.

Erickson: Next February, the following February, or the February following that? Suppose you tell me.

Subject: You'd better wait a while.

Erickson: How long? How old do you want to be when I see you again?

Subject: I guess I'll be—do you want to wait until I'm in high school?

Erickson: I'll see you any time you want me to—any place you want me to. I could even become an October Man.

Subject: I like you as the February Man.

Erickson: You're getting a little tired of talking, aren't you? You can rest now.

Erickson: That's a total bind ["But if anything unpleasant or unhappy did occur, do you think you could tell me—any time, any place, anywhere?"] She answers "Sure"; she's bound to tell me no matter what it is.

Rossi: So you're getting her to say "sure" to a very general, all-inclusive statement. You're binding her to tell you about anything unpleasant. This functions as a bind for her because she is a moral person who keeps her word. You are utilizing her moral attitudes to effect this bind. Her "moral attitudes" are internal response tendencies that function as a metalevel to double-bind her into telling you anything unpleasant.*

---

*See "Varieties of Double Bind" (Erickson & Rossi, 1975/1980).

I also notice in this section that you "leave well enough alone" regarding her early habit problem of nail biting. I assume you did this because she is able to say in her age-regressed condition that she will not bite her nails when she is older (and, in fact, she does not). In this kind of personality reconstruction utilizing age regression, you deal as much as possible with the issues most directly related to adult problems—in this case, her fear of water. You don't deal with the nail biting since you already know that it takes care of itself. Is there anything else you want to say about this section?

Erickson: No. I'm surprised at the amount of caution I show there.

Rossi: Yes. This took place back in 1945 [when Erickson was in a creative period of transition from hypnotic research in the laboratory to this new process of hypnotic exploration in clinical work. Caution was indeed an important attitude in such exploratory work.]

Erickson: I ask, "When shall I see you again?" I've gotten her total trust as the February Man, and she wants to keep it that way when she says, "Better come back in February." Then I give her the illusory choice: "Next February, the following February, or the February following that? Suppose you tell me." When I offer her the October Man, I'm making her recognize by her own response, "I like you as the February Man," that she prefers the February Man.

Rossi: She prefers the safety of that choice.

Erickson: Yes. I'm giving her freedom but she really isn't getting freedom.

1.41   Sixth "Visit" of the February Man: New Patterns of Psychological Understanding in Adolescence; Minimal Cues, Reframing, Symptom Prescription, and Time Binds; Metalevels in Children

Subject: Why, you won't even speak to me!
Erickson: Oh, yes I will. I'm just wondering what month this is.

Subject: October.
Erickson: Am I late?
Subject: I guess you are.
Erickson: What year is it?
Subject: Don't you know?
Erickson: I just asked you what month it is.
Subject: You don't know what year it is? 1939. [*It is actually* 1945.]
Erickson: [*Administers handshake cue*] How old are you?
Subject: Thirteen.
Erickson: Where abouts are you in school?
Subject: I'm a freshman. You know, it's too bad. I'm the second
              youngest in the class. That's bad. Everybody else is older.
Erickson: Oh, I don't know. **They will be practically old maids
              while you are still young.**
Subject: Oh, people aren't old maids anymore.
Erickson: What are they?
Subject: **Bachelor girls, I guess.**

Erickson: To be the youngest girl in the class gives all the
other girls the prestige of being older. You can tell that
age is the important thing. A 15-year-old girl describes a
25-year-old man as old. So when I bring in, **"They will
be practically old maids while you are still young,"** I'm
bringing in doubt. That leads her to eventually say, not
"old maids" but **"bachelor girls."**

Rossi: Another subtle language distinction that is a minimal cue about her developing maturity. Her generation
has new psychological attitudes, and she is telling you
about them. This has interesting implications for the
reason why language changes gradually over the generations. The newly emerging awareness and unique
patterns of understanding in each generation are encoded
in these linguistic shifts. The new ways of describing
situations, status, and relationships are not mere euphe-
misms but rather new patterns of psychological insight
and understanding. To inhibit these new language patterns (i.e., *slang*) is to inhibit the new awareness that is

emerging. Thus the "purists" of language really are "old fuddy-duddies" when they deride the new, although they do provide a very important function in insisting upon the still useful meanings and distinctions in words that past generations labored to create.

Erickson: [*Erickson tells stories and anecdotes about the minimal cues of language and behavior that shaped events in his family.*]

Rossi: And a lot of your hypnotherapy is just a continuation of those changing concepts that emerge naturally in everyday life.

Erickson: Uh-hum. [*Erickson now continues with a further illustration in the case of Jimmie, a little boy who sucked his thumb. Jimmie's parents wanted Erickson to use hypnosis as treatment.*] I sat down with Jimmie and said, "Now Jimmie, your father and mother want me to stop you from sucking your thumb." Jimmie nodded; he knew that. I told him, "All little kids six years old should be able to suck their thumb and nobody should interfere! Of course, when they reach seven years old, all kids stop sucking their thumbs. Your birthday is coming soon, *so you'd better do plenty of thumbsucking.*" This was just before his seventh birthday—it was just six weeks away. [This was a use of] *changing concepts!*

Rossi: You are also illustrating the use of *reframing, paradoxical symptom prescription,* and a kind of *time bind* in this charming example.

Erickson: [*Erickson now regales us with further humorous examples of his grandchildren's "precocious" remarks revealing their metalevels of understanding (the ways in which they comment on their own mental experience). For example, one granddaughter said, "But, Mama, I haven't had enough experience at six years old to know about that!"*]

Rossi: [In 1987] Again and again, these preoccupations with family everyday life remind us that these interests were at the source of Erickson's creative vision. His therapeutic work was an application of the natural processes of psychological growth he witnessed in his family and in those around him. He learned from these experiences rather than from books and theory. If we are to learn to emulate something of the *process* of his creative work—rather than merely copying by rote the *contents* of his therapeutic method—the lesson is clear: *Take delight in your growing awareness of how people all around you develop in everyday life; enjoy the surprise and humor inherent in helping your "patients" learn to recognize and utilize these life lessons; and cherish the birthright of each succeeding generation to create its own unique patterns of consciousness and understanding.*

1.42 Displacing and Discharging Resentment and the Negative; Two-Level Communication to the Cognitive and the Literal-Concrete; Implication as the Vehicle for Indirect Suggestion; Polarizing Yes and No Responses

Erickson: Well, let's see. Why should I come in October?

Subject: I don't know. Maybe you like October.

Erickson: Now, how shall I explain my arriving in October? Or am I to become the October Man? Shall we say my train was late?

Subject: That's a good excuse. But it's an old one.

Erickson: What old **excuses** do you know?

Subject: There are lots of **excuses** for everything.

Erickson: What old **excuses** do you use that you don't like to use? [*Pause*] Aren't you going to answer me?

Subject: When the kids go swimming I always say I have a cold. I don't have a cold. That's just an **excuse**.

Erickson: **Getting tired of that excuse? Want a better one?**

Subject: **Sure. That one is getting worn out.**

Erickson: How long will it take to wear it out?

Subject: I don't know.

Erickson: Do you think you'll ever want to go swimming?

Subject: I want to right now.

Erickson: **Do you think you ever will?**

Subject: I hope so.

Erickson: **Do you think you ever will?**

Subject: You're just like the teachers. You got to answer yes or no. Yes.

Erickson: It's pretty cold to go swimming right now, isn't it?

Subject: Couldn't it wait until next summer?

Erickson: It could possibly happen next summer. But we don't know, do we? Is there anything else that's troubling you? Is there anything else that troubles you?

Subject: Maybe you'll think I'm awful.

Erickson: No, I'm very sure I do not.

Rossi: What's all this dialogue about *excuses*?

Erickson: "Getting tired of that excuse? Want a better one?" [*The subject responds*] "Sure. That one is getting worn out." You let excuses get worn out! You let habits wear out.

Rossi: In other words, people naturally outgrow their limitations and you're simply facilitating that naturalistic method of psychological growth?

Erickson: Uh-hum.

Rossi: She says she doesn't know how long it will take to wear out her excuse for not swimming. This type of response is very typical of the way we naturally give up old limitations and bad habits: they are replaced by new abilities that have been synthesized on an unconscious level in such a way that we are usually surprised to find ourselves doing better. In fact, we usually don't know why we are doing better. This *not knowing* is often the signature of unconscious work.

Erickson: Notice the resentment in: "You're just like the teachers. You got to answer yes or no." But she does answer yes!

Rossi: What are you doing with that?

Erickson: [Erickson reads the dialogue out loud, building up to the subject's final yes when she says, You got to answer yes or no. Yes."]

Rossi: That's why you ask twice, "Do you think you ever will?" To get that "Yes"?

Erickson: Yes!

Rossi: You have an almost fanatical insistence that the subject really say yes when you ask an important question. You require a clear commitment, is that it?

Erickson: She gave the yes reluctantly here: that's what teachers always do when they make you say yes or no. Then I say, "**It's pretty cold to go swimming right now, isn't it?**" So I'm taking over her negative attitude and intensifying it. What she doesn't notice is that I'm implying that *she can swim when it's warm!*

Rossi: She obviously gets that implication when she answers with, "**Couldn't it wait till next summer?**" You displaced her negativity and thereby polarized her into the opposite yes response tendency that she could go swimming later.

Erickson: That's right.

Rossi: You discharged and displaced her negativity so that it became possible for her to take a step in a therapeutic direction!

Erickson: She asks, "**Couldn't it wait until next summer?**", and I'm happy that "**It could possibly happen next summer. But we don't know, do we?**"

Rossi: You are again using implication when you add, "**But we don't know, do we?**" The implication is that her unconscious does know. Implication is the vehicle for that important indirect suggestion.

Erickson: When she ends by saying, "**Maybe you'll think I'm awful,**" I think she may be displacing onto herself the awful feeling when you have to answer yes or no to teachers.

Rossi: So you have to reassure her by directly answering, "**No, I'm very sure I do not.**" Again you say the no and hopefully displace it away from her.

[In 1987] Once again we may be witnessing how Erickson communicates on two levels simultaneously: on a purely cognitive level he is giving the subject positive reassurance with the words, "No, I'm very sure I do not." At the same time on a more primitive-literal level he is "taking over" the no so that her system does not have to "carry" it. Addressing this more primitive-literal-unconscious-concrete level appears to be a peculiarly unique feature of some forms of Erickson's two-level therapeutic communications.

1.43 *Trance Writing Versus Automatic Writing; The Best Set; Therapeutic Analogies to Deal with Emergent Sexual Concerns; Depotentiating and Reframing Transference on a Literal-Concrete Level: Speculations on the Many Meanings of "Nice"; Learned Limitations and Denial; Two-Level Communication*

Erickson: It's awfully convenient, isn't it, to have this pad here? Suppose you write whatever it is that you think might make me think you are awful—right there. Hold it, of course, so you can read it yourself. And make up your mind if it is all right for me to know. I think it would be very important for you to learn that, too, before you tell me anything. Do you think that's a good idea? Suppose you just write it. Hold it so I can't read it. Suppose you do a lot of fast thinking to see if you want me to read that.

Subject: [*Subject writes the material seen in Figure 1 and frowns.*] I guess you can read it.

Erickson: I can read it. But can you want me to read it?

Subject: I guess you may.

Erickson: I may read it. But would you like to have me read it?

Subject: I think so.

Erickson: Just keep on doing a little thinking, until you're real sure. Because I rather believe you want me to and at the same time you wish I wouldn't. Is that right? So let's do it the best way so that you can either not let me read it at all, or you can decide I may read it and that you really hope that I will read it.

Subject: I think you better read it.

Erickson: You think I better read it. All right. Now, your reason for

I wonder about so many things that no one wants to talk about things like dates, boys, sex, religion, why some things are right and then wrong, and why people don't want to talk about things they all want to talk about

Sex

Figure 1. The subject's first trance writing during the sixth visit of the February Man, when she writes the forbidden word "sex." "I wonder about so many things that no one wants to talk about. Things like dates, boys, sex, religion. Why some things are right and others wrong and why people don't want to talk about things they all want to talk about."

	saying that is that you expect me really to understand it and really to help you to understand better.
Subject:	Yes.
Erickson:	All right. Shall I take it now?
Subject:	Yes.
Erickson:	I haven't looked at it yet. Are you worried?
Subject:	No.
Erickson:	Is there anything bad about that?
Subject:	No.
Erickson:	Have you got any special worries about any of it?
Subject:	Forbidden word.
Erickson:	Would you like to write that forbidden word?
Subject:	[Subject writes the word sex below her paragraph in Figure 1.]
Erickson:	But that isn't a forbidden thing, is it? It's an awfully important thing, isn't it? And it's a very necessary thing,

isn't it? And it's something about which you are going to learn. Don't you hope so? And I hope you learn the easiest way. What do you suppose I mean by the easiest way?

Subject: By what people tell us?

Erickson: By the easiest way I mean the way in which the fewest mistakes are made. Because it's like a little baby learning to walk. When he first learns to walk, he picks up his right foot and moves it one step ahead. And then after that he has had the experience of moving his right foot, so he moves the right foot again and takes another step ahead. He doesn't learn to walk all at once, by putting one foot up and then the other, so he learns to walk this way and then he tumbles. But the baby has to learn to do it, one foot after another. They make mistakes in learning to walk, and they learn how with the fewest possible tumbles and without trying to hurry too much. Now you are going to learn about all of these things. But there's something I want to say to you right now to remember, and that is this: I can't tell you about these things too much right now. But there will come a time when you are older when I will be able to tell you the answers to all of these questions, but that means you will have to wait for the answers. I can't explain to you now why you will have to wait, but you will have to wait. And even though you have to wait, there's one thing you can really do that will help you a great deal. Remember all of the questions you have right now, so that sometime in the future when I see you again and answer these questions, you will remember all of them. You will remember all of them, and you will ask them of me without any hesitation, any uncertainty, any worry or concern. You have known me quite a long time now and you are going to realize that in all this time I have known you, I have helped you. Isn't that right?

Subject: Yes.

Erickson: And a little bit of help here and a little bit of help there counts up, doesn't it?

Subject: Yes.

Erickson: Do you mind if I put this sheet in my pocket now?
Subject: No.
Erickson: And keep it until some time, maybe years from now, I can take it out and show it to you?
Subject: Yes.
Erickson: Is there everything there?
Subject: I think so.
Erickson: **How do you think you will like me three or four years from now?**
Subject: **It will be nice.**
Erickson: **I think it will be nice to meet you then. Why do you suppose I came here this October?**
Subject: School? Maybe you wanted to know what I thought of it.
Erickson: What do you think of it?
Subject: It's all right.
Erickson: **What do you think you will be when you grow up?**
Subject: Oh, something awfully complicated. **I hate school teaching.** All those foolish women running around. I would like to be a secretary, only I don't want to sit at a typewriter all day.
Erickson: But you are beginning to think about it, aren't you?
Subject: I'm going to take all the hard subjects.
Erickson: Are you going to take swimming?
Subject: We don't have swimming.
Erickson: When shall I see you again?
Subject: **I'm not going to make a date with you** for a couple of years. When do you want to come back?
Erickson: Whenever you think I may be helpful or useful.
Subject: I'll be a junior in two years. Maybe you should come then.
Erickson: All right. Isn't it nice to meet once in a while? And it will really happen, too, won't it?
Subject: Always does.
Erickson: It always does.

Rossi: In this lengthy multilevel interaction you help the subject express her emergent adolescent concerns about dates, boys, sex, and religion through the trance writing.

I'll call it *trance writing* because she's writing it in trance and it is expressive of her concerns in her age-regressed condition. But it does not appear to have the typically dissociated character of *automatic writing.*

Erickson: Yes. In automatic writing subjects don't know what was written. In trance writing they know what's written on a cognitive level, but are not able to deal with it emotionally yet.*

Rossi: The word *sex* that was written a short time after the main paragraph, however, does have more of the disso- ciation characteristic of automatic writing. You accord this trance writing the same respect as you give to regular automatic writing, however. You carefully ask her permission to read it, and you respect her wishes in this regard. There is no "rape" of the unconscious here; you always permit material to emerge at a rate and manner acceptable by the patient's state-of-being. In this age- regressed state of emerging adolescence, you allow the subject to write the word *sex* instead of making her talk about it in a bold and blatant fashion. She still doesn't feel ready to deal with the swimming issue, so you don't pursue it.

Erickson: I ask her here about how certain she is that she wants me to read her trance writing: "**I may read it. But would you like to have me read it?**" It's purely her choice.

Rossi: Why are you giving her all those choices in such an elaborately puzzling way in the paragraph that begins with, "**Just keep on doing a little thinking,**" and ends with, "**... you really hope that I will read it.**" Is that a yes set?

Erickson: Not a yes set—a *best* set: "**So let's do it the best way...**" Merely giving permission that I read it and having the *hope* that I will read it are two very different things.

---

*See Section 4 in Volume III of Erickson, 1980, "Automatic Writing and Drawing" (pp. 143-187).

Rossi: So you are moving her from *reluctantly* giving you permission to read it to the *expectant hoping* that you will read it. You're making it a positive thing on her part. So she finally says, "**I think you better read it.**"

Erickson: A positive thing on her part!

Rossi: A person doing something with reluctance is really not doing it.

Erickson: They are *not* doing it. . . . In the trance writing she is allowed to express her unconscious mind and her emerging adolescent feelings at the same time.

Rossi: Yes, that's right.

Erickson: And my hesitation in reading it literally compels her attention to the emotional aspect, so it alters the writing! [*See Figure* 1 *where the word* sex *is written with a style different from the rest of the writing.*]

Rossi: I see. You make it more emotionally loaded when you treat it with such respect.

Erickson: *Sex* is a bad word.

Rossi: Yes, that was her problem.

Erickson: It's a learning problem. I put together *sex* and *walking*—a therapeutic analogy.

Rossi: You use learning to walk step-by-step as a therapeutic analogy for learning about sex step-by-step.

Erickson: Um-hum. She knows about walking, and sex can be learned like walking—by making the fewest possible mistakes. I'm laying the foundation for her future life attitudes. [*Erickson now tells an anecdote of how little Johnnie asked a little girl to take down her panties in a hidden place in the yard and then exclaimed, "So that's how Catholics are different from Protestants!"*]

Rossi: It's funny, you're working on so many levels at once here!

Erickson: And you're working on the levels that occur naturally. And you grow up. [*Erickson now tells a poignant story of how one of his daughters, feeling she had grown too old for an imaginary playmate, regretfully disposed of it.] . . . .* Then when I change my identity to October. . . I'm facing a different situation. October is older than February. It's increased my age. I'm becoming more her *confidant.*

Rossi: Your respectful attitude toward her trance writing is not only an ethical approach; it's also an indirect suggestion for her to be deeply involved with it in an emotional manner to facilitate the therapeutic process.

Erickson: And I increase my age from February to October to emphasize that. I'm getting older, which implies *she* is getting older. I'm confirming her growing up. I ask, **"What do you think you will be when you grow up?"**, and she responds with, **"I hate school teaching."** Our attitudes toward school change with every state. After grammar school some are too afraid to go on and so they drop out; at the end of high school some are too afraid of college and so they drop out; at the end of college some are too afraid of graduate school and so another bunch drops out.

Rossi: These dropouts are all victims of learned limitations.

Erickson: When I ask, **"How do you think you will like me three or four years from now?"**, I've got good rapport with her. She answers with, **"It will be** *nice.***"** I come back with, **"I think it will be nice to meet you then."** I've depotentiated a little girlish crush.

Rossi: I see. I had no idea you were working on the transference at this point.

Erickson: **"Why do you suppose I came here this October?"**—to downplay my February Man identity.

Rossi: To diminish the transference?

Erickson: Um-hum.

Rossi: You do these things in such a literal-concrete way!

Erickson: And so very easily!

Rossi: [In 1987] Although I agreed with Erickson at the time, I am now uncertain about the actual dynamics he believed he was using to depotentiate the subject's transference at this point. I can speculate as follows:

The word *nice* has many levels of meaning depending upon the way it is said, to whom it is said, and the different levels of context in which it is said. Apparently Erickson felt the subject's response, "**It will be nice**," was said with either a connotation of a girlish crush, or with a note of ambiguity in her intonation of the word and her accompanying facial and body gestures that suggested the possibility of a sexual transference. We can suppose that there were many competing parts of her developing personality that were all striving for expression in this ambiguous situation: she is in part a little girl thankful for the security and support of a fatherly February Man, and at the same time she is a developing adolescent with sexual impulses that are seeking an uncertain expression. In all probability her conscious mind would not be aware of these different parts contending within her and expressed in the way she used the word nice. Erickson was aware of these ambiguities, however, and protected her with the response, **I think it will be** *nice* **to meet you then**." The vocal and gestural connotations that accompanied his response thus resolved, reinterpreted or reframed her *ambiguous nice* into a definitely *nonsexual nice*. To reinforce that nonsexual connotation, he then further depotentiated the transference by threatening to change his February man identity by coming in October. In spite of this she later gives another two-level response when she says, "**I'm not going to make a** *date* **with you**. *Date,* of course, has romantic connotations which her more conscious response level denies by saying, "**I'm** *not* **going to make a date with you**."

If these speculations have any plausibility, they again illustrate the tremendous subtlety and skill with which Erickson received communications on many levels and responded to them on corresponding levels.

1.44   Seventh "Visit" of the February Man: Trance Writing
        and Speculations about Multiple Levels of Meaning in a Parapraxis;
        A Phobic Symptom of a Lifestyle; Reinforcing a New Perspective

Erickson: [Administers his usual handshake cue.]
Subject: Hi.
Erickson: How are you?
Subject: Fine. How are you?
Erickson: I'm fine.
Subject: You said you'd come back.
Erickson: I said so, and I did. What month is it?
Subject: October.
Erickson: Train schedules again. What do you suppose ran that
             train?
Subject: I don't know.
Erickson: I have a special name for that train. And I hope it was
             well loaded. What's going on?
Subject: Oh—parties, studies—just everything.
Erickson: How are the hard subjects?
Subject: They don't give us any hard ones.
Erickson: Do you like school work? When you look back over your
             hard freshman days, what do you think now?
Subject: I don't study now.
Erickson: What kind of grades do you get?
Subject: I have been on the honor roll all the time.
Erickson: Let's see. By the way, do you remember my last visit?
Subject: Yes.
Erickson: [Taking paper from pocket] Could you guess what's on that?
Subject: Sure. I know what's on it.
Erickson: Suppose you write what's on that paper, and hold it up
             so I don't see it. And let's see if you have changed at all
             since those freshmen days. [Erickson calls attention to cata-
             lepsy of her left foot.] All set?
Subject: All set. [Subject writes the upper paragraph in Figure 2.]
Erickson: Is that the way you remember the page you wrote before?
Subject: No, but I remember it, though.

*I wonder about quite a
few things yet. World affairs,
the future, marriage, & how
to get the most out of life
without too much pain &
at the same time giving
for a reason.*

*I wonder about so many things
boys, dates, sex, religion, why
some things are right & others
wrong & why people don't
want to talk about the things
they want to talk about.*

Figure 2. Trance writing from the seventh "visit" of the February Man. The first (upper) paragraph reads: "I wonder about quite a few things yet. World affairs, the future, marriage, & how to get the most out of life without too much pain & at the same time living (diving, giving) for a reason." Notice the "error" in the fourth word from the end, in which the subject has combined the words living, diving, and giving.

The second paragraph reads: "I wonder about so many things boys, dates, sex, religion, why some things are right & others wrong, & why people don't want to talk about the things they want to talk about."

Erickson: Is there anything omitted?
Subject: Yes.
Erickson: What is it?
Subject: Boys and dates and sex.
Erickson: [*Pointing to her writing in the upper paragraph of Figure 2*] That's a very charming thing, isn't it? How would you read it now—just as it looks there? Just as anybody who didn't know it was a mistake might read it? How do you think they would read it?
Subject: "**Living, giving, diving.**"
Erickson: What do you think about that mistake? That makes it read **diving**.
Subject: I can't see anyone diving for that reason.
Erickson: Do you suppose you are going to sometime dive for a reason?
Subject: Probably just to prove to myself I'm not scared.
Erickson: Anyway, you remember what's on this sheet [*holding up Figure 1, but in a way that she cannot read it*]. Write it, as best you can remember it—whatever is on this sheet. [*The subject writes the lower paragraph in Figure 2.*] May I take that?
Subject: Yes.
Erickson: How do you feel about this paragraph now? Do you feel as concerned over these feelings as you did when you were a freshman?
Subject: **They were kind of childish.**
Erickson: **You feel a lot more grown up.** Do you think I could actually explain a lot of those things to your benefit and satisfaction?
Subject: You probably could.
Erickson: Sometime later I will explain them.
Subject: By that time I'll know all the answers.
Erickson: You will?
Subject: I think so.

Rossi: Her trance writing in the fourth word from the last in the upper paragraph of Figure 2 illustrates an interesting parapraxis where the words *living, giving,* and *div-*

ing are all combined. At this point we could read into it as follows: *diving* (coping successfully with her swimming/ water phobia) is related to *living* a full life, involving an appropriate balance of getting and *giving*. Would you agree?

Erickson: You dive into life; you take a fling.

Rossi: So her water phobia has something to do with her manner of participating in life?

Erickson: Um-hum.

Rossi: Her water phobia is a kind of metaphor for her withdrawal from life. So dealing with one symptom can have ramifications for a person's whole existential state of being.

Erickson: You take a plunge; you dive into the business of life; you dive into marriage. I think this should be understood as a question. One can only speculate: diving can be equated with plunging, and that equated with the folk language of plunging into work and plunging into marriage. But this is only speculation.

   She is also getting a new perspective when she says, **"They were kind of childish."**

Rossi: And you reinforce that by saying, **"You feel a lot more grown up."**

1.45   *Therapeutic Analogies and Reframing: Exercises with Multiple Meanings of Words; Words as Symbols, Metaphors, and "Bricks in the Therapeutic Tower of Babel"*

Erickson: How many times can you pick up your feet and put them down in the water?

Subject: Not very many times.

Erickson: You won't take a step forward without lifting your feet first, will you? But we must not forget the word *diving*.

Subject: **What would I be doing diving?**

Erickson: What about swimming?

Subject: What about it?

Erickson: How do you feel about swimming?
Subject: **It's all right.**
Erickson: Do you enjoy it?
Subject: **I can't swim. I'm not that brave.**
Erickson: Do you think you ever will?
Subject: Maybe, someday.

Rossi: Therapeutic analogies and reframing appear to be two basic approaches you use in this case.

Erickson: Yeah.

Rossi: Back in 1945, did you think of these two approaches as definite therapeutic techniques, or were you just doing what you were doing without labeling it?

Erickson: I was labeling. That first sentence [of this section] says, "*Wading in the sea of matrimony.*"

Rossi: Where [how] do you get that?

Erickson: "**How many times can you pick up your feet and put them down in water?**" *Water* is a symbolic word there. You come down the "mountain of life" to the "sea of matrimony."

Rossi: But how do you get matrimony in here? She hasn't been talking about marriage!

Erickson: No, but she is talking about diving. When you examine words—the word *run* has a hundred meanings—I think 140 meanings, or more.

Rossi: So when a person hears the word *run*, he can go into any one of 140 associative directions.

Erickson: That's right!

Rossi: And you utilize that to tap into all kinds of associative areas—problem areas.

Erickson: You see, the first book I ever really read was the unabridged dictionary.* That made me tremendously aware of the meaningfulness of words.

---

*See "Autohypnotic Experiences of Milton H. Erickson," in Erickson & Rossi, 1977/1980.

Rossi: The multiple meanings of words.

Erickson: I once went over with a Russian psychologist over 100 words meaning *intoxicated*.

Rossi: So you've done this as an exercise for yourself, which probably has enhanced your own flexibility in the use of words and in making contact with different associative areas in your patients. Do you recommend this as an exercise for all of us to increase our verbal facility?

Erickson: [*Erickson describes "A Word Book Preparation" that is the theme of two doctoral dissertations he is apparently a consultant on.*]

Rossi: So her doctoral dissertation is on the multiple meanings of words?

Erickson: [*Erickson discusses how his son Robert, a grade school teacher and a dictionary buff, is helping with the doctoral dissertation by illustrating how he is teaching children about the multiple meanings of words.*] I think she's attaching multiple meanings here; that of "getting her feet wet."

Rossi: What do you see as the clue to multiple meanings?

Erickson: [When she says,] "**It's all right,**" "**I can't swim,**" and "**What would I be doing diving?**"

Rossi: You mean *diving* has more than one meaning?

Erickson: In her very answer!

Rossi: What do you mean, "In her very answer?"

Erickson: [When she says,] "What would I be doing diving?"

Rossi: How do you explain that?

Erickson: Taken simply, what you do when you dive is plunge into water. But she asks what would she be doing diving? She must have a different kind of [meaning] in mind [than literally plunging into water].

Rossi: Ok, but that's *your inference* from the way she frames the question!

[In 1987] My rather sharp and disbelieving final response to Erickson's explanation in this section reflects my inability to fully comprehend—much less accept—

what he is proposing. His inferences about the use of the symbolic and metaphorical meanings of words here struck me as utterly fantastic stretches of his imagination. In the last section he sensibly labeled my interpretations of the parapraxis *diving-living-giving* as speculative. Yet in this section he seemed, to my understanding, to be going off the deep end in his inferences about the multiple significances of the subject's question, "**What would I be doing diving?**" In my view, the subject's question was a fairly straight-forward reflection on her long-established swimming/water phobia: if she were afraid to even get in the water, what indeed would she be doing *diving*!

Such is the "Tower of Babel" we are in. The multiple meanings of words lead each person to draw different levels of confidence about the inferences, implications, frames of reference and belief systems he or she creates as a function of his or her particular life experience with these words. Thus one person's reasonable inference can be ludicrous to another. This is the basic problem in all efforts at creating consensual belief systems as well as consensual psychotherapeutic approaches.

1.46 *Reframing, Implication, and Therapeutic Analogies Bonding and Depotentiating Psychological Trauma with Love; Indirect Resolution of Psychological Trauma; Depotentiating Fears by Associations with Strong Abilities: Not Knowing and Unconscious Learning*

Erickson: Tell me, how would you like to learn how to swim?

Subject: Well, I think the best way would be to get an instructor. But Linda learned just by being pushed off a raft. That's a good way.

Erickson: I remember every year a boy I knew named Jason used to go down to the swimming hole by the dam and sit down on the pier. He would be down there every day and he would say, "Just as sure as God made little green apples, I'm going to learn to swim this summer. Just as sure as God made little green apples! Yes, I'm going to learn to swim this summer!" He hasn't learned to swim yet. What do you think should be done for him?

Subject: I suppose you could push him in. But that would scare him. Somebody should have helped him.

Erickson: How should they have helped him?

Subject: They should have told him that the water was nice, and he shouldn't be afraid of it, and that it was fun to swim.

Erickson: Just telling him not to be afraid wouldn't help him, would it?

Subject: No.

Erickson: Now I can tell you another story about a woman. This woman was very, very afraid of water, and she wanted to learn to swim very, very much. And yet she got so scared every time she went near the water that she couldn't go in water over her ankles. Then one day her sister went out in the water. The sister could swim, but she got a cramp, and the very scared sister on the shore saw her sister about to be drowned. And she was so scared about her sister that she forgot how scared she was about water, and she rushed out and dog-paddled and half-waded in the deep water and got her sister and brought her back. And then after that she learned to swim. What happened to her?

Subject: I guess she forgot about being scared. She had to do something important.

Erickson: She had two fears. One was a very, very bad scare, and the other was a disabling fear. But the very bad scare took her mind off the disabling fear, didn't it? A very unpleasant way to learn how to swim, wasn't it? But a very nice way at the same time. Awfully unpleasant, but awfully good. Wouldn't you have a lot of respect for that woman—a lot of liking and admiration for her? One other thing I would like to have you understand. **That disabling fear of hers that kept her from walking in the water was really a way of measuring her strength.** Isn't that right?

Subject: Yes.

Erickson: And it showed her that no matter how terrible was her fear, that she possessed so much more strength than fear that she could actually meet it and overcome it in the right situation. And of course that disabling fear of hers could be utilized in another way and in a helpful way. Remembering how afraid she was and realizing that she had actually gone out in deep water successfully when she didn't know how to swim made her understand **she could take that fear and transform it into confidence.** And that's what she did. **I wonder what you will do with your fear of water?** One can, under strong stimulation and emergency, do unexpected things. Sometimes one can do these things in an unexpected situation that calls for only pleasant feelings. **One can do something out of a sense of love,** a sense of appreciation of one's self. Just as some babies learn to walk all at once, because they suddenly discover, "Well, why worry about it? I have to take so many falls and so many bumps." And they go ahead and walk. **You don't know how you are going to learn to swim. But wouldn't it be a delightful feeling sometime to be able to swim?**

Subject: Yes.

Erickson: **Now I wonder if what I have said to you has helped you in any way?**

Subject: I think so.

Erickson: **We will have to wait and see, because I'm going to be around again.** When shall I see you again—do you know? I'll be around again. Have you anything more to say before I leave? **This is the February Man signing off for a while.**

Erickson: [*Erickson points to the word* instructor *in the subject's first sentence of this section:* "**I think the best way would be to get an instructor.**"]

Rossi: She wants an instructor to learn how to swim. What do you see in that now? What implications does that have for you?

Erickson: Well, she wants to get another person in her swimming.

Rossi: So the word has a sexual connotation you say? And further, someone who could teach her?

Erickson: [*Nods tentatively and examines the transcript very carefully with total concentration.*] The word *love* in there . . .

Rossi: You brought in the word, what . . . ?

Erickson: *Love!* And I depotentiated her fear in relationship to Helen [*referring to her sister Helen's near drowning*].

Rossi: How did you do that?

Erickson: I pay close attention in the situation after I said, **"I wonder what you will do with your fear of water?"**.

Rossi: It's like a therapeutic analogy?

Erickson: Uh-hum.

Rossi: And you brought in the association for love in case she would want to bring that up again.

Erickson: **"Now I wonder if what I have said to you has helped you in any way?"** *I'm bonding Helen and love.* Now that's a passing thing—you tend to overlook it!

Rossi: Right, there are inner connections in her mind that will bring it up to response strength.

[*In 1987*] Erickson is emphasizing how it is easy to overlook his strategy in this section wherein he reinterprets the subject's psychological trauma of her younger sister's near drowning and then bonds it to a more adaptive resolution of the incident. He achieves this in an indirect manner by associating a similar traumatic situation with the qualities of confidence (**"she could take her fear and transform it into confidence"**) and love (**"One can do something out of a sense of love"**).

Erickson: When she says, **"I think so,"** I say, **"We will have to wait and see . . ."**

Rossi: You're implying that those associations of confidence and love will continue developing?

Erickson: Yeah, **"because I'm going to be around again."**

Rossi: In summary of this section: You give the subject a

series of therapeutic analogies depicting some of the possible ways people learn how to swim. You initiate some interesting reframing when you point out, **"That disabling fear of hers that kept her from walking in the water was really a way of measuring her strength."**

Erickson: And reinterpreting that tragic incident with Helen.

Rossi: You later use *not knowing* coupled with a positive suggestion when you add: **"You don't know how you are going to learn to swim. But wouldn't it be a delightful feeling sometime to be able to swim?"** You are thereby giving primacy to unconscious learning which the conscious mind can also enjoy. Is that right?

Erickson: Yes, and I think you ought to mention that in reference to *love*.

Rossi: Right, and you bring in that reference to *love* to pick up any other associations with *diving, sexuality,* and *love*.

Erickson: Yes.

Rossi: Fantastic! You're probing—that's your way of exploring and facilitating indirect, therapeutic resolutions of psychological traumas.

Erickson: Yes, and now her fear of **"walking in the water was really a way of measuring her strength."** She knew she could walk and the strength of that ability is associated with her fear of water.

Rossi: So you depotentiate her fear of water by diluting it with her strength and ability to walk.

1.47 *Subtle Reorientation to Apparent Awakening with Amnesia for Trance Work; Psychotic Insight and the Multiple Meanings of Words: Slang and Sexual Associations*

Subject: [*Now apparently awake*] **Why doesn't somebody say something?** *Gott in Himmel!* Where have I been? **Dead silence!**

Erickson: **Not dead.**

Subject: Well, silence anyway. I'm definitely getting the once over —**once over lightly.**

Erickson: **Won't you have a cigarette?**

Subject: Thank you. **All right, you fellows, what have I been doing?** What have I been doing for all this time? **You all look so self-satisfied and happy—every one of you!**
Fink: You don't look particularly unhappy.
Subject: I'm not particularly unhappy. Why the smirk?
Erickson: Do you think you could be hypnotized?
Subject: I don't know.
Erickson: Do you think you would like to be?
Subject: **Not right now.**

Rossi: She is subtly reoriented to a state of being apparently awake with your last remark (in the last section), "**This is the February Man signing off for a while.**" You did not tell her to awaken, so she still could be in a somnambulistic state, but she now includes everyone present in the room within her attention when she says, "**Why doesn't somebody say something. . . . Dead silence!**"

Erickson: I respond with, "**Not dead.**"

Rossi: She has an obvious amnesia for the trance work you have been doing when she says, "**All right, you fellows, what have I been doing?**"*

Erickson: How do you react to that?

Rossi: Well, she has an amnesia for her trance work. What else do you make of it?

Erickson: She's been somewhere "**not dead.**" She's really been living it up!

Rossi: Again a sexual implication via a two-level communication?

Erickson: [She says,] "**once over lightly.**"

Rossi: Definitely a sexual association there? Without her realizing it?

Erickson: Uh-hum. "**Once over lightly**" . . . Where was

---

*For the theory and further examples of this use of hypnotic amnesia, see Section I in Part II of Volume III of Erickson, 1980 (pp. 35-90), particularly the paper, "Varieties of Hypnotic Amnesia" (pp. 71-90).

that used commonly back in those days [1945]? You go to a barber and say, "**Once over lightly.**"

Rossi: That implies a preparation for going out on a date?

Erickson: When you go on a date you go "**once over lightly.**" That was the slang of that day.

Rossi: In fixing her makeup, a woman could say she's going "**once over lightly.**" In the last section you introduced the word *love*, and in this section she's responding to some of the implications of that word, perhaps unconsciously. Would you say that?

Erickson: Yes.

Rossi: So this is multiple levels of communication we are getting into here again.

Erickson: And she's offering it, too. "**Once over lightly**" was used by women when they fixed up their makeup. [The phrase] "freshen up" came later.

Rossi: So we really have to keep abreast of the slang of our day, don't we?

Erickson: And my question was, "**Won't you have a cigarette?**"

Rossi: "What are you doing with that?"

Erickson: A round phallic-oral pleasure.

Rossi: Did you have these associations in mind back then when you said that?

Erickson: Oh, yes!

Rossi: This wasn't just casual conversation?

Erickson: [*Shakes head no.*]

Rossi: Nothing is casual conversation!

Erickson: Cigarettes were so handy, and I smoked back then. In 1938 I used cigarettes extensively for research.*

Rossi: I'd like to ask you a question about one of my patients who went through a mild psychotic episode for

---

*See Section 5, "Mental Mechanisms," in Part II of Volume III of Erickson, 1980 (pp. 188-228).

about a week. She thought she was the greatest sinner in the world, and what not. During this time she was a bit paranoid, and she said than I was doing a lot of things to her; that there were a lot of implications in my remarks; that I was not being entirely straight with her; and that I was being underhanded in the way I was suggesting things. Now on a conscious level I was not implying anything. Do you think that during this period of psychotic sensitivity she picked up more multiple levels of meaning than I realized I was using? Is that what we mean by "psychotic insight"?

Erickson: Yes.

Rossi: So psychotic patients are not entirely crazy—they're hypersensitive to the multiple levels of meaning in words. We should really respect that and learn from it.

Erickson: Yes. To quote from actual memory: A very disturbed patient said, "I was very underhanded—I gave my sister a cigarette." His history was that he had [sexual] intercourse with his sister. His case history showed that.

Rossi: In his psychotic ideation he transformed the intercourse into, "I was very underhanded—I gave my sister a cigarette." This certainly bears out the Freudian theory of phallic objects and their sexual associations.

Erickson: Yes, but it was "poetic theory" long before Freud. You set down a lot of those disjointed remarks of psychotic patients and go through them and select out the folklore, the folk language; and you often get a very nice picture of what they really mean.

[Then the subject says,] **"All right, you fellows, what have I been doing?"**

Rossi: A sexual connotation in that, huh? And she adds, **"You all look so self-satisfied and happy—every one of you!"**

Erickson: When she says, **"Not right now,"** she means *yes*.

> *Rossi:* It implies there will be a yes later. All her responses in this section strongly suggest she has a complete amnesia for her trance experience in this session.

1.48 Sexual Slang and the Obscene: A Dynamic Theory of Their Psychosocial Evolution and Function

Erickson: Miss Dey looks rather sleepy.

Miss Dey: I have worked rather hard today.

Subject: [*Reaching for pad*] There's something under here I've got to see. You know there is. You told me not to let you forget about it.

Erickson: What do you suppose is there?

Subject: I don't know. I wrote something. I must say my writing has definitely gone to the dogs. [*Turns paper*] Wow! You see what I mean when I say my writing doesn't mean anything. It looks like 75 different forms of January!

Erickson: It doesn't mean a thing, does it?

Subject: I wrote it in a very sketchy manner.

Erickson: Would it be fun to find out how you wrote it, just a little bit at a time, so that you would enjoy finding out? Perhaps you would like to have the pad and pencil, and see if you can discover just how you did that writing.

Subject: No wonder they complain about my charting. This looks like the stuff I do when I'm about ready to go to sleep in the morning. **I must have written it with my left hand.**

Erickson: **Which one?**

Subject: I don't know. They are all such a mess.

Erickson: Can you write with your left hand?

Subject: I have tried it a couple of times, but it was such a mess. This one must have been written with my left hand.

Erickson: Is that all you can tell me?

Subject: **I sure got humps on the r's.** That's all I got to say.

> *Erickson:* [She says,] "**I must have written it with my left hand,**" [and I ask,] "**Which one?**"

Rossi: What do you mean by that question?

Erickson: There is a left hand in the waking state, and a left hand in the trance states.

Rossi: She would write different things in the waking and trance states.

Erickson: [*Erickson notes another use of sexual slang in the word* humps *when the subject says,* "I sure got humps on the r's."] I know it was used that way [back in the 1940s].

Rossi: You mean people actually put more humps on their r's for the sexual connotation of it?!

Erickson: Um-hum

Rossi: That's very hard to believe!

Erickson: Slang changes so much!

Rossi: The word *humps* is out of fashion today—and is really considered kind of "gross."

Erickson: Oh yes! [*Erickson now playfully mentions a few other old-fashioned slang terms for sexual intercourse.*]

Rossi: As soon as a slang term for sex gets too popularized, it becomes too gross. Then people have to invent a new slang term that has fewer associations to sex so that it is more titillating.

Rossi: [*In 1987*] This suggests the basis of an interesting new theory of the function of slang. *Slang terms* are ever-new linguistic inventions that give fresh expression to impulses in a manner that frees them from the inhibiting weight of past unfortunate associations. *Obscene terms*, on the other hand, are an aggressive attack on the listener's associative structure: obscene terms disrupt and break down the listener's attitudes and world view so that the speaker can impose his own. Slang actually begins as a delicate creative effort to express new or socially suppressed impulses. Once the slang term becomes popularized, however, it becomes so loaded with the negative associations society attaches to the referent impulse that the term becomes gross—or obscene.

As an obscenity the term is then used socially for a period of time in an entirely different function: it serves as a club to attack and break down the listener's psychological defenses. As the obscenity ages and in turn becomes too popularized, most people build up adequate defenses against it. The obscenity now loses its disruptive potency, tends to become less used, and eventually dies a natural linguistic death by becoming archaic.

This could be considered a new dynamic *psychosocial* theory of the evolution and function of slang and obscenity. It is *psychological* insofar as it deals with the intrapersonal associative structure within an individual; it is *social* insofar as it deals with the dynamics by which emotionally charged impulses are transmitted from one person or group to another. The evolution of slang and the obscene as presented here could have implications for a more general theory of the evolution of new linguistic forms, their functions, transformations, and eventual demise. Language is not a static communication tool, as some would like to believe. Rather, *linguistic invention is a manifestation of the evolution of consciousness and its struggle to perpetually free itself from the limitations and constraints of past usage.*

1.49   *Further Sexual Associations Predictive of Future Behavior; Covert Hypnotic Induction via Object Placement and Associated Slang*

Erickson: I would like to suggest that you point out the one written with your left hand, and that you know it was written with your left hand.

Subject: I think that one, but I wouldn't swear to it. Is it that one?

Erickson: I would like to have you point to one, and to tell me and be absolutely correct. And as soon as you have done so, you will suddenly realize—you won't know how to prove it—something else.

Subject: [*Holding cigarette in left hand*] Does that go under file X?

Erickson: X marks the unknown.

Subject: I got it.

Erickson: Got what?

Subject: The unknown.
Erickson: Do you like that pencil?
Subject: [*After changing pencils*] This is a fairly good pencil. I'll stick
with it.

Erickson: [*Holding cigarette in left hand*] "Does that go under
file X?"

Rossi: Both the cigarette and the X have sexual associations?

Erickson: X for kiss.

Rossi: So all these sexual associations were not talked
about consciously during the therapy. Did you do any
follow-up on this?

Erickson: I do know she had an affair after this.
"X marks the unknown."
"I got it."
"Got what?"
"The unknown."
Now I ask, "Do you like that pencil?" Then after chang-
ing pencils [she answers,] "This is a fairly good pencil."

Rossi: So you ask that question about liking the pencil to
focus the sexual connotation?

Erickson: I used that for induction....It's a covert use....

Rossi: [In 1987] In this and other conversations with Rossi,
Erickson described how he would use slang associated
with certain position-placements of a cigarette or pencil
to induce hypnosis and at the same time evoke particular associative pathways within the subject.*

1.50 *Writing Forwards and Backwards: Word Association Research
Methods for the Right and Left Hemisphere; Evoking Learning Sets
as the Essence of Erickson's Indirect Approach*

Erickson: Why don't you pick up the other one?
Subject: I would look silly with two pencils. They would be calling

---

* See Section 5, "Mental Mechanisms," in Part II of Volume III of Erickson, 1980.

out the men with the little white jackets. [Holds *both pencils*] I think I wrote them both at the same time.

Erickson: How do you know?

Subject: I don't know. That's impossible. It can't be done!

Fink: It's amazing.

Subject: I'll say it is. I'm stupefied!

Erickson: Which two did you write at the same time?

Subject: You're trying to confuse me. [*Points to two words*]

Erickson: You are so right and so wrong.

Subject: You make the darndest statements.

Erickson: You are so right. If I were trying to find out something like that, with a pencil in each hand, what do you think I would do?

Subject: You would try to write? Are you kidding? Did you ever see me try to write with both hands at the same time?

Fink: Yes—but yes!

Erickson: Now suppose just for the fun of it, you put your hand here, and this hand here. Now copy this just as you wrote it.

Subject: You're joking, of course. You wouldn't want me to commit that the second time.

Erickson: Yes, I would. I think you will enjoy watching yourself. Go ahead. The other hand, too.

Subject: Are you kidding? The other doesn't even wiggle. That doesn't look like anything I ever saw before. I am forgetting how to spell.

Erickson: You certainly make a mess out of it.

Subject: I have to explain this as I go along. It doesn't look like it was, but it was!

Erickson: Now just stop and try to see what you have here before you finish.

Subject: So I wrote it backwards.

Erickson: Yes, this one. This one you have written backwards, and this one you wrote forwards—both at the same time. What do you think of this?

Subject: **That is out of this world!**

Erickson: See this bottom one. When I turn it over it will be the top one, won't it? You see, you can read it now, can't you? But this way the *Y* is bottom side up; the *N* is bottom side up. You see, you just happened to write it bottom side up—backwards.

Subject: Am I accomplished!

Erickson: Yes, you certainly are. You can write bottom side up and backwards and for some reason you know this is your writing, too.

Subject: Oh, yes! Nobody else could make such a mess!

Erickson: And this mess, seen properly, is January.

Subject: Oh, brother!

Erickson: A little light on it makes it perfectly legible; doesn't it?

Subject: **I'm astounded!**

Erickson: She actually did write with two pencils at the same time.

Rossi: The reason why you're doing all this backwards and upside down writing is to give her something to do that she's never done before—to awaken a new learning set, is that right? Did she really write backwards and forwards at the same time? Did she actually do that?!

Erickson: Try it yourself!

Rossi: Impossible! I can't do that. [*Rossi now makes an effort to write simple letters—an A, X, and R—forwards and backwards.*] Fascinating! But we don't actually have a record of how she did that, do we?

Erickson: No.

Rossi: It was unfortunately lost. [*Rossi continues trying to write other letters forwards and backwards at the same time and giggles at his own awkward efforts.*]

Erickson: You impress me as being awfully naive. [Is Erickson here referring to the fact that he is now deliberately evoking a new learning set in Rossi without Rossi's awareness of it?]

Rossi: I impress you as being awfully naive? Others have

said that about me too! I can *print* backwards more easily than I can *write* backwards.

Erickson: How did you learn to write—by printing first?

Rossi: I think so, yes. So the real purpose of this backward writing is to give the subject a new learning set. You're trying to activate pathways in her mind that have not been used before, for the purpose of helping her to learn something new.

Erickson: Pathways which are there!

Rossi: You are utilizing patterns for new learning that are already there. You are evoking new learning sets by presenting her with tasks that require her to inhibit her usual way of writing and explore new and unusual ways. This also becomes a metaphor for giving up old ways of dealing with personal problems to explore the new— and for her, unusual. Is this correct?

Erickson: Um-hum.

Rossi: So this can be a part of any therapy session in which the therapist wants to facilitate an inner change. You achieved the same thing with your use of puzzles to evoke thoughts and efforts that had never been used before. This helps patients think about their problem in a new way. Do you agree?

Erickson: [*Nods yes.*] You know the Kent-Rosanoff [Word] Association Test? [*Erickson now describes how he would have patients write word associations with both hands at the same time, and then get separate verbal associations to each in a way that seemed to have tapped into left- and right-hemispheric associations long before Sperry's research (Sperry, 1968.) Erickson describes how rigid many psychologists were in their standardized method of using the Kent-Rosanoff Test, and how shocked they were when Erickson introduced his "two-hand writing" with separate verbal associations.*] I got into an awful lot of trouble at Worcester [*where he began as a junior physician and ended as Chief Psychiatrist between the years of 1930 and 1934*] because I never did things the same way as others—the right way—the orderly way!*

Rossi: It's a pity so many psychologists were shocked. Research on your left-right word association approach may have anticipated some aspects of Sperry's cerebral hemispheric research by a generation.

Erickson: Yes. [In this section] I'm teaching the subject the things she can do without knowing in advance that she could do them. And it really surprised her when she said, **"That is out of this world!"**, and, **"I'm astounded!"** And that's going to help her assimilate more and more of the trance work.

Rossi: She's done all this previous trance work depotentiating her fear of water and facilitating psychological work for which she has an amnesia. But before this session ends, you want to make sure she has a mental set for assimilating all that new trance learning.

Erickson: Yes, that total learning.

Rossi: You don't give her a series of direct posthypnotic suggestions merely telling her to assimilate, learn and grow; you actually evoke a new learning set by facilitating a performance of her unrealized abilities. You are thereby proving to her that she can learn and do things without knowing in advance that she had the ability.

We might say that this is one of your innovations in hypnotherapy: you evoke certain mental sets or processes for learning and for reexperiencing without telling the patient what you are doing. Indeed, *evoking these mental sets to do the appropriate inner work at the appropriate time* is the essence of your indirect approach. You're actually using the *generalization of learning* principle: most people are afraid of new situations, but you help them generalize

---

* For details on Erickson's use of the Kent-Rosanoff Word Association Test, see Huston, Shakow, and Erickson, 1934/1980.

their success from past learnings to their new situations. *Erickson: [Erickson gives a colorful example of a learning situation from his boyhood days on the farm: farmers would train a new horse by hitching its right and left sides to well-trained horses; as the well-trained horses went through their paces, the new horse would be automatically trained!]*

Rossi: OK, enough of horses! Can we get on with humans? But this is where you really learned your therapeutic approaches—back there on the farm—no fancy laboratory for you!

1.51 *Eighth "Visit" of the February Man: Distraction to Depotentiate Resistance and Facilitate Trance Reinduction; A Spontaneous Two-Year Age Regression; Somnambulistic Trance Training*

Erickson: Do you think you can be hypnotized?

Subject: No, probably not now. I'm too wide awake.

Erickson: **Do you want to keep this** [*indicating the trance writing*]?

Subject: No, not particularly. I would just as soon not. **It's amazing.**

Erickson: **What is your technique in taking a pulse?** [*Erickson reaches toward her hand, as if to take her pulse.*]

Subject: You got one. That's all that counts.

Erickson: [*Shaking hands with patient*] Hello.

Subject: Hi.

Erickson: What date is this?

Subject: February.

Erickson: What year?

Subject: 1943.

Erickson: And who am I?

Subject: The February Man.

Erickson: Simple childish thing, isn't it? **Anytime, anywhere, I can shake hands with you in this way, but only I can do it. Only I can do it, and only for a legitimate purpose. Sometime I am going to shake hands with you, and it will be March 30, 1945.** Would you like to see me then?

Subject: Sure.

Erickson: All right. And then I want you very much as you are in general right now, on March 30, 1945. Can I say goodbye now?

Erickson: "What is your technique in taking a pulse?"

Rossi: Why do you ask that question at this point, after she has just denied that she can be hypnotized because she is too wide awake?

Erickson: "Do you want to keep this?" meant *keep you in the [trance] writing*. She says, "It's amazing." Well, let her be amazed. I reach to take her pulse.

Rossi: I see. The question about taking a pulse allows you to get your hand closer as if to take her pulse. But you actually surprise her by shaking hands with her and reinducing another trance with another "visit" from the February Man before her resistance can block it.

[In 1987] This very brief reinduction of trance by using the distraction of apparently taking a pulse while actually shaking her hand was probably Erickson's response to her statement of being "too wide awake," which he would recognize as possible resistance. Her unconscious needed a demonstration that it indeed had been conditioned to go into hypnosis upon administration of the proper cue of handshaking. Erickson thus reinforces the trance induction here and uses this final brief trance to strengthen the handshake cue with a direct posthypnotic suggestion about it: "Anytime, anywhere, I can shake hands with you in this way, but only I can do it. Only I can do it, and only for a legitimate purpose." We should note the implied ethical injunction with Erickson's use of the work **legitimate** here. It is a casual, fairly indirect suggestion, but it is a very important reassurance to the patient's unconscious that its integrity will always be respected.

But also note that Erickson ends this session in a very subtle and non-traditional manner. Nowhere does he tell the subject that she is going to awaken from trance.

He ends this February Man visit with the pseudo post-hypnotic suggestion: "Sometime I am going to shake hands with you, and it will be March 30, 1945"; and after she agrees he adds: "And then I want you very much as you are in general right now, on March 30, 1945. Can I say goodbye now?"

Apparently this posthypnotic suggestion is being used to end this hypnotherapeutic session—yet she is never really asked to awaken from trance. On the contrary, she will still be in trance when Erickson next shakes hands; she will merely be reoriented in time to the current date of March 30, 1945. At that time she will remain "very much as you are in general right now." That is, she will be reoriented to correct time but she will remain in trance—a somnambulistic trance: she will act normally in everyday life, appearing to be awake and well oriented; but she will remain in the profoundly close trance relationship with Erickson whereby the hypnotherapeutic processes he has initiated will continue autonomously on many levels within her. This is one of Erickson's typical approaches in training patients to experience somnambulistic trance.

He then ends this visit of the February Man with a question which is actually a direct suggestion, "Can I say goodbye now."

1.52 Ratifying the Continuation of a Trance Relationship While Apparently Awake; Two Simultaneous Levels of Communication: A Structured Amnesia and Trance Ratification via Time Distortion

Erickson: [Administers the handshake cue] How do you do?
Subject: Hello.
Erickson: Remember me?
Subject: Yes.
Erickson: And what is my name?
Subject: You have a couple of dozen of them.
Erickson: What are they?

Subject: Sounds awful foolish! The February Man!
Erickson: You see, I'm not too tall—and February is a short
             month.
Subject: Oh, brother!
Erickson: By the way, I have enjoyed meeting you very much. **You
             have done a tremendous amount of work tonight,
             intended entirely for your profit and ultimate interest.
             And that's why the time has passed so quickly. And
             now I suppose it's time to get you back to the hospital.**

Rossi: [In 1987] Upon administering the handshake cue
for her to reorient to current time while remaining in
trance in relation to him, Erickson tests her state by
asking, **"Remember me?"** and **"And what is my name?"**
She replies ambiguously, **"You have a couple of dozen
of them."** When pressed further she says, **"Sounds awful
foolish! The February Man!"** This remark indicates that
she is now capable of responding on at least two levels.
On her normal everyday level of awake consciousness, it
"sounds awful foolish" because she has a hypnotic amnesia for her visits with the February Man. Since she does
mention "the February Man," it indicates that a trance
level of responding is simultaneously available to her in
relation to Erickson. He then responds with a two-level
communication in the form of a non sequitur pun that
satisfies both aspects of her current two levels of responding. **"I'm not too tall, and February is a short
month,"** is apparently a poor effort at a pun that enables
the subject to respond from her awake state of consciousness with the groan, **"Oh, brother!"** To her simul-
taneous trance consciousness in relation to Erickson,
however, this poor pun contains Erickson's indirect
acknowledgment that, yes, I have a special relationship
to February—that is, yes, I am the February Man to you in
our trance relationship.
     The poor pun and the response it evokes in the sub-
ject further serves as a reintroduction and continuation

of the kind of games, puzzles, puns, and emotionally confusing situations that characterized the beginning of this lengthy session. As such, the pun structures an amnesia that further facilitates her hypnotic amnesia for all the February Man "visits," and helps her reestablish her normal everyday personality in conscious relation to Erickson.

Since the subject is now well established in responding simultaneously to two levels (her "normal awake personality" and her new hypnotherapeutic trance relationship with Erickson), he uses his final closing remarks to give her normal personality the reassurance that it has "**done a tremendous amount of work tonight, intended entirely for your profit and ultimate interest. And that's why time has passed so quickly**" [a ratification of trance via the experience of time distortion].

He gives her everyday identity as a nurse a pointed and final send off with, "**And now I suppose it's time to get you back to the hospital.**" For all practical purposes she will now function as well as she normally does in everyday life. In addition, however, her hypnotherapeutic relationship to the February Man continues simultaneously on another level. We may suppose that the inner therapeutic work set in motion by her "visits" with the February Man continues to take place on a more unconscious level, while she goes about her normal everyday life.

Thus concludes the subject's first hypnotherapeutic session with Erickson. The session lasted about two hours, and involved some eight uniquely separate "visits" with the February Man. The subject's second hypnotherapeutic session (Session II), which will extend and deepen the work established here, occurs approximately two months later.

Multiple Levels of Communication and Being

2.0 *Two Levels of Being and Responding: Confusion and Conflict as Multiple Levels of Being and Indicators of the New*

Fink: Shall we tell Dr. Erickson your first complaint? She is not learning anything.

Erickson: And no flowers tonight.

Subject: No, no flowers.

Erickson: Is there anything here you don't like?

Subject: No, I don't think so.

Erickson: So you haven't learned a thing? What do you mean by that?

Subject: I thought I was going to learn something about psychiatry or psychology, but so far I haven't learned anything.

Erickson: Do you want to bet?

Subject: No.

Fink: I asked her that. I don't think she wanted to bet even with herself.

Erickson: Why not? Do you think perhaps you have learned something?

Subject: There it goes again. **I want to think no, and say yes.** But you can't think two things at the same time. Or can you?

Erickson: So you have learned something?

Subject: Yes, I suppose that's one of the things I have learned.

---

*Present for the second session in 1945: Dr. Milton H. Erickson, Dr. Jerome Fink, the subject (who is also referred to as "Miss S" and "Jane"), and Mr. Beatty. Present for 1979 commentaries: Dr. Milton H. Erickson, Dr. Ernest L. Rossi, and Dr. Marion Moore.

Right? That it's possible for people to think two things at the same time, in direct opposition.

Erickson: She has learned something on an unconscious level but she doesn't know it consciously yet.

Rossi: Yes. This session takes place two months after the previous one, and Miss S apparently has an amnesia for your work with her as the February Man. Her complaint that she has not learned anything comes from the conscious level that "wants to think no," but something else within her wants to "say yes." So she certainly is experiencing at least two levels or two opposite response tendencies at the same time.

When this sort of thing spontaneously happens to people during everyday life, they tend to experience it as a disturbance or conflict. It might better be understood as an opportunity to tune into their own different levels of being rather than simply identifying with their most superficial persona experience of apparent conflict. Confusion and conflict are actually manifestations of the new states of being that have developed spontaneously within on an unconscious level, and are now interfering with (conflicting with) the old established attitudes, states, and identities of ego consciousness.*

2.1 Not Knowing Indicating a Source Amnesia for Previous Trancework with the February Man

Erickson: I wonder if you know why you came here tonight?
Subject: Dr. Fink asked me to.
Erickson: Did you have any reason?
Subject: Yes. I wanted to see you so I could see how the thing worked.
Erickson: What thing?
Subject: Hypnotism.

---

*See Rossi, 1972a/1985, for a detailed development of this concept.

Erickson: Have you ever been hypnotized?
Subject: Yes.
Erickson: By whom?
Subject: Dr. Fink and oh, yes, by Miss Jones.
Erickson: Anybody else?
Subject: No.
Erickson: How do you feel about hypnosis?
Subject: I think it's a very good thing.
Erickson: Would you like to be hypnotized?
Subject: Definitely.
Erickson: Do you have some special purpose to achieve?
Subject: Nothing except to know a little more.
Erickson: And you really mean that—to know a little more?
Subject: Yes.
Erickson: Could I hypnotize you?
Subject: I don't know.
Erickson: Is there any other answer in your mind?
Subject: **It's yes. But I don't know why.**

Rossi: Her remarks in this section clearly indicate a conscious amnesia for her previous hypnotherapy with you. Is this just because she's an exceptionally good hypnotic subject, or does it have more to do with her very real need for therapy?

Erickson: No, once you receive your therapy, you allow it to become yourself.

Rossi: She has a source amnesia for her previous hypnotic work with you when she responds to your query with, "**It's yes. But I don't know why.**"

Erickson: That's right.

2.2 *Trance Induction via Hand Levitation and Implied Directive: Utilizing the "Hidden Observer"; Self-Monitoring Trance Experiencing; Behavioral Signaling and Trance Depth*

Erickson: How ought I to go about it?
Subject: Let's see. There are various approaches, aren't there? The first time Dr. Fink hypnotized me, I lifted my hands.

Erickson: [*Lifting subject's hand*] Can you sleep now?
Subject: I think so.
Erickson: Would you like to do so?
Subject: Yes.
Erickson: All right. You can go ahead. You can go to sleep. You can close your eyes and go way, deep, sound asleep. You can go to sleep feeling comfortable. You can go to sleep feeling comfortable and you can enjoy your sleep, so that you are very comfortable. Relax and feel comfortable all over. Relax till you are comfortable and sleeping deeply, deeply, and soundly. Easy, deep, sound sleep. And sleep deeply and soundly. **And to let me know you are sleeping soundly, your left hand will slowly rise.** When you are sleeping soundly, but not until you are easily, deeply, soundly asleep. And to let me understand that you will sleep **continuously and deeply,** that you will sleep **continuously and deeply,** as I suggest to you, your right hand will lift up. And now your left hand has lifted up to let me know that you are sleeping deeply and soundly. And your right hand is lifting to let me know that you will sleep continuously. And that's right, is it not? And you are comfortable about that? All right. From now on you can feel your arms relax. Relax and be comfortable. And I can talk to myself or anybody else without it meaning anything to you, can I not? [*Subject nods. Erickson now outlines the subject's actions to Dr. Fink.*] Left hand raised first, and then right hand raised. The suggestion was given that it could lower. Left hand having raised first, lowered first; and then the right hand lowered. [*Back to subject*] **Was I speaking to anyone?**
Subject: **Yes.**
Erickson: **Did you pay attention?**
Subject: **Yes.**
Erickson: Are you pleased with what I said? One does like to do a thing well. There's something for you to learn, is there not? Do you yet know what it is? Will you be willing to learn even if it's hard? **It's been a long time since I saw**

you, has it not? [*Subject nods.*] Months have passed—
weeks, months. Is that right? Can you tell me how
long? It has been a long time, hasn't it? Can you tell me
what day it is?

Subject: Sunday.
Erickson: What month is it?
Subject: June.
Erickson: And what year?
Subject: 1945. [*Miss S is correct and well oriented to current time.*]

Erickson: .... Say Mr. A and Mr. B are in a closed room,
arguing a controversial question. How many people are
in that room? Betty [*Erickson's wife*] promptly answered,
"Six: Mr. A as he is; Mr. A as he thinks he is; Mr. A as Mr. B
thinks he is; and the same with Mr. B." I laid the founda-
tion for that right there [with the sequence]:
"Was I speaking to anyone?"
"Yes."
"Did you pay attention?"
"Yes."
I'm [indirectly] telling her to learn to disregard.

Rossi: You're telling her conscious mind to disregard,
while another part picks it up?

Erickson: Yes—what Hilgard calls the "hidden observer."
(Hilgard & Hilgard, 1975). Here the hidden observer is
used deliberately.

Rossi: To summarize this section. You use your typical
approach to trance induction by guiding her left hand
upward; you give her suggestions for sleep and comfort;
and you use the implied directive, "**And to let me know
you are sleeping soundly, your left hand will slowly
rise,**" so that she can signal when she is in trance. You
then add another implied directive to signal when she
will sleep "**continuously and deeply**" by lifting her right
hand. She gives these signals and then responds with a
head nod to your statement-question, "**It's been a long
time since I saw you, has it not?**" She seems to be in an

appropriate trance condition so you then give the age regression cues: "Months have passed—weeks, months. Is that right? Can you tell me how long?" You were hoping that she would spontaneously regress to your last "visit" with her as the February Man so you could set up your current "visit" a few months after that. But no such luck. She responds to your questions by indicating she is still in current time—no age regression has taken place yet. Is this perhaps because it's been a couple of months since you last saw her, and she needs a bit more time to get reacquainted with trance work before she can manage the age regression?

Erickson: No, she's monitoring herself.

Rossi: How do you mean, she is monitoring herself?

Erickson: She is becoming aware that she is asleep and I'm letting her know she is going to sleep continuously, constantly, and comfortably.

Rossi: So is this self-monitoring in the hypnotic induction a stage that comes before the age regression?

Erickson: Yes. She has to monitor herself so that she knows where she is. Then she can monitor herself. . .

Rossi: . . . for age regression *per se.* Can you say anything more about this monitoring, Milton? Is this the ego watching the process of going into trance? Is the ego helping to manage the process of hypnotic induction?

Erickson: Once you climb a hill, is halfway up enough? Do you want two-thirds of the way up, three-quarters? Eighty percent? She's got to know how far I want her to go. That's self-monitoring to make sure she responds fully.

Rossi: So self-monitoring takes place all the time in trance. Would you say that?

Erickson: No, only at the assignment of a task.

Rossi: When you assign a new suggestion, the ego comes in to help the process, or what?

Erickson: She has to measure how deep she is in the

trance. And when she is deep enough, then she can do certain things.

2.3 Approaches to Age Regression Utilizing "Seeming," Amusement, Forgetting, Uncertainty, Not Knowing, and Confusion; Counting One to 20: One of Erickson's Favorite Inductions: Trance Without Awareness of It

Erickson: And that's the date. But time can change, can it not? And I want you to forget something. I'm not going to tell you just what it is. But you are going to forget something gradually, slowly, easily, and comfortably. **It almost seems as if it might be Monday, or perhaps it might be Saturday, or as if it might even be Friday.** And I want it to seem that way, and I would like to have you feel a bit amused as you begin to get confused about the date, and enjoy it. [Subject smiles.] It's nice, isn't it? [Subject laughs.] And since you don't know what day it is, it will be hard to tell what week it is. It has to be this week, but what week is this week? Is it the last week in May or the first week in June? Or maybe it isn't either one. I want you to enjoy that. [Subject laughs again.] June, May, May, June, and the first thing you know the thought of April will come in to your mind; and it can't be June, it can't be May, it can't be April. And now as you experience that feeling, I want you to realize you have forgotten something else. You forget it is May, and if you think it is April or March, or even if you think it is February—March, April, May, and June are forgotten, and now I want you to discover you are not certain whether it is 1944 or 1945. [Subject frowns.] And keep sleeping comfortably. And you will be able to tell me what month it is in 1944. As soon as you are ready to tell me, go ahead.

Subject: I don't know.

Erickson: That's surprising, isn't it? It almost terrifies you. And yet you can feel comfortable because you are going to remember me. Can you tell me what year it is?

Subject: Yes, 1942.

Rossi: In this section she age-regressed three years. How was that accomplished? You seem to be using forgetting, confusion, and not knowing.

Erickson: **"It almost seems as if it might be Monday, or perhaps it might be Saturday, or as if it might even be Friday."** Friday comes before Saturday, Saturday comes before Monday. I'm going backwards in time.

Rossi: This is your way of facilitating age regression.* In everyday life the experience of "seeming" (imagination), amusement, uncertainty, and confusion are processes or responses that we usually do not presume to control. We think of these processes as our natural responses to outer life situations which we do not control. But here, in trance, you have your subject utilize these natural responses in a controlled way to facilitate age regression.

Erickson: And the important thing is that fact that Monday doesn't come before Saturday. Saturday comes before Monday, when you add another day like Friday.

Rossi: Just talking about these things facilitates regression?

Erickson: Um-hum.

Rossi: The words cause a shift in meaning?

Erickson: The way you use the word. Monday can be a Monday *before* a Saturday, but when you add Friday it has to be the Monday that comes *after* Saturday.

Rossi: [*Re-reads the bold face section of the trance induction dubiously.*]

Erickson: When you count to 10, you have 7, 8, 9, 10. Try this: 1, 7, 2, 5, 8, 8, 4, 6, 9 10.

Rossi: Try that over again.

Erickson: 1, 7, 2, 5, 8, 8, 4, 6, 9, 10.

Rossi: I don't see it.

---

*For the theory and examples of Erickson's age-regression techniques, see Section 3 in Part II of Volume III of Erickson, 1980 (pp. 102-142).

Erickson: I counted from one to 10. I began with one and ended with 10.

Rossi: But with a shifted order—

Erickson: —in between one and 10.

Rossi: What are you trying to illustrate with that?

Erickson: I demonstrated how you can go from one to 10 without letting other people know. They will all recognize [be distracted by] the other numbers between one and 10.

Rossi: What's the purpose of that?

Erickson: To count to 10 without letting the person know consciously.

Rossi: As in the situation where you have conditioned the patient to go into trance when you count from one to 10? If you disguise the counting from one to 10, the patient will go into trance without awareness of it.

Erickson: The patient is still trying to figure out some other relationship [among the numbers].

Rossi: The patient slips into trance unconsciously while the conscious mind is distracted by trying to figure out the puzzling relationships among the numbers between one and 10. So this is a trance induction without the patient's awareness of it!

Erickson: It's one of my favorites. "I can count to 20 and you will go into trance." Then sometime later I say, "So-and-so has 8 kids, and *they come cheaper by the dozen.*"*

Rossi: The reason you like this type of trance induction is because the conscious mind cannot interfere with it.

---

*See Erickson's variations on hypnotic induction and awakening by counting from one to 20 in Erickson, Rossi, & Rossi, 1976; and in "A Transcript of a Trance Induction with Commentary" (in Volume I of Erickson, 1980, pp. 206–257). Erickson might count from one to eight and then curiously ask, "Do children really come cheaper by the *dozen*?" to get the count from one to 20 in a covert manner. Eight plus one dozen equals 20! The patient's unconscious puts that puzzle together (and is thus cued to enter trance) *before* the answer (8 + 12 = 20) reaches consciousness. Thus the patient is in trance before the implications of the answer become conscious.

The conscious mind does not even know the trance is being experienced.

Erickson: That's right. When you're trying to solve a problem and you've had years of experience in avoiding that problem—you cut down on the patient's defenses [with this covert induction].

Rossi: So patients can go into a hypnotherapeutic trance without their habitual patterns of avoidance. And they might be surprised to discover that they've dealt with the problem and not even known they were in a trance. A lot of good research could be done on this approach of trance without awareness of it.

Erickson: [Erickson gives illustrations of patients going into trance without awareness of it simply because they were conditioned to the therapist's vocal alterations when inducing trance. Whenever the therapist used that particular tone of voice, the patient would go into trance without awareness of it.]

2.4   Ninth "Visit" of the February Man: Trance Writing to Facilitate Comfort and Deepen Age Regression

Erickson: 1942. And who am I? [Subject very distressed.] Do you remember me?

Subject: Yes. You're the February Man.

Erickson: What are you so shaken about? Can you tell me? You can really tell me, can't you? Do you want to tell me now?

Subject: It isn't anything very important.

Erickson: I would like to help you. It wasn't comfortable, was it? It really wasn't comfortable. And I don't want you to have anything in mind that isn't comfortable. I think you ought to share it with me. Do you want to tell me? You can think about it a bit longer. Here's a pencil. You might not want to say it, but you can write it. You might not like to say it, but you might like to write it. Can you do that? All right. Write it rapidly. Now listen carefully to what I have to say. I'm the February Man. Just what that means is not quite certain. But one thing it means is that you can tell me many things so that you can reach a better understanding of a lot of things. Is that clear? Things that you could have told me about when you were a little girl and told to me yesterday and last year or the year before. Do you understand? Now, do we need to discuss this matter? [*Subject shakes head.*] Now listen carefully to me. It's 1942, is it not? And time is changing, changing, and soon it won't be 1942. Soon it won't be 1941. Many things are slipping from your mind, and you are forgetting and forgetting and forgetting and forgetting, and you are just a little girl—just a little girl and feeling happy. Now you can talk to me. Hello.

Subject: Hi.

Erickson: How old are you?

Subject: Six.

Erickson: How long have you been six?

Subject: About a month.

Erickson: Do you know who I am?

Subject: Sure.

Erickson: Who am I?

Subject: The February Man.

Erickson: How many times have you seen me?

Subject: Lots of times.

Erickson: Are you going to see me some more times?

Subject: Sure. You said I would.

Rossi: You extend the spontaneous three-year age regression she fell into by first giving her an opportunity to write anything she cannot express verbally. You are obviously picking up facial cues from her indicating some discomfort, so you give her an opportunity to express and clear up any difficulty she may be having in progressing to a deeper age regression. You then give more direct suggestions reacquainting her with the February Man, and she does then age regress to six years old.

Would you agree that's what happened here essentially?

Erickson: [Nods yes]

2.5 Multiple Age Regression; Somnambulistic Trance Training; Reassurance at Different Age Levels; Denial and the Negative as the Guise of New Awareness and Abilities

Erickson: That's right. And what shall I call you?

Subject: I got lots of names.

Erickson: What would you like to have me call you?

Subject: I'd like to have you call me Jane.

Erickson: Why should I call you Jane?

Subject: Because nobody calls me that.

Erickson: All right, Jane. That's what I am going to call you. So you are six years old. Would you like to see something that I have that is crystal? I've got a very, very smart watch. Tell it to open.

Subject: Open. [Erickson snaps his watch open; subject laughs.] That's cute. Do it again. You push a button on top.

Erickson: That's right. Pretty smart little girl, aren't you?

Subject: Sure.

Erickson: So you don't think that watch is very smart. It's just a good watch, is that it? What color is the watch?

Subject: It's either gold or silver. I guess it's gold. Gold or silver, that's what Larry said.

Erickson: Who is Larry?

Subject: My brother.

Erickson: What do you think is going to happen to you when you grow up?

Subject: Oh, I don't know. I won't know that for a long time.

Erickson: Who else is here? Is there anybody else here?

Subject: No.

Erickson: Just you and me?

Subject: Yes.

Erickson: Sometime when you are bigger, and when you are older, maybe sometime when you are bigger and older, and feel badly or unhappy about something—maybe you can tell me about it. Is that right?

Subject: Sure.

Erickson: If something makes you unhappy, what would you do about it?

Subject: I would probably be mad.

Erickson: Suppose it made you very unhappy. Then what would you do?

Subject: Keep it inside.

Erickson: You would really keep it right inside yourself and not tell about it. Would you tell me?

Subject: Sure.

Erickson: Everything?

Subject: **Maybe.**

Erickson: Suppose it was something I could help you on.

Subject: I'd want to know you can help me. **Maybe** you are kidding me.

Erickson: I don't kid. When things are like this, I don't kid. Would you tell me?

Subject: **Yes.**

Erickson: You are sure of that?

Subject: **Yes.**

Erickson: Well, I'm going to leave you, Jane. I'll come back and see you. That's a promise. I don't know just when, but when I come back to see you, I'm going to take you by the hand, like this, and count your fingers—1, 2, 3, 4. Now, nobody else will ever shake hands with you that way, but I will. And I'll come back and see you sometime because I'm going to leave you now to rest. When I come back and shake hands and count your fingers, that's the way you'll know I'm back. Now I'm going to ask you to do something very interesting. I'm going to ask you just quietly to go to sleep for a minute. And sleep. And sleep. And sleep. And sleep. And sleep soundly. And you will know it is 1945. [Pause] By the way, Miss S, what is the date today?

Subject: [Gives correct date.]

Erickson: Are you asleep?
Subject: No, am I supposed to be?
Erickson: What do you suppose is the object of having you come out here?
Subject: You want to help me, I guess, but I don't need any help.
Erickson: What might I want to help you with?
Subject: I don't have any idea.

Rossi: You reestablish an age-regressed trance condition with her in this session, and talk again about the themes (growth, unhappiness) that connect her back to your previous eight sessions. You end the age-regressed part of this minivisit by reorienting her back to the current date after reinforcing your handshake cue with an added finger counting signal. But while you reorient her back to current time, you do not really awaken her from trance. When you ask, "**Are you asleep?**", and she answers, "**No, am I supposed to be?**", the casual observer might assume she was awake and well oriented to current time. But since you did not tell her to awaken from trance, she is now in a somnambulistic trance: she acts as if she is normally awake, but she is actually in a trance relationship with you. This is one of your favorite methods of somnambulistic trance training, and also as a means of assessing trance reality as a state that is discontinuous with waking reality. Do you agree with that?

Erickson: Uh-hum. Any lingering doubts about my willingness to help her—all this reassurance I'm giving her at different [age-regressed] levels.

Rossi: And yet she ends by saying, "**You want to help me, I guess, but I don't need any help.**"

Erickson: She's beginning to recognize—maybe I do need help.

Rossi: When we really need something, the conscious mind's first recognition of what is needed is often through the defense of denial. We say, "*I don't need it.*"

Erickson: Um-hum.

Rossi: Often when I'm writing I will say to myself, "No, *that's not it,*" precisely when a new idea is coming to me. The new often comes in the guise of the negative.

Erickson: Little Becky [*one of Erickson's granddaughters*] is two years old, and at her two-year-old birthday party she was thoroughly in her "terrible two's." Everything she said, "is mine, mine, mine, mine." The next thing was, "let me, let me, let me, let me." She defined what was hers, and then she defined her ability to cope.

Rossi: So when new abilities are becoming manifest in children, it is important for them to establish that fact by claiming the new abilities as their own, and by denying (using the negative) they need any help. That reminds me: one of the first important discriminations for a newborn infant is to say no by turning its head away from the breast when it has had enough (the origin of headshaking to mean no?).

Erickson: I got the subject past that **maybe.** [*The subject said* **maybe** *twice in the middle of this section, before she said* **yes** *twice to Erickson's offer to help.*]

Rossi: So we frequently use these very primitive defense mechanisms of denial against others as well as against the new in ourselves.

Erickson: Very early.

2.6 Facilitating Commitment to Therapeutic Work and Expectancy of Cure: Questions Evoking and Utilizing Favorable Unconscious Channels

Erickson: Now let's see. June is here. July is coming soon. Then August. Did you ever go swimming?

Subject: Not if I can get out of it peacefully. I'm not too fond of water.

Erickson: Why not?

Subject: I don't know. It sort of makes my heart jump around. I just feel terrified, and I don't know why. But I just get absolutely terrified.

Erickson: How terrified?

Subject: Pretty gosh-darned scared. I feel like running like mad
            in the other direction.
Erickson: What do you do about it?
Subject: It all depends. If I can't get out of it, then I go and very
            gingerly put my foot in the water, and then make an
            excuse, and then run and get in the car.
Erickson: How long have you been afraid of swimming?
Subject: Gosh, I don't know.
Erickson: Would you like to swim?
Subject: I think I would. I hate being afraid of something. It gripes
            me.
Erickson: How did it start?
Subject: I don't know.
Erickson: How long have you been afraid like that of water?
Subject: I can't remember. Mother says we went when we were
            little kids, and we used to go out in the water till it was up
            to our ears before she would be able to chase us back.
Erickson: When did you quit going out in the water?
Subject: I don't know. All I know is that now it is really an effort to
            go into the water. I just don't get any happiness out of it
            at all.
Erickson: What did you do after you went swimming last time?
Subject: Dried myself off and went home.
Erickson: How did you feel?
Subject: Pretty darn scared.
Erickson: How long did that feeling last?
Subject: Not very long. We went from the Nurses Home down
            to—where is it?—Henry Hall, and all the way down I
            could feel my old heart just banging away. But then after I
            got out of the water and on my way home, I felt very
            refreshed. That water was swell.
Erickson: Would you like to get over that scared feeling?
Subject: Sure. I think everybody should know how to swim. I have
            just about learned several times, and then I run like
            mad to get away from it.
Erickson: You mean you really run like mad?
Subject: Yes. I jump out of the water and go a good long ways
            away from it.

Erickson: All right. Now would you really like to learn?
Subject: Sure.
Erickson: Do you think you can?
Subject: I don't know. I have tried just about everything. I have lectured myself and told myself I shouldn't be afraid, but that didn't do any good.
Erickson: No, it didn't do any good, did it?
Subject: No.
Erickson: Lecturing yourself won't help, will it? All of your talking to yourself won't help, will it?
Subject: Sometimes it does, but not on that.
Erickson: What do you suppose could help you?
Subject: I guess I'll have to spend three or four thousand dollars and be psychoanalyzed.
Erickson: But talking to yourself about it won't help.
Subject: Apparently not. Unless I haven't been stern enough with myself.
Erickson: Do you want to make a bet with yourself?
Subject: I'm game.
Erickson: Will you bet that there's a way to get over that?
Subject: There undoubtedly is.
Erickson: Are you sure of that?
Subject: Yes.
Erickson: Positive?
Subject: **Absolutely.**
Erickson: How much time do you think it will take to get over it?
Subject: I don't know.
Erickson: And you would like to get clean over it, wouldn't you?
Subject: **Oh, absolutely!**
Erickson: Have you any particular help in mind? Any help that you would like to receive?
Subject: According to Mr. Menninger, there must be something that caused it in the first place.
Erickson: Yes.
Subject: And if I could only think of what it was, it might help.
Erickson: Would you like to think of what it is?
Subject: Yes, but I can't. I mean I just can't.
Erickson: By yourself. But perhaps you can, but not by yourself.

Subject: Maybe. But who else can help me remember something? **Maybe I'm suffering from repressions.** Would
you say that I was, Dr. Fink? He's a sphinx!

Erickson: It rhymes with Fink. Either you can remember or you
can't. Either you can or you can't, or you can or you
can't, or you can. What would you do if someone helped
you to remember that?

Subject: Maybe I could analyze the situation and realize it was
something that shouldn't have made me afraid.

Erickson: But maybe there was something in the situation that
would make you afraid.

Subject: Then I guess I would be scared. If there was something
that scared me I should remember it, because you remember most of the things that you have been scared about.

Erickson: You should remember it and understand it. Isn't that
right? Do you want to take another step? Perhaps you
should remember, but don't want to remember.

Subject: But I've tried.

Erickson: **You can try, but would you like to succeed?**

Subject: Yes.

Erickson: You are sure of that?

Subject: Yes.

Erickson: Would you like to finish your cigarette first?

Subject: Yes. I may not get another cigarette for a while. [*Finishes
cigarette.*]

Rossi: This section indicates that the swimming phobia is
still in full force. She is aware that she is "**suffering from
repressions**," so you initiate a line of inquiry that will
heighten her expectation that further therapeutic work
will help her remember and thus resolve her problem.
You finally get her to commit herself to actually succeeding, in contrast to merely *trying* ("**You can try, but would
you like to succeed?**"). I've noticed that you frequently
have your patients first make a strong commitment to
wanting *cure* or *change* before you give therapeutic suggestions. Is this commitment a necessary part of the
hypnotherapeutic process?

Erickson: A definitive frame of mind [*pointing to the subject's response of,* "**Absolutely**"].

Rossi: You want a more definitive frame of mind, so she responds with, "**Oh, absolutely!**" Why do you want her to be so definitive here?

Erickson: She's got to get over her fear!

Rossi: So here again you are trying to evoke and utilize certain mental mechanisms. You're facilitating a *certainty process* rather than an *uncertainty process*. To get over the symptom she has to be certain, and she has to make a strong commitment.

Erickson: Yes. You may have a simple toy. You keep it behind you. The child might not like the toy, so you make her guess which hand it's in.

Rossi: That initiates an expectation and a fun guessing game so that the child will want the toy. There is an analogy here: getting over the swimming fears is a puzzle the subject can wonder about.

Erickson: She gets cathected to wanting a cure.

Rossi: She gets cathected, curious, and committed to wanting the cure. So this is an expectancy set for cure that you develop before trance work and therapeutic suggestions. This expectancy set is the prepared fertile "soil" into which you will drop the therapeutic "seed" suggestions. You're heightening her unconscious activity around the traumatic associations, and you're activating unconscious channels for therapeutic work.

Erickson: Favorable unconscious channels!

2.7　An Interrupted Trance Induction: Solidifying Trance with Repeated Inductions and the Zeigarnic Effect

Erickson:　Let me shake hands with you.
Subject:　All right.
Erickson:　One, two, three, four. One, two, three, four. [*Dr. Fink passes paper to Erickson.*]

Subject: Let me see it. I want to see what he had on that piece of
          paper there in his hand.
Erickson: Whose hand?
Subject: Dr. Fink's. Well, I want to see it.
Erickson: Wake up. Wide awake. Would you like to see this? [*Shows
          subject paper.*]
Subject: You don't make any more sense than anybody else.

Rossi: At the moment you give her the handshake cue for
a hypnotic age regression visit with the February Man,
Dr. Fink unwittingly gets her attention by handing you a
sheet of paper. You quickly reverse your induction suggestions to "wake up, wide awake," and allow her to see
the paper containing some notes she evidently cannot
understand ("You don't make any more sense than anybody else"). You handle this interruption by telling her to
wake up, lest the handshake cue conditioning process
be partly extinguished by the failure of trance to immediately follow the cue.

Erickson: Yes. I didn't want to lose that conditioning. But
since it was an interrupted task, there was going to be a
tension in her to complete it.

Rossi: Yes, that is called the *zeigarnik effect.**

Erickson: And the more inductions you can do, the more
you solidify the trance.

2.8 Evoking and Utilizing Mental Mechanisms and Processes as the
       Essence of Erickson's Approach; Establishing Reassurance by Evoking
       and Radiating Comfort

Erickson: Sleep now. As you go deeply asleep, **I want your hand
          to come to rest in your lap.** Go way deep sound asleep.
          And as you sleep deeply, I want your hand to come to
          rest in your lap. Sleep deeply and soundly, and you will

---

*The *zeigarnik effect* refers to the tendency to return to a completed task after it has been
interrupted. See Woodworth and Schlosberg (1954).

continue to sleep, will you not? Continue, will you not? Continue to sleep, will you not? And you will sleep continuously and soundly. Now I would like to ask you to tell me about something. Can you do that? I want you to sleep and tell me about it. Can you do that? Take your time and get all set to tell me about it.

Subject: There isn't anything to tell, except that I get scared. I just have horrible visions about turning blue and drowning. Not myself, altogether, but of people turning blue and drowning.

Erickson: Horrible visions of people turning blue and drowning.

Subject: Yes.

Erickson: And your heart beats fast.

Subject: It usually does—with a plausible excuse, of course.

Erickson: And you don't like that excuse?

Subject: No.

Erickson: Do you think that perhaps we can discover why?

Subject: Maybe.

Erickson: Would you like to have us do that?

Subject: Yes.

Erickson: Do you think it will be easy? Do you think it will be comfortable? [Subject nods.] Do you think it will be comfortable?

Subject: Maybe not.

Erickson: Are you game to do it?

Subject: Sure.

Erickson: You really are.

Subject: Sure.

Erickson: Do you have a feeling of guilt or regret in relationship to me tonight?

Subject: Yes.

Erickson: Why? **You need not have any feeling of regret or guilt about that. I want to be very careful to do just exactly the right thing in the right order.** And I did something not really comfortable, didn't I? And so you needn't regret that you have a vague feeling that something was not quite right, because that will help. Do you know what

I am talking about? You probably don't, but I do. I want you to feel comfortable about that.

Rossi: In this section you again build up her expectancy for doing some good hypnotherapeutic work. You reinduce trance with sleep suggestions, after which you question her about her swimming fears. She admits it may not be easy or comfortable to overcome them. You apparently feel that she is not as relaxed as usual because of the interrupted induction, so you assure her that she need not feel regret or guilt and you will "**be very careful to do just exactly the right thing in the right order.**" Is this referring to your order of first inducing trance with these sleep suggestions, and then administering the hand-shake cue for age regression as you do in the next session?

Erickson: Only in part. "**I want your hand to come to rest in your lap.**" I wanted her hand in comfort.

Rossi: Why?

Erickson: She may be miserable, but one part gets comfortable and at ease.

Rossi: You can initiate and radiate comfort throughout her system by getting one part comfortable. Here again your approach is to evoke and utilize mental mechanisms and processes to facilitate the therapy. In all of your work, Milton, I'm noticing more and more something which most professionals do not understand: you're always dealing with mental processes, mental mechanisms—

Erickson: —within the person!

Rossi: Within the person in a very peculiar way that almost seems concrete! Even after studying intensively with you for eight years and writing *Hypnotic Realities* and *Hypnotherapy,* I'm still kind of naive, as you said earlier today. It's difficult to comprehend this way of working. *You don't just analyze and understand; rather, you actually evoke and utilize the mental processes within the person.* Most professionals don't have an understanding of this approach, even after reading most of your work. You're really evoking and utilizing mental mechanisms and processes rather than just talking, analyzing and understanding! This is the essence of your approach, isn't it? We might say that you are a mental mechanist—you're always dealing with mental mechanisms. Would you agree?

Erickson: Yes.

Rossi: Then this is the essence of the therapist's work: utilizing, facilitating, transforming, or evoking different mental processes, right?

Erickson: [*Nods yes.*]

Rossi: Tell us something more about this approach. This is really a different world view of therapy. Most therapists usually analyze and explain what they understand *about* the patient *to* the patient.

Erickson: I think I've asked you this before: How do you get from this room into that room?

Rossi: Right—all the different ways. I can go out this window, go to China, and come back through that door. There are an infinite number of ways. Why are you asking me that again?

Erickson: Because [professional] people are so rigid in their thinking.*

Rossi: Yes, and most psychotherapy is just talking. Most therapists think their job is to analyze and understand what's happening in the patient's life so that they can then tell the patient, "This is what's happening in your life." But that's not therapy!

Erickson: No. Therapy is getting a patient to use his own processes!

Rossi: Therapy is getting the patient to use his own mental mechanisms and processes. It's not for the therapist to be the

---

*See "The Limiting Preconceptions of Most 'Schools' of Psychotherapy," in the General Introduction to Volume IV of Erickson, 1980.

answer-man or the wise one who understands the patient and hands down that understanding to the patient. Ridiculous! That is often only the therapist's prejudices and projections. It's not for the therapist to give his philosophy of the world to the patient.

Erickson: Every individual has a different background.

Rossi: That's right. Every person has his own unique world he is living in. You cannot ask the patient to discard his phenomenological world and adopt yours. You can only help him work within his world. This is a very big paradigmatic shift—a fundamentally different way of doing therapy. It's so different from everyday life. A lot of people interested in psychology say: "Oh, I like to talk with people. I understand people. I think I'll become a psychotherapist because people love to talk to me and I understand them." But just understanding people—understanding their life patterns—is not enough. We must learn to evoke processes that will help people change their own life patterns. *That* is the essence of psychotherapy. Do you agree?

Erickson: [Nods yes.]

Rossi: The essence of therapy is to work with those mental processes.

2.9   Tenth "Visit" of the February Man: "Sleep" Facilitating a Deep Age Regression to Age Six; The Therapeutic Rationale for Age Regression

Erickson: Now I'll shake hands with you. One, two, three, four. All right, now. How old are you?

Subject: I don't know.

Erickson: Don't you know? How old do you think you are?

Subject: I don't know.

Erickson: Do you know who I am?

Subject: Yes.

Erickson: Who am I?

Subject: The February Man.

Erickson: Are you six years old?
Subject: I don't think so.
Erickson: **Just close your eyes and sleep a moment. I want you to be six years old, to be six years old.** And I want you to talk to me.
Subject: Hi.
Erickson: How old are you?
Subject: Six.
Erickson: What month is this?
Subject: February.
Erickson: It's February.
Subject: You always come to see me in February.
Erickson: That's right.

Rossi: I'm really interested in all the little things you do that add up to a sound hypnotic induction and age regression. She is age regressed to her hypnotic reality with you as the February Man, but you want her at age six so you simply ask her to close her eyes, sleep a moment, and be six years old.

Erickson: When I *ask* her to be six years old she can disagree with my *question*. When I *tell* her, "**Just close your eyes and sleep a moment. I want you to be six years old,**" she is *doing* something.

Rossi: Her unconscious is doing it in the "sleep" state; she's not doing it with her conscious intentionality.

Erickson: That right.

Rossi: This is the hypnotic modality: when the unconscious is able to operate autonomously under the guise of sleep. She is not really asleep. *Sleep* is just a cue word, a metaphor for her unconscious mind to take over and do something.

Erickson: A six-year-old can really believe anything.

Rossi: I see. That's an interesting reason for doing hypnotherapy in an age-regressed state. A child's receptive state of mind can believe and make therapeutic suggestions work a lot more readily than the adult skeptical state of mind.

Erickson: But you're not talking about *belief* for a child. It *is real!*

2.10   A Naturalistic Approach to Gradually Overcoming a Swimming Phobia: Growth from Ambivalence to Certainty; Juxtaposing Speculation with Reality

Erickson: Tell me, Miss S, did you go swimming last summer?
Subject: Yes.
Erickson: Did you like it?
Subject: **Sort of.**
Erickson: **I don't understand "sort of."**
Subject: **I guess I did.**

Erickson: "I don't understand 'sort of'"; "I guess I did." She's making a concession to her own reality past when she says "**sort of.**" I pursue that until she says, "**I guess I did.**" I did!

Rossi: You allow her to savor the positive aspects of the experience so that she can say, "**I did**" . . . like it!

Erickson: Um-hmm. That's a natural growth process.

Rossi: A step-by-step process of gradually coming to a full acknowledgment of something new she can enjoy—getting over her water phobia. This is your naturalistic approach—imitating a natural growth process.

2.11   Desensitizing Traumatic Experience Via Repetition: Utilizing Time, the Future, and "Promise" to Facilitate Recall; Sweeping the Rattlesnake Out the Door

Erickson: What makes you say you guess you did?
Subject: It sort of scared me sometimes.
Erickson: Why?
Subject: People get drowned.
Erickson: Did you ever know of anybody who got drowned?

Subject: No.
Erickson: Never?
Subject: No.
Erickson: Did you ever know of anybody you thought drowned?
Subject: Once I thought Helen was drowned.
Erickson: Who is Helen?
Subject: My sister.
Erickson: When did that happen?
Subject: Not here.
Erickson: Where did it happen?
Subject: Over on the other street.
Erickson: How did it happen?
Subject: I told you.
Erickson: Tell me again.
Subject: I tried to pick up Helen and I tipped her over into the water.
Erickson: Then what happened?
Subject: Mother came and pulled her out.
Erickson: How did she look?
Subject: She was all blue.
Erickson: How did you feel?
Subject: I felt terrible. I thought she was dead.
Erickson: You thought she was dead.
Subject: Yes.
Erickson: Jane, I'm coming to see you again many times. And sometime when you are older and bigger, I want you to tell me this. I want you to remember everything about it and tell it to me. Will you do that for me? Sometime when you are older and bigger, I want you to remember this, very carefully. Sometime when you are older and bigger, I am going to speak to you. I'm going to call you Jane, and I'm going to tell you, "Jane, tell me all about that. Everything." Will you be sure to do that? I want you to tell me. Do it not now, but sometime when you are older and bigger, when you are grown up. And I want you to talk just as fast as you can when you tell it. Just as fast as you can. Like "Peter-Piper-picked-a-peck-of-pickled-peppers!" Did you

ever learn to say that? I want you sometime when you are older and bigger to tell me this story, every bit of it, even some of the things you have forgotten now you will remember then. Even things you have forgotten now you will remember then. Is that a promise?

Subject: Yes.

Erickson: Now, what shall I do when I call you Jane, so you will be sure to tell me that?

Subject: You can remind me by asking me.

Erickson: And you will tell me, when you are older and bigger, all about Helen, and tell me fast. And you will surely do it. That's a promise? You will tell me even those things you have forgotten now.

Subject: I might not remember.

Erickson: But you will remember, even if you have to tell me two or three or four or five times. Isn't that right? [Subject nods.] And it might be a very good thing, when you tell me about that when you are older and bigger, not only to tell me the things that happened but to tell me your feelings. You didn't feel so good when it happened, did you? I want you to tell me those feelings. You will do that?

Subject: Yes.

Erickson: Shall I let you sleep a little while now?

Subject: Yes.

Erickson: And get all the memories back.

Subject: Yes.

Erickson: And then sometime when you are older and bigger I'll come and see you, Jane, and I'll say, "Jane, tell me about Helen." And you will tell me about it, if you are 10 years old, or 12 years old, or 16 years old, or 19 or even 25.

Subject: Maybe I'll forget by then.

Erickson: I think when a little girl makes a promise, she ought to keep that promise. Shouldn't she?

Subject: Yes.

Erickson: This entire narrative is much less painful.

Rossi: She has progressed therapeutically to this point where she can review the entire near-drowning of her sister with more objectivity. At this point why did you choose to give her a posthypnotic suggestion to talk about her swimming phobia later? Why not ask her about it now when she is in good rapport with you and an excellent age-regressed condition?

Erickson: In general if you ask for something now people become anxious, so you put it into the future when they can be prepared—but you get a promise. When you promise to do something in the future, the future adds weight to her promise.

Rossi: The more time that passes the heavier that weight gets so that expectancy and motivation build more and more.

Erickson: You're utilizing time and the future.

Rossi: That's fantastic!

Erickson: "Familiarity breeds contempt." The more times patients tell a traumatic thing, the less traumatic it becomes.

Rossi: You're desensitizing her by these repetitions of telling the traumatic story.

Erickson: Desensitizing it so it becomes "old hat." [Erickson now tells a story of how his 30-year-old mother came upon her one-year-old daughter sitting on the floor of the cabin looking at a coiled up rattlesnake right in front of her.] And my mother said, "So I grabbed up the broom and I swept Mr. Rattlesnake out of that cabin so fast he never knew what happened." Forty years later, 50 years later, 60 years later, she still said she swept "Mr. Rattlesnake" out of the cabin. She always put in that respectful "Mr." And her voice got more rigid as she talked about grabbing that broom. That was a traumatic experience, and she was never entirely desensitized from it.

Rossi: So the stirring quality of a good, real-life story (or oral history) is that the person is *not* desensitized to all its original emotional elements. In telling the story the original emotion grips the speaker, and it is that emotion that the listener receives and responds to.

2.12   Two-Level Communication: Illusory Choice to Naturalistically Cope with Upset; A Time Double Bind; Evoking a Mental Set to Talk Fast without Interruption

Erickson: All right. Just go to sleep, because I'm going to leave. And just sleep. Sleep until June, 1945, so that it is June 3, 1945 [the current date then]. [Subject awakens] Same old faces.

Subject: Never change.

Erickson: Would you like a cigarette?

Mr. Beatty: Here we are.

Subject: You're sure you have another package?

Erickson: Yes.

Mr. Beatty: I'll furnish the light.

Subject: Too bad you don't smoke.

Erickson: Notice the way she said that!

Mr. Beatty: You didn't open the window wide enough for me to smoke my pipe, did you? My wife always makes me sleep or smoke in my own room.

Erickson: I hope you enjoy your cigarette.

Mr. Beatty: Do you mind my pipe?

Subject: No, my grandpa has blown smoke all over me ever since I was a little kid.

Mr. Beatty: Now there—I mentioned smoking my pipe in my room, and I started out by saying I slept in my own room. Now I do sleep in a separate room because I snore so much. Is there a psychological or psychoanalytical meaning there?

Erickson: One problem at a time is enough.

Subject: Are you solving another one for him? You have lots of problems?

Mr. Beatty: Yes, I have lots of problems.

Erickson: You will be pleased to know that I have made a great deal of use of my acquaintance with you, while I was at the Menninger Foundation.

Subject: Hallelujah! I'm of some use.

Erickson: I was lecturing there and I took my notes on you.

Subject: Well, I'm good for something. Isn't that wonderful? I was telling [my friend] tonight, after I got [here] wouldn't it be

	funny if you waited for me to be hypnotized and I just sat there and laughed? She said, "Don't be funny."
Mr. Beatty:	Do you work at Menningers?
Subject:	No, I'm a student nurse at Providence. Some day I hope to finish and get out of there.
Erickson:	Can you tell me something about this swimming of yours? Can you, Miss S?
Subject:	I don't know what I could tell you.
Erickson:	Is it connected with anything that you know of?
Subject:	No.
Erickson:	Your hand is here [indicates], and you say you don't know when that fear was started, when it began. Were you afraid of swimming when you were eight years old?
Subject:	I don't remember. All I know is that I have been afraid of the water ever since I can remember. I used to go anyway, but I don't like it. Of course I can go if I have to. You can do lots of things when you have to. But I don't like it.
Erickson:	How fast can you talk?
Subject:	Depends on how mad I am.
Erickson:	**How fast can you recite "Peter-Piper-picked-a-peck-of-pickled-peppers"?**
Subject:	"Peter-Piper-picked-a-peck-of-pickled-peppers." But I don't like that one.
Erickson:	Maybe you like this one better: **"How-much-wood-could-a-woodchuck-chuck-if-a-woodchuck-would-chuck-wood?"**
Subject:	I like that one. When we were little kids, my grandma used to say that over and over to us. I never could understand why.
Erickson:	**Tell me, are you getting all set?**
Subject:	What should I get all set for?
Erickson:	Are you?
Subject:	Sure.
Erickson:	What do you mean by "sure"? Is that just a polite answer, or do you mean it?
Subject:	Well, I don't know what I am to be all set for, if that's what you mean. Just mention it, and **"I'll be set for it.** Is that all right?

Erickson: Yes, it's all right. But we will wait until you finish that
cigarette.

Subject: I'll be all set by the time I finish my cigarette?

Erickson: That's right.

Erickson: Again I'm speaking at different levels: "**Tell me,
are you getting all set?**" [*And she finally says,*] "**I'll be set
for it.**"

Rossi: She's in a very accepting frame of mind.

Erickson: She's in good rapport with me and in good
rapport with Dr. Fink, and she's all set in relation to
something else—and not just to please us.

Rossi: That "something else" is important to her personally.

Erickson: Um-hmm. She'll be "all set" when she finishes
her cigarette. She'll be "all set" in relation to her own
comfort in smoking. Her hand is comfortable, her mouth
is comfortable; she's "all set."

Rossi: She's "all set" to do some important therapeutic
work. This sequence is highly characteristic of your two-
level communication approach (Erickson & Rossi, 1976/
1980). You are addressing her awake conscious mind
(she's actually still in a somnambulistic trance in relation
to you), and yet many of your remarks about "**How fast
you can recite . . .**" and getting "**all set**" have meaning
only for a more unconscious earlier age level.

Erickson: Yes.

Rossi: When you ask her to recite, "**Peter-Piper-picked-
a-peck-of-pickled-peppers,**" is this actually a cue which
you hope will evoke the earlier suggestions [in the previous section] to tell more about the swimming problem?

Erickson: No, but I did give her that "**Peter-Piper-picked-
a-peck-of-pickled-peppers**" as a cue that she follow
the actual process of removing upset from what I said to
what she would like.

Rossi: How does that remove the upset?

Erickson: Peter Piper was my idea. I gave her the opportunity to go to something she liked better with, "How-much-wood . . . woodchuck-would-chuck-wood?"

Rossi: So you're giving choice to her?

Erickson: Um-hmm. With "Peter Piper" she would be responding to my direction. When I offer her another way, I give her choice.

Rossi: You're implying she can have her choice because you want her own inner dynamics to activated. That's the importance of giving people choice: it gets their inner worlds activated even if it is an illusory choice: they are still going to do what you want them to do.

Erickson: The fast talk with these games is to prepare her to have no difficulties or interruptions when she tells me about the traumatic materials.

Rossi: So your fast word games are another example of how you evoke certain mental sets to facilitate therapy—in this case, a "talking-fast-without-interruption-set" when she has to talk about something that is difficult. Again you're evoking a process to facilitate therapeutic responsiveness.

Erickson: It's a double bind!

Rossi: What's the double bind?

Erickson: She's binding herself when she says, "**I'll be all set by the time I finish my cigarette.**" I set her up for it when I said, "**But we will wait until you finish that cigarette.**"

Rossi: It's what we originally called a *time bind* (Erickson & Rossi, 1975/1980).

2.13   Utilizing Two Mental Sets to Evoke a Complete Traumatic Memory: A Time Bind, and Fast-Talking Set

Erickson: Is there anything else you can say about your phobia for water?

Subject: [*Frowning*] Oh, Dr. Fink was going to solve the problem. [*To Dr. Fink*] Remember, you came up in the hall when I was in O. B.? [*Back to Erickson*] He came in and talked about all those fears that people have, and I told him I was afraid of water. He was going to fix it—just like that.

Erickson: Anything else you want to say?

Subject: Maybe I inherited it. My dad never wanted to swim. But he wasn't afraid of the water—he had bronchitis, and asthma, and a million other things, and he couldn't swim. Too bad he couldn't swim. In fact, Mother used to get angry with us when we used to insist that Daddy would take us out in the water when we were little kids. We used to tease him to take us out, and she got disgusted with us. We used to want him to go way out with us.

Erickson: How did you learn?

Subject: To swim? I didn't. Oh, I just about learned several times. We had a neighbor, a Mr. Smith. He was a stinker. We went swimming one time—I can't remember whether I was scared. I don't know where we went, even, but there was one of those big long docks. So he said to me, "Do you want to learn to swim?" And I said, "No." So he said, "Come on out with me and we'll look at the water." So he took me by the hand and we went out on the dock, and the first thing I knew I was in the water and so was he. Mother scolded me afterwards, but he made me so mad I kicked him and scratched him and just about killed the guy. I tried to bite him and everything else. So he brought me out of the water. I guess he thought I was hopeless.

Erickson: Why did you kick and bite him?

Subject: I don't know. I was just mad at him. I didn't expect him to pull me in the water that way. He wanted to teach me to swim, but that wasn't the way to do it. So I just got mad at him.

Erickson: Your cigarette is getting short.

Subject: Yes. But you would be surprised at how short you can smoke them.

Erickson: I won't be surprised.

Subject: In fact, I have the reputation for leaving the shortest butts in the solarium. It always seems like a mortal sin to me not to. We have an hour for lunch, and it takes about 10 minutes to eat the food they set in front of you. Then after combing our hair we have about five minutes left for a smoke. So the girls smoke about so much of the cigarette, and I just sit there and watch them and get sicker and sicker.

Erickson: You aren't smoking that. You're just dusting the ashes off. Don't you think you'd better take a puff?

Subject: Oh, I don't know. The more drags you take the shorter it gets. It's sort of wasteful to let it go like that, though. There are at least three puffs left on that.

Erickson: Will you get them?

Subject: I hope so. Wasn't it in the Sahara that they took a pin—one cigarette for six fellows? To think I used to take shorthand. If I go back without any fingers, you can explain to my mother.

Erickson: Perhaps you will go back without something else.

Subject: You mean some of my memories will be left here? What would you do with them?

Erickson: Straighten them out.

Subject: Without me being here?

Erickson: Perhaps. [Subject finally puts out cigarette.] Jane, I want you to tell me all about Helen. Quickly, rapidly, hurriedly, tell me about Helen, Jane.

Subject: Helen. Let me see.

Erickson: Quickly, with all the feelings you had.

Subject: But—maybe that's connected with water. One time when we were little kids, I can't remember where we lived, but mother was scrubbing up the floors, and she used one of those big—not basins—tubs, I guess you'd call them. It seemed to me she was always scrubbing floors. Helen was a little baby, but she was about as big as I was. Mother went into the other room and left the tub on the floor and Helen was playing in it. I told Mother that Helen was in the water and she said, "That's all right." So I told her Helen would get all wet, and she said, "Oh, leave her alone, for heaven's sake." So then I tried to pick her up. I put my arms around her waist and tried to lift her, but she was too heavy for me, and she sort of did a somersault backwards and landed in the water. I called to Mother that Helen was in the water, but she didn't pay any attention. I called her again, and then **I started to yell my head off.** Then Mother came in to see what was the matter, and she dragged Helen out of the water.

Erickson: Go on.

Subject: There was water coming out of her nose and mouth. Then Mother slapped her on the back. Then I guess she slapped her on the back. And I cried.

Erickson: Now really tell me the story about Helen.

Subject: She didn't breathe for a long time. I felt horrible.

Erickson: What did you think you had done that was horrible?

Subject: I picked her up and wanted to help her, but she almost drowned.

Erickson: Were you a bit mad at Helen?

Subject: I was mad at her for being so heavy. She had her hands around [the tub]. She wouldn't let go.

Erickson: All the feelings. All the feelings.

Subject: She wouldn't let go. I should have dropped her but I didn't. I guess I sort of lost my balance.

Erickson: I want you to remember all of that. Tell me the rest, Jane, about Helen.

Subject: She had a pink dress on. I didn't want anything to happen to her that day. She looked so pretty that morning. People used to come to the house and say she was so pretty and so beautiful, and that pretty little kids like her might die, so you have to be careful of them.

Erickson: Were you jealous of Helen?

Subject: No.

Erickson: Tell the truth.

Subject: A little bit, maybe.

Erickson: Were you jealous?

Subject: Yes.

Erickson: Go ahead. Go ahead.

Subject: It's silly.

Erickson: What has all that got to do with swimming? Now start thinking and start understanding. What has that got to do with your fear of swimming?

Subject: The water was dirty. There was soap in it. Soap was all around the sides of the tub. And Helen had bubbles coming out of her mouth.

Erickson: What's that got to do with your fear of swimming?

Subject: I must be afraid I'll push somebody in and drown them. That must be it. Maybe I'm afraid I'll push myself in. I'm afraid somebody is going to get drowned.

Erickson: This is her first complete description of the traumatic situation.

Rossi: This full description finally comes at the exact point when two of your indirect approaches to utilizing mental sets are activated: (1) the double bind (or time bind) comes into action automatically when she finally finishes her cigarette; and you seize that crucial moment to (2) cue the "fast talking without interruption" set you introduced with your Peter Piper game in the last section. The time bind and fast talking sets are two mental sets that together finally collected and channeled her traumatically scattered associations into one complete coherent story. I believe this may be *the clearest verbatim demonstration on record of your utilization of two mental sets simultaneously to recover a lost traumatic memory upon which a phobia is based.*

Erickson: Yes, and it allows her to bring in visual memories which complete it more. She lays it all out for the first time in a way that she can begin to separate the trauma from water and swimming.

Rossi: So what really happened is that Jane was a misunderstood hero and Mother was really at fault for Helen's near drowning. Jane tried to warn Mother that Helen was in the water but Mother did not come. Jane tried to lift Helen out of the water, but Helen then accidentally somersaulted back into the water. It wasn't until Jane

"started to yell my head off" that Mother finally and be-
latedly came to help.

2.14   *Trance Reinduction with Arm Catalepsy: A Fuller Recall of Early Loss*
         of Love as Source of Sibling Rivalry; Comfort and the Implied
         Directive as Biofeedback Mechanisms

Erickson: [*Erickson gently guides both her arms up in the air.*] Now go to
             sleep. Go to sleep. Go to sleep. Way deep, sound
             asleep. As soon as you are sleeping soundly, let your
             left arm come to rest on your lap, and you will keep
             sleeping, will you not? [*The subject's left arm comes to rest in
             her lap.*] Do you know what you have been doing? Do you
             remember what you were telling me?
Subject: Yes.
Erickson: Do you know why I wanted you to tell me that?
Subject: No.
Erickson: You were awfully scared in telling me, weren't you? And
             you held something back, didn't you? Now I want you to
             tell me again while you are asleep, and this time tell me
             everything. And tell the whole truth. And you will really
             do a good job. You will do it comfortably so that you can
             understand this fear of yours about swimming. You don't
             want that anymore, do you? And as you tell me that
             occurrence, I want every other thing that is connected
             with your fear of swimming to come forth. Are you
             willing? Now as you sleep, would you like to sit for a
             while and think about it? All right. **And when you are
             ready, you can put your right hand down.** Do you think
             you will have enough courage to do that, or shall I help
             you? [*Subject nods.*] All right, I'll help you. And this time
             you won't hold anything back, and you will pass it off and
             laugh it off. You won't push things out of your mind, and
             you will say them completely. Isn't that right? And it is
             right, too. Now is there anything special you would like to
             have me do in order to help you? Any special thing? Or
             will you just have simple trust and faith that I will do
             everything I can, and will that be satisfactory?

Subject: Yes. [*Pause*] One time when Helen was **real little**, she was sitting in the high chair playing with clothes pins. Mother was hanging up stuff in the backyard, and Helen wanted to get closer to the door so she could see her out in the yard. I wanted to move her closer to the door. So I asked Daddy to come in and move her closer to the door. He said no. Then I asked Mother if she could come in and move her to the door, and Mother didn't do it. So I tried. I tried to push her. I was pulling on the chair and it tipped over on me. It hurt my arm, and Helen fell out of the high chair. She cried and cried. Daddy came out to see what had happened, and he asked what I had done. I told him I was trying to move the high chair closer to the door. He said, "You shouldn't do things when you're told not to." He was awful mad. So he spanked me. He never had spanked me before. He never had spanked me before that.

Erickson: And that hurt, didn't it?

Subject: [*In tears*] He never spanked me after that. **I think I hated him for a while.**

Erickson: You did hate him for a while, didn't you?

Subject: Sure did! That was wrong. But **I wanted to kill him.** He was so blind he couldn't see that I was just trying to help.

Erickson: Go on.

Subject: Mother was crying. She told me to go to my room and stay there. **I hated all of them.** * **I wanted to kill all of them.** I felt bad. I never wanted to kill anybody before. But I wanted to kill them then.

Erickson: Go on.

Subject: [*Pause*] Daddy used to play with me. We used to have a lot of fun. But then Helen came and after that he didn't play with me anymore. And then he got sick, too. I guess I was too little to see he was sick. Mother kept telling us he was sick and that we shouldn't bother him. We used to go upstairs and put our heads on him and turn somer-

---

*Jane is the third-born child of the family, with a brother and sister (Lisa and Larry) preceding her, and Helen following as the youngest.

saults into his lap. He wouldn't let us do that anymore after Helen came. But he used to go in and play with Helen. Then when we gave him a workout he would be all choked up.

Erickson: You used to be mad at him when he played with Helen.

Subject: **I used to be awful mad.**

Erickson: Keep on talking. Tell all those things.

Subject: She was the youngest and Grandma said the youngest always gets babied. Helen was little and had to have more attention. I know that. When we got older we used to run away from her. We would hide upstairs and she would look for us and not be able to find us. She would cry, and we would just let her cry. We would sit up and listen to her cry and just laugh. Then I got older and I thought how silly it was. **It wasn't Helen's fault. It was all Mother's fault.**

Erickson: Tell me about that.

Subject: Oh, it isn't that. Mother wasn't to blame. Grandma used to say if Mother gave a damn about us she would come out and see us, but she never did. Mother didn't scold me when I dropped Helen in the water. **She just looked at me as if I were awful, just awful wicked.** But I wasn't. Then I used to sneak in the door and look at her—at Helen, I mean. I would look at her and feel sorry for the way I felt, but I couldn't help it. **I used to get awfully mad at everybody.** I used to go off by myself and cry, but I didn't want anybody to see me cry. I don't ever want anybody to see me cry.

Erickson: Go on. With all the feelings. All the feelings. Go on.

Subject: One day when Helen was bigger, it was summer. Mother and Daddy and the people next door—they had a girl named Dotty, and she was cute and nice to us kids—we all went down to the lake. Helen was just big enough to walk around, and Mother asked me to watch her. But I was scared. I was scared to watch her.

Erickson: Why?

Subject: I thought, what if she would get all **blue again.** Mother was out swimming and there was nobody near except Larry. But Larry was playing ball, and if Helen got drowned

I wouldn't be able to do anything about it. She would just be dead. And it would have been all my fault. So I didn't let her go in the water. But she cried, and Mother scolded me and said I was silly and that I should take her in the water. So I watched her while she was playing in the water. I stood right beside her with my arms around her waist, so she couldn't get hurt.

Erickson: Go on.

Subject: Larry came over then and took care of her. He took her way out in the water and let her ride on his back. She liked that. I went over and played with Lisa, and she said, "What's the matter? Don't you like to watch Helen?" I said, "No, I hate her." Then I felt bad to think I had said that, because I didn't hate Helen—I liked her.

Erickson: Is there something about Helen in the washtub you haven't told me?

Subject: Mother wouldn't come when I called her. She just wouldn't come. I called her and I told her Helen was all wet. I said she will get sick. When I started to cry so loud she said, "Well, don't cry about it." Then she came in to see what the matter was, and when she saw Helen in the tub she just looked at me.

Erickson: Go on.

Subject: Helen coughed all day. I was so scared to think I had done something I shouldn't have done. I just didn't want her to get hurt.

Erickson: And yet you were mad at her for getting you in this trouble.

Subject: I don't know why she hung onto the tub. I think I could have lifted her if she had let go. But she wouldn't let go.

Rossi: In the beginning of this section you reinduce a deeper hypnotherapeutic trance by lifting her hand and arm and suggesting, "Go . . . way deep, sound asleep." This is one of your typical catalepsy inductions.* You then follow up with an implied directive when you add,

---

*See Erickson and Rossi, 1981, for detailed exposition of Erickson's use of catalepsy for trance induction deepening.

"As soon as you are sleeping soundly, let your left arm come to rest on your lap." When that arm does come to rest in her lap, you take it as a signal from her unconscious that it is ready for you to proceed with further hypnotic work.

You then use the implied directive again on her other arm when you say, "And when you are ready you can put your right hand down." This is a signal for her to tell you the whole story again "comfortably." Repeating the recall of the trauma with comfort is important in the continuing process of desensitization, as well as in your continuing effort to elicit all significant details.

The implied directive is a very useful indirect approach that functions like a biofeedback signal, letting both of you know when her mind-body system is ready to continue with optimum comfort.

Erickson: For formalized theory the interweaving of all these memories is important.

Rossi: Yes. Freud talked about the "multiple determination of symptoms" whereby a psychological symptom such as the swimming phobia is the result of a concatenation of many interweaving psychological sources of stress. We learn in the session that when Jane's younger sister was "**real little**," Jane wanted to help her see Mother. Tipping over Helen's high chair was truly an accident. Jane's father and mother did not understand this and began to suspect that she wanted to harm Helen. Because of this misunderstanding, they punished Jane and withdrew love. And for the first time in her young life, Jane hated and wanted to kill her father and then "all of them" ("**I hated all of them. I wanted to kill all of them.**").

Even before this accident, however, things were greatly changed when Helen came into the world. It was a time when Daddy stopped playing with Jane and having fun. It was also the time that Daddy got sick. In relation to her mother Jane says, "**It wasn't Helen's fault—it was all Mother's fault**" that attention was withdrawn from Jane upon Helen's arrival. When the accident of Helen's near drowning took place in the bathtub, it was actually Mother's fault for not coming when Jane originally called out a warning. By this time, however, both Mother and Father had a suspicious frame of reference regarding Jane's relation to Helen. So although Jane was trying to help Helen in the near drowning, it resulted in Mother blaming her and looking at her "as if [she] were awful, just awful wicked."

One summer when Helen was a bit bigger, Jane again found herself in a position in which she felt responsible for Helen's safety near a body of water (the lake). Jane naturally didn't let Helen go into the water out of fear that she would get "blue again" and "just be dead." But again Jane was misunderstood and chastised for her thoughtful and well-intentioned actions. We can assume that Jane then generalized her fear of water to herself, and this resulted in what we call her "swimming phobia."

From the account thus far we can conclude that it was parental withdrawal of love and attention that led to a series of misunderstandings culminating in Jane's being "awfully mad at everybody" for being wrongfully accused of trying to hurt her baby sister. In this case at least, it seems as if the so-called sibling rivalry was a direct consequence of the parents' unwitting withdrawal of attention from the older sibling when the younger sibling was born.

[Some of these interweaving sources of psychological stress that led to the formation of Jane's "swimming phobia" are diagrammed in Table 1 at the end of the following section.]

2.15   The Multideterminants of the Swimming Phobia: Sources, Reinforcement, and Generalization of Fears; Not Knowing and Unconscious Processes

Erickson: Is there something else you would like to tell me? Tell all the rest.

Subject: Mother told me that if I went swimming with Mr. Smith, he would show me how and I would be a real good swimmer. Then when she told me, I didn't want to do it. I just didn't want to do anything she told me to, or anything anybody asked me to do. When Mr. Smith asked me to go out and look at the water, it was deep and black. I wondered where Helen was, and I looked for Mother but I couldn't see anybody. Then when he asked me if I would like to learn to swim, I said no. He asked if I would like to put my feet in the water, and then he pulled me in the water and tried to teach me how to swim. **I got scared and kicked him. I was so mad I wanted to kill him**, but I couldn't. I was too little. He never ducked anybody. He said it wasn't nice. But he pulled me in when I wasn't looking, and that was just as bad. I'm not afraid of being ducked. It's fun to watch the bubbles going up.

Erickson: Just like you watched the bubbles from Helen?
Subject: That wasn't funny. **I thought she was dead.**
Erickson: What else is there connected with your fear of swimming?
Subject: I used to go way back on the Rouge River where there was a big cable wire, sort of—one at the top and one at the bottom. The big guys used to walk across, hanging onto the cable. I was too little to do that, but I used to follow Larry all around. He didn't care. One time he went down there and I followed him. He said he was going across on the cable, and he said he would take me if I would hang on to his belt. Halfway across I got real scared, but he got [us] over to the other side. We played over there and picked flowers, and then we had to throw them away because we couldn't carry them back. I was scared to go back by myself. **I was scared to put my foot in the water.** Larry had to carry me. He didn't care. He thought it was funny. But I told him not tell anybody about it. **I felt like crying but I didn't cry.** I didn't want anybody to know I was so scared.

Erickson: And what else. What else?
Subject: A couple of years ago—about three years ago—before Carl went into the Army, I went out with him and another couple. We went to a lake near Pontiac. We were just sort

of horsing around. I was scared but it was sort of fun. Carl was pulling me around in the water. He didn't care if I was scared. Finally Paul got a boat so that we could go out on the lake. It looked as if a storm was coming up, but they said it wouldn't rain for a long time—probably not before evening. It was about three o'clock in the afternoon. We went way out, and it started to rain; it was thundering and lightning. I always loved that, but the waves were real high. We weren't making headway against the waves at all. I was scared. **I was shaking like mad.** Carl asked me if I was cold, but I wasn't cold. **I was just scared to death.** Finally we got back to shore and I told them I wanted to go home. They wanted to go to a show that night, but I didn't care. I guess I ruined their night. But I told them flatly I just wouldn't go.

Erickson: **Have you held back some of your feelings?**

Subject: **Yes. I don't know what they are, though.**

Erickson: Listen to me, Jane. You are still asleep, are you not? Now, there's something I want you to understand very clearly. You came out here for serious reasons tonight; for very serious reasons, reasons that are meaningful to you. There is no good purpose in having a fear of swimming, is there? This fear of swimming has troubled you a lot more than you have admitted, isn't that right? So that even when you see flowers in a vase of water it makes you uncomfortable.

Subject: Sometimes awfully uncomfortable. And I always buy flowers for people, too. I don't know why.

Erickson: Because flowers are connected with funerals. Is that why?

Subject: I don't like funerals.

Erickson: Now we're getting close to the whole story: her mother and father and others condemming her.

Rossi: Only now in this deeper and more comfortable trance state do you get a clear and comprehensive picture of the many factors that combined to form and

reinforce her fear of water and of swimming. The generalization of this fear to many other things accidently
associated with it, such as water in a vase to flowers and
funerals, is also becoming evident.

Erickson: The |innocent| connection of flowers with her
problems may have happened when she and Larry threw
away the flowers they had picked because they could
not carry them over the dangerous water.

Rossi: She doesn't know why she always buys flowers for
people because she remains unaware of the multiple
associations in her mind between flowers, water (trauma),
and death. When she answers your question, "**Have you
held back some of your feelings?**" with "**Yes, I don't
know what they are, though,**" her *not knowing* is again an
indicator of autonomous unconscious processes striving for expression in behavior.

The dangerous activity of crossing over the river on a
cable wire with Larry reinforced her fear of water, which
was then generalized to the flowers they had to discard
in order to cross. The connection between death and
water was reinforced still further years later when she
was "**just scared to death**" when caught in a boat during
a dangerous storm with Carl and the other couple. These
stages in the formation, reinforcement, and generalization of her fear of water are diagrammed in Table 1.

2.16 *Awakening from Trance and Working Through Resistance on the Conscious Level: Left-Right Hemispheric Speculations; Ambivalence as a Two-Level Response Shifting Between Symptom and Cure*

Erickson: Now, you came out here for a very serious purpose:
reaching an understanding of your phobia for water, of
your fears and your anxieties. Now do you want really
to get over those fears and anxieties? Do you think you
have taken a step? Now I am going to ask you to take
another step. Are you willing to do that? **I am going
to have you awaken shortly, and I want you to remem-**

Table 1

The Multideterminants of Psychological Stress Leading to Jane's Swimming Phobia: Seven Stages in the Formation (Stages 1–5) and Reinforcement (Stages 6 and 7) of the Fear of Water and Dying

Originating Traumas	Interpersonal Reactions	Psychological Consequences
1. Birth of the subject's younger sister, Helen	Mother & father withdraw attention from Jane; father becomes ill and withdraws attention from Jane.	"I used to be awful mad."
2. The subject's high chair accident with Baby Helen	Mother & father believe Jane has ill will toward Helen and therefore punish her.	Jane wants to kill mother and father; hides from Helen.
3. Helen's near drowning in bathtub at hands of her sister, Jane	Mother & father feel confirmed in blaming Jane and believing her "wicked."	Jane gets "mad at everybody" and does not want anyone to see her cry.
4. Jane responsible for Helen near the lake	"She [Helen] would just be dead. And it would have been all my fault."	Fear generalizes to all situations involving Helen and water; water becomes associated with death.
5. Mr. Smith tries to force Jane to swim	Jane "got scared," kicked Mr. Smith, and "wanted to kill him."	Bubbles, water, and swimming again associated with death ("I thought [Helen] was dead")
6. Dangerous cable-walk with Larry over the river	"I was scared to put my foot in the water. . . . I felt like crying but I didn't cry."	Fear of water reinforced and generalized to flowers that are discarded.
7. Stormy boat-crossing on lake	"I was shaking like mad. . . . I was just scared to death."	Death associations with water further reinforced and generalized to funerals.

ber everything you said while you were asleep: how you hated your mother, and hated Helen, and hated your father, and all those things. And I want you to **really try to discuss them with me intelligently and understandingly.** Will you do that? I want you to remember every one of those things and talk about them. Will you do that?

Subject: All right.

Erickson: **Wake up, now. Wake up now.** How do you feel? Tired?

Subject: Exhausted. **I feel as if I had lost a war single-handed.**

Erickson: **You certainly are incredibly clever.** So you lost the war single-handed. **What is this war you lost?**

Subject: God only knows. But I lost it. I'm sure of that. Or maybe I won it. I don't know. Anyway, either side would be tired.

Erickson: Why did you come out here tonight?

Subject: I guess I wanted to see you again.

Erickson: What about?

Subject: **I don't know.** I mean—you told me you were going to see me again.

Erickson: Do you think you will go swimming this summer?

Subject: **I don't know.** I might.

Erickson: **Are there two answers in your mind?**

Subject: **Yes and no, as usual.**

Erickson: Have you ever had that experience of thinking yes and no in connection with swimming before?

Subject: No, I usually answer an emphatic no. Then occasionally it turns out that I have to, because I can't always get out of the situation gracefully. Here, smoke my cigarettes.

Erickson: When you go to psychoanalysis week after week with nothing happening, they call it *resistance*. I'm circumventing the resistance by having her recall [these traumatic incidents] in relation to the waking state.

Rossi: You give her a very direct posthypnotic suggestion "to remember everything you said while you were asleep" and "really try to discuss them with me intelligently and understandingly."

You then very directly have her "**Wake up, now.**" No more somnambulistic trance; she is just plain awake so she can intelligently discuss all her recently recalled traumatic material in a fully awake state. If I may continue my speculations about the right-left hemispheric responses in your approach, I would say that you are now having her "work through" her traumatic memories by having her ego consciousness—her more detached, analytical and logical left-hemispheric process—receive and integrate what was formerly locked into her more unconscious or right-hemispheric processes. In these right-hemispheric processes, her traumata could only "act out" via the swimming fear and its generalizations to her fear of flowers, death, funerals, etc.

Erickson: She knows she has been through a war but has an amnesia for the trance work she has just done.

Rossi: Yes, after awakening she answers "**I don't know**" to your question of why she came tonight. To your crucial question about going swimming this summer, she again answers with "**I don't know.**" She then responds to your pointed question, "**Are there two answers in your mind?**" with the ambivalent, "**Yes and no, as usual.**" I believe this ambivalence is the first real evidence that you are entering a wedge into the iron curtain of her defeatist attitude toward swimming.

Erickson: Yes.

Rossi: This ambivalence is a classical indication of another attitude or potentiality developing within her.

Erickson: [*Nods yes vigorously.*]

Rossi: Her answer of "**Yes and no, as usual,**" means there are two levels of response simultaneously pressing for expression within her: her usual habitual attitude of no, together with the new therapeutic possibility of yes. *She is at this moment suspended halfway between symptom and cure.*

When she makes the seemingly sarcastic wisecrack upon awakening, "**I feel as if I had lost a war single-**

handed," you reply rather cryptically: "You certainly are
incredibly clever. . . . What is this war you lost?" What
was that all about?

Erickson: [*Erickson points to a passage* (*Section* 2.23 *below*) *when
Jane automatically writes the letters* **t-e**, *which when added to
war make* **wa-te-r**. *Even at this point, however, Erickson had the
remarkable perspicacity to recognize that her wisecrack about
losing the* **war** *was really a cryptic reference* (*a two-level response*)
to losing her symptom to **wa-te-r**.]

2.17   *A Fully Conscious Integration of Traumatic Memories: Direct, Open
Communication Regarding All Hypnotherapeutic Processes; The
Realization of Death*

Erickson: Now, you came out here for a certain purpose tonight.
Have you been in a trance so far this evening?

Subject: Yes.

Erickson: Do you feel tired as a result?

Subject: Yes. I'll never forget the night that Dr. Fink hypnotized
me, and afterwards I blamed my headache on the drink
you gave me. Then that night when you asked me if I had
pain from here down or here up [*Section* 1.6], I said no but
I thought, "That's a lie." It was my unconscious, I guess.
Nurse Dey said afterwards that I was telling her I couldn't
go on duty, and she said it must have been something in
the drink. I said, "Just wait, wait till I see him." Then I
forgot about it.

Erickson: Well, now, there's something further I want you to do
tonight. **You have been in a trance and you have also
been awake.** And while you were awake, you have told
us about your anxiety about swimming, and you also did
a much better job discussing it when you were in a
trance state. **Now I want you to really remember completely every one of the ideas, thoughts, and feelings
that came to your mind, as well as those you have
described. And I want you to review them and discuss
them openly and honestly and completely, and to do
it wide awake.**

Subject: Where shall I start?
Erickson: Where will you start?
Subject: He won't even designate an area. Well, let's see. First, I realize I was insanely jealous of Helen. It was asinine but natural, probably.
Erickson: Rather than asinine.
Subject: Yes, if you will.
Erickson: If you will.
Subject: If I will. Up until the time she was born, I was the youngest child. I was undoubtedly babied. I must have been—the youngest child always gets a bit of babying. Say, maybe Larry hates me. I'll have to ask him about that. And I used to get awfully mad at Helen. She was so little. And you're not supposed to get mad at babies. But I used to get mad at her, mad enough to strangle her. Don't take me literally. I was mad enough to kill her, but I don't think I would have, though, even if I was tempted. The affair about the high chair—I don't think I'll ever forget that. I was thoroughly disgusted with life and people. Maybe that's why I am still disgusted with people most of the time. It's so foolish. People refuse to see the obvious things, and they see everything that isn't obvious. And everybody gets all confused. I don't remember Daddy ever saying a cross word to us until that time. We could almost pull his hair out by the roots and he wouldn't say anything. But when I tipped Helen out of the high chair, he got mad. And I can understand that. You don't go around dumping babies on the floor. But he shouldn't have let his temper run away with him. I was so indignant to think he couldn't see I wanted to help Helen to see Mother so she would stop yelling her silly head off. Then when Father spanked me I thought, "Nobody loves me. I'm an outcast." I proceeded to hate everybody including Helen. I don't think I had any feeling toward Lisa and Larry. I was immune to them, or they were immune to me. But when I bounced Helen on her head that time...
I remember the neighbors used to come and say, "She is such a beautiful child. She looks just like a picture. She

looks just the way a baby ought to look." I remember
one of the ladies said, "You have to be careful because
such a beautiful baby could not live." And I thought,
"She never will live if I keep this up." I guess that's why
they thought I was trying to kill her. Maybe I was. Yes, I
guess I was. I was pretty young to murder people. Then
in rapid succession came the affair with the washtub
and the scorching look Mother gave me. Even after
Helen was all right I kept thinking she would die. She
coughed all day and all night. I guess she kept Mother
awake. But I was an outcast after that—for a very limited
time, of course. But then I always seemed to have an
affinity for doing things I was told not to do.

Then the affair with Mr. Smith—he was quite the character. Of course, now that I remember it, he was probably a pretty good egg—but I didn't think so then. He had
twins, and they were real little. Of course we were little,
too, but they were younger than we were. They were six
then—must have been six—we used to go over and play
with them. I remember Mother telling us Mr. Smith was a
German. Before the babies were born he wanted his
wife to go back to Germany so the children could be
born in Germany and be German citizens instead of
Americans. That immediately made me think he was the
worst thing that ever walked on shoe leather. But it was
natural, I guess, because he was born in Germany. He
was very angry with his wife because she wouldn't go
back there then. He was always fairly nice to us kids. He
used to take us out and play with us, but I used to sort of
stay out of his reach.

Rossi: She is now fully awake, and for the first time in this
entire therapeutic encounter, you are seemingly open
and direct in telling her, **"You have been in a trance and
you have also been awake."** You want her to now **"really
remember completely every one of the ideas. . . . and
discuss them openly and honestly and completely,**

and to do it wide awake." This one-level, open, honest and direct approach is very characteristic of you at the end of the difficult periods of hypnotherapeutic work when you will "tell all" to your patients—the way you indirectly worked on them, etc.* It is very important to directly emphasize that she **"do it wide awake"** because you do not want her to fall back into your conditioned pattern of somnambulistic trance as she reviews these trance events to you. That also was the purpose of your posthypnotic suggestion in the last section when you told her, "**I am going to awaken you shortly, and I want you to remember everything you said while you were asleep. . .**"

By the way, I really like the way you very directly and concisely do not allow Jane to put herself down by calling her feelings asinine.

So here for the first time she gives conscious expression to a clear and emotionally well-balanced understanding of herself and her early family relations. Do you feel that this is the sort of self-understanding that you have been striving to help her reach?

Erickson: She's only part of the way there now.

Rossi: What more needs to be done?

Erickson: The realization of what death is.

Rossi: Why is that realization important at this point?

Erickson: When Grandma is mentioned in relationship to it, Jane wasn't allowed to understand what death really was.

Rossi: She is integrating this important understanding of what death is. That is the total picture you are integrating.

Erickson: And it is related to her realization of what the war now means.

---

*See the various case studies in Erickson and Rossi, 1979, for further examples of Erickson's "telling all" approach.

2.18   A *Conscious and Unconscious Assessment of Therapeutic Work:*
        Ideomotor Signaling for Trance Induction

Erickson: Are you satisfied with your present performance?
Subject: No.
Erickson: Let your hand write the answer. Are you satisfied with
            your present performance?
Subject: [*Writes automatically no.*] Let's go, Harry. But I can't think of
            anything else.
Erickson: Can Jane go swimming? Let your hand answer that. I
            want it answered rapidly.
Subject: [*Writes yes*] It doesn't make sense. That's what happens
            when I ask myself the names of those three men. Dr. Fink,
            do you want to start writing notes again?
Fink: Can you write better with this pencil?
Subject: No. I thought maybe you were going to write something
            again—some of that silly Ann Arbor-Grand River stuff.
Fink: You know something about Ann Arbor, don't you?
Subject: I've been through there.
Fink: Have you ever been around there?
Subject: Not for a long time.
Erickson: **Let your left hand drop if I may interrupt you, Jane.**
Subject: [*Left hand slowly lowers.*] I'm glad I don't have to—transcribe
            this.
Erickson: "I'm glad I don't have to—transcribe this!"
Subject: What does that mean? Come on—educate me.
Erickson: [*To Mr. Beatty*] Now do you understand why I said it was
            not a very simple process?
Subject: What does that mean?
Erickson: You don't have to worry about it.
Subject: I never have to worry about anything. Silence is golden.
            What does that mean?
Erickson: We'll find out.
Subject: This reminds me of when Helen used to write letters
            before she could write—all this doodling [*referring to paper
            passed between Dr. Fink and Erickson*]. I take it I'm not sup-

posed to look at that, either. Tomorrow I'm going to hate you.

Erickson: I see your left hand is going down all right. Wouldn't you say so?

Subject: Yes.

Erickson: All right. [To Dr. Fink] The answer is yes but the letter s was accomplished through a disguised motion of the pencil. It follows the word *Monday*, and then a scrawl about which she made the remark about transcribing. She previously mentioned that she used to take shorthand.

Subject: Continue. This is very interesting.

Erickson: What is to happen tomorrow?

Subject: Tomorrow?

Erickson: Yes.

Subject: I am to scrub with Dr. Young. You know Dr. Young. Two of them, in fact.

Erickson: What else is to happen tomorrow?

Subject: I am to return a book to the library. Thanks for reminding me.

Rossi: You are now careful to assess her satisfaction with the therapeutic work on the conscious and unconscious levels. On a conscious level she says no, she is not satisfied; and on the unconscious level she uses automatic writing to answer no also. Yet she is able to automatically write yes to your question about being able to go swimming. Some therapeutic gain has been made, but more work needs to be done.

You then, in effect, ask her unconscious to signal if it is all right to interrupt her conscious mind when you say, **"Let your hand drop if I may interrupt you, Jane."** Her left hand does lower slowly in the manner characteristic of unconscious ideomotor signaling. This, of course, is also a way of beginning to reinduce trance without her quite being aware of it.

2.19   *Trance Induction, Doodling, and Automatic Writing for Further*
       Desensitization and Reassurance

Erickson: Just go to sleep. Go to sleep. **Easy, deep, sound sleep.**
            Are you sleeping now? Sleep deeply, soundly, and you
            are, are you not? All right. Now I want you **freely and**
            easily with this hand to rewrite what you were writing
            previously. Write it **freely and easily.** [*Subject writes.*] May
            I read it?
Subject: Yes.
Erickson: "Yesterday was Monday. The walk to Cusic was most
            boring. Think again, Jane. There must be a way." Are you
            trying to introduce something else? Or are you staying
            on that water problem? Or are you trying to introduce
            something else? Will it be all right to remain asleep but
            discuss that for me so that I can understand it better?
            Keep sleeping and discuss it freely.
Subject: I used to go to school at Romulo, and we used to walk
            out to Cusic two or three or four times a week. Some-
            times we used to go out there and go swimming.
Erickson: Go ahead.
Subject: I used to get awfully scared. I think it was perfectly silly
            because there was nothing to be afraid of. The kids used
            to laugh at me and I used to laugh, too, because it was
            funny. They would take me out with them and one would
            get hold of me on each side and walk out in the water
            with me until I was in water up to my neck. But that time I
            don't think I was really scared, but somehow I just had to
            get back to the shore. I would break away and run like
            mad for the dock. I was always thinking, if I could just
            make myself go out and make myself swim. I devised
            ways of doing it. Once I went out by myself. Cusic was
            very beautiful, and that night it was very dark. The water
            looked ugly, but I thought, "No time like the present." So I
            went in and I went out quite a ways and was just walking
            along in the water until it was up to my shoulders, and I
            don't know why but I thought about people drowning,

and I thought, "Maybe I'd better go back." But I didn't, I went on, because I thought if I could make myself do it, then I would learn how to swim. The next thing I knew I was right back on the shore.

Erickson: Go on. [Pause] Do you know what your hand is writing?

Subject: M-e-r-c-y.

Erickson: All right. Tell me about that.

Subject: That doesn't mean anything.

Erickson: Do you know what the rest of it is going to be now?

Subject: It's going to be reason.

Erickson: Can you explain it now?

Subject: No.

Erickson: Are you afraid to know what that means?

Subject: I am.

Erickson: Does that *mercy* mean something?

Subject: I don't think so.

Erickson: Let's see what the hand says, Jane. Does that *mercy* mean something? [*Subject writes.*] Do you know what your hand has written? [*Subject nods.*] Can you tell me what it means? Are you afraid to know? Are you afraid to know because of others being present?

Subject: No.

Erickson: Are you afraid to let me know? [*Subject breathing heavily and greatly distressed.*] Are you afraid to let me know? Are you afraid to know? [*Subject nods.*] Would you like to have me do something so that you would have the courage to know? [*Subject nods.*] All right. Suppose you get a vague, glimmering idea of what it is—not too good an idea but just a faint glimmer of an idea. Have you done so? [*Subject nods.*] Can you feel the idea a little bit more? [*Subject nods.*] You may feel it still a bit more. Just a little bit more. [*Subject nods.*] Until you get the whole idea completely. And it isn't so frightening as you thought, is it?

Subject: No.

Erickson: It is distressing, yes. But that's all right, isn't it? And you can really know what it means, can you not? Well, are you willing for me to know what it is? [*Subject nods.*] All of

it? [*Subject nods.*] Would you like to tell me now? Would
you like to tell me now? [*Subject nods.*] All right, Jane, tell
me. You can do it safely. You can tell me, can you not? All
right. Go ahead. Go ahead.

Subject: Yesterday Ann (Dey) came to me and said her folks had a
cottage in Mexico for about three weeks. Our vacations
are at different times. We have always been ranting
about that, and about how unfair it was. But she said her
dad and mother wanted me to come up for a weekend.
We get every other weekend off, and she said, "You can
come up and we'll go swimming." When she said that I
felt as if she had thrown cold water in my face. Here I've
been thinking about it—I've got to go. I can't just tell her I
don't want to. I don't even have any reason for not going.

Erickson: Yes. Now what has mercy got to do with that?

Subject: I don't know. Ann can swim, and with her I feel better.

Erickson: Why was it such a frightening idea?

Subject: It wasn't really frightening. I just thought so.

Erickson: Is that just doodling you are doing, or are you trying to
tell me something else?

Subject: It's just doodling.

Erickson: Do you think it's doodling? Do you still think it's doodling?

Subject: It must be.

Erickson: See what your hand writes here. Is it doodling? It wasn't
doodling, was it? Now do you think you'll have the
courage to understand what that doodle really was? Do
you think you will? Do you think you will have the courage to know? All right, that will be very interesting to
search your memories and discover. Or would you like
to have your hand surprise you and write the most
meaningful word that would give you the key to what the
doodle was? Just bring your hand up here and let it write
the meaningful word that defines the doodle. I think it
ought to be interesting to see what your hand writes.
Because you don't know, do you? And your hand does.
[*Subject writes.*] Can you tell me what the word is?

Subject: Trying.

Erickson: Now let's put in another word that is meaningful and see if this time your hand can write it more rapidly and more easily. Now what is that word? [Subject writes, "**failure.**"] Now write something more rapidly that is informative. Now what is that doodle a picture of? [Subject writes, "**girl in bathing cap.**"] Then you are really asking me a question, aren't you? Do you mind verbalizing that question?

Subject: I know if I don't try to swim I won't get scared. If I do, it will be effort gone to waste again.

Rossi: Having received her unconscious ideomotor signal that it's all right to interrupt her conscious mind, you now proceed to reinduce a deeper trance in the beginning of this section with direct suggestions to go "**easy, deep, sound asleep . . . freely and easily.**"

Erickson: She has a lot turning over in her mind. There is turmoil developing over something; I have to be right there to comfort her so she can give it "**freely and easily.**" She can go through all kinds of turmoil because I am supporting her.

Rossi: In spite of the apparently satisfactory insight and conscious working through of her swimming phobia in the awake state a few sections back, we again find a kind of emotional resistance to even trying. Why is this? Was she rationalizing while awake, and now in trance her fears overwhelm her again? Or is this just part of the typical process of gradual desensitization by repeating the recall and partial reliving of the trauma?

Erickson: Maybe you [Dr. Marion Moore, M.D.] can answer that, with your experience of going into combat with younger soldiers.

Moore: I would show myself as stronger than they were. You bring yourself to a point where you do better than you ordinarily might do in order to show the young soldiers what they have to do to not be a coward, or whatever.

Erickson: The first time you entered combat, you had fear?

Moore: No. Quite a few men did, but I didn't.

Rossi: You Southern gentlemen seldom do feel fear [Dr. Moore is from Tennessee]!

Erickson: So you'd say something like that to reassure the younger soldiers.

Rossi: So in this section, you [Erickson] are reassuring and doing further "working through." Your questions, doodling, and automatic writing all help to reevoke unresolved material about her fears of "**failure**" and of the "**girl in the bathing cap.**"

Erickson: Yes, it's reassurance.

2.20   Interpersonal Aspects of Recovering from Phobias: Breaking Through Persona Behavior By Sharing Fears with Others

Erickson: You don't want it to go to waste again, do you?

Subject: No.

Erickson: All right. Now I'll say a few things to you, Jane. I asked you verbally when you were awake to discuss all the things you had said to me in a trance. And you didn't really like that, did you? And yet you wanted to be polite and courteous and to observe all of the laws of etiquette. Isn't that right?

Subject: Yes.

Erickson: And you can't quite understand why, when I am doing therapy, I bring in strangers, isn't that right? And it's very distressing to you. It doesn't seem quite fair or honest, isn't that right? Now perhaps this will help you to understand a bit. This fear, this anxiety about swimming, is observed in relation to other people. This gentleman who is here tonight is a total stranger to you. He doesn't mean anything to you nor you to him, except that you are both interested in many of the same things. You don't know what my purpose is in having him here, but there is a purpose. I can't explain it to you, just as you have been unable to explain to yourself a lot of things.

You need to get over some of these fears and anxieties—that are manifested in relationship to other people and concealed from other people—by bringing them out so that it can be realized that one can live even if others do know. Do you see? And so we make use of these people in that way. You have said things to us tonight that you didn't even dare to remember to yourself, isn't that right? And you have made yourself the more likable in our eyes, because we can see clearly that there is a very human person behind all of that charming behavior. And one wants more than just charming behavior in a person. One wants to know that there is a human being behind the charm, and that there is something real—that there isn't just quick wit and ready words and a gay answer and ready laughter—something just for show. We like people best when we know that they are real in a lot of little things. And you are really going to believe what I say, because you know it's true, and you know everybody listening to me knows it's true.

Erickson: In formal psychotherapy you have to keep things so secret. A husband and wife were in psychoanalysis separately for over a year, and each was trying to keep it a secret from the other. I told them they could save a hell of a lot of money just being open with each other about what was common knowledge to everybody.

Rossi: So you really believe what you are saying here about the importance of the subject sharing her fears with others—even strangers. Because her fears were learned in relation to others, she can best give them up by sharing them with others.*

Erickson: [*Erickson now gives further illustrations from his secret work with Margaret Mead and Gregory Bateson for the U.S. Office of Strategic Services during World War II, interviewing*

---

*The interpersonal component of Erickson's work has been well documented by Jay Haley in his books, *Strategies of Psychotherapy* (1963), *Uncommon Therapy* (1973), and *Conversations with Milton H. Erickson* (3 vols.) (1985).

Japanese and German prisoners of war. This information is still classified top secret, however, and cannot be publicly reported at this time.]

2.21 Emotional Catharsis and Reframing as an Essence of Erickson's Approach: Not Personality Restructuring But "A More Complete View"; Failure as a Part of Successful Living

Erickson: Now, about this fear of yours about swimming. You are making one very grave error in handling it. You are going to have to correct that error. Because you are trying and trying and trying again to go swimming, and you want to go, and yet you have some fears too strong for you. Isn't that right? Now you are going to handle it in a totally different way. You are not to let it compel you to try and try again. The first thing you need to do is, by yourself, to remember all those things you told me, and remember all of them, and remember them with full understanding. And remember that as a little child, you were much more honest and sincere in your feelings than you have been since childhood—because you didn't let people see you cry, and that really wasn't honest, because you did cry. And crying wasn't a sign of weakness as you thought it was. **And when you think about it now, you realize that the strong as well as the weak cry at times. You will realize that the strong must have their happy moments and their sad moments,** isn't that right? And so you have been putting up a front pretending that you never cried, and that you don't feel bad, and that you don't feel miserable. And you don't want to face the fact that you were awfully jealous of Helen, and that you did hate your father and your mother. But you don't quite understand about that, Jane. You don't understand, and it is really very simple. What you don't understand is this: That you like some of the things your father and mother did, and you hated some of the things that they did, and that's a lot different than hating them. You hated some of the things your father and mother did, and you liked some of the things they did. **And there's a lot of difference between what people are and what people do.** And there's a lot of difference between what people want to do and what they succeed in doing. And you are going to respect and admire honesty of intention. **And you are going to respect fully and appreciatively people who fail in some things here and there and elsewhere.** Are you beginning to understand that?

You need really to sit down and not try to argue with yourself that you can go swimming. You don't need to do that sort of thing. You do need to sit down by yourself and really, honestly and completely and appreciatively, look over your memories—look over your understandings. And be awfully pleased that you had so much character as a little child, and to not condemn yourself because that little child, unable to understand the implications and significances, did things and wanted to do things that didn't have a real meaning to you. What did being dead mean to you then? It meant to be away for a while—to be in a different place. But it didn't mean death as you as a grown-up understand it. **Being jealous of Helen when you were a little baby had one meaning. Now when you are grown-up, it has another meaning entirely.** Wouldn't you want a little baby to appreciate its own worth and its own personality and its own needs enough to defend them in any way it understood? All of these years you have been condemning yourself, have you not?

Subject: Yes.

Erickson: Why? Perhaps so that you could reach a still better and larger understanding of yourself. Perhaps by sheer accident. But whatever has happened to you is something that you can use for yourself. I want you to look back upon that jealousy of Helen as constituting the nucleus of a sense of personality—of personal appreciation of the self. A little child's sense of its own worth. And when you tipped her over in the high chair and she fell on you and hurt your arm, when you were motivated by perfectly good reasons, it was disgusting, it was aggravating, it was maddening to have a good turn attempted for Helen result in pain to your arm and a spanking from your father whom you loved, and who betrayed you in that spanking by something that he didn't understand. Actually, when you look back over it, it was a very miserable return on your good deed. You failed, your father failed. **But then there are failures in life. They constitute a part of successful living.**

Rossi: Here you do some very comprehensive reframing of her childhood patterns of understanding regarding failure and jealousy. You reframe her jealousy of Helen into the nucleus of a more positive, mature personality development. This idea is fairly common now, with the development of humanistic psychology, but it was innovative back 1945. Would you agree that we are now seeing how emotional catharsis and a reframing of childhood misunderstandings are an essence of your hypnotherapeutic approach? That's it: catharsis and helping a person reframe and restructure the personality, right?

Erickson: Not restructuring. You give them a more complete view!

Rossi: So hypnotherapy is not magic. It simply facilitates a more complete, comprehensive point of view that frees one from the limitations and literalism of childhood.

Erickson: Yes, as when I say: **"And when you think about it now, you realize that the strong as well as the weak cry at times. You will realize that the strong must have their happy moments and their sad moments . . ."** It is a shift from her oversimplified child's level to a more mature adult understanding. **"But then there are failures in life. They constitute a part of successful living."**

Rossi: When you say, **"There's a lot of difference between what people are and what people do,"** and, **"you are going to respect fully and appreciatively people who**

fail in some things here and there and elsewhere,"
you are using the childhood trauma as a steppingstone
to enhance her more adult understanding. So the trauma
in her memory becomes reframed into a new nucleus of
personality, in a positive way rather than the old hurt-
ful way.

Erickson: Yes, as when I say: **"Being jealous of Helen
when you were a baby had one meaning. Now when
you are grown-up it has another meaning entirely."**

2.22   *Prescribing the Symptom: Evoking a Yes Set and Implication to
Reinforce Posthypnotic Suggestions*

Erickson: When you say that you don't know what to do about that
trip to Mexico—well, that can be fixed up for you. **I can
solve it for you very neatly.** Do you think I can?
Subject: Yes.
Erickson: I can solve it in a number of ways. But I'm not going to
specify the way yet. I'm going to have another interview
with you, because you have a lot of work to do. Now
when is that trip to be?
Subject: Sometime in July.
Erickson: And you will be in Detroit until then?
Subject: Yes.
Erickson: Do you feel we have enough time to solve it?
Subject: Yes.
Erickson: Dr. Fink wrote me a note that he wants you to reply to. Do
you want Miss Dey with you next time we have a session,
or do you think we can get along without her?
Subject: Yes, we can get along without her.
Erickson: Well, now to summarize things. You have uncovered a lot
of forgotten memories, forgotten fears. I indicated to
you some ways in which you can view those things, and I
think you are beginning to agree with me. Isn't that right?
**And next time we can work on this problem of your
fear of water. Does it already look smaller to you?**
Subject: Yes.

Erickson: Now there's one bit of instruction I want to give you, and that is this: **Until the next session there must be no effort on your part to go swimming. That has to be a promise, do you understand?** No trips to Webster Hall. You can accept Miss Dey's invitation to Mexico and disregard entirely the question of swimming. That doesn't have to enter into your thinking any more than you will now think about what you will eat when you get to Mexico. And you won't worry about that. Neither do you need to worry about the swimming side of it. The eating side of the trip is one thing, and you don't have to think about that, or about what bed you are going to sleep in. And in precisely the same way you need not think about the swimming. Now is there anything you would like to say to me?

Subject: No.

Rossi: She still has unresolved fears by the end of this session, so while she is still in trance you utilize her feeling of *not knowing* to *apparently* take over responsibility for dealing with her fear of swimming on the projected Mexican trip (**"I can solve it for you very neatly"**). Before you do this, however, you introduce an important posthypnotic suggestion in a casual, passing, and indirect way by saying, **"And next time we can work on this problem of your fear of water."** With equal casualness you then have her admit that the problem looks "smaller."

Next you relieve her fears by *directly prescribing the symptom:* **"Until the next session there must be no effort on your part to go swimming. That has to be a promise, do you understand?"** This seems to be a perfectly direct and straightforward posthypnotic suggestion. But what it accomplishes indirectly by implication is what is most important to you. It certainly will be easy for her to carry out this posthypnotic suggestion since it is in fact her symptom, and it has all the force of her lifelong swimming phobia to support it. The very ease of carrying out this posthypnotic suggestion opens a yes or acceptance set in her that tends to positively reinforce the other very important therapeutic suggestions you gave her so casually just a few moments ago (doing further work on the phobia, and the phobia looking smaller). The important relief her conscious mind gets from your symptom prescription now absorbs all her attention so that these two more important but casually administered therapeutic suggestions tend to fall into her unconscious. Here they can lay the groundwork for future healing without any interference from her conscious mind's distortions and fear.

On another level symptom prescription also has the implied effect of giving you control over the symptom: if she can activate the symptom upon your suggestion, she can presumably learn later to deactivate it upon your suggestion.*

2.23   Not Knowing and Prescribing the Symptom in Therapeutic Work: A Wisecrack Revealed as a Form of Cryptic, Two-Level Communication

Erickson: Is this doodle down here anything you want to discuss? Let your hand write the answer. [Subject writes, no] Are you sure of that? **Now after you awaken, I want you to prefer a Lucky Strike cigarette.** Will you do that?

Subject: Yes.

Erickson: Also after you awaken, I want you to have a very thorough appreciation of how very capably you have worked tonight. It is awfully hard for me to tell you how capably you have worked. You haven't the background and understanding to realize that you have done a tremendous amount of work tonight. As a nurse you can appreciate that when the surgeon does a colostomy, he has done a

---

*See Rossi's volume, The Psychobiology of Mind-Body Healing (1986b), and Rossi and Cheek's volume, Mind-Body Therapy (1988) for many illustrations of how symptom prescription can be used to facilitate patients' control over their own symptom reactions.

tremendously important piece of work, but you also have your own professional appreciation of the fact that behind that successful operation lay many years of training and experience; that behind that operation lay a foundation of talent and training and ability. Isn't that right?

Subject: Yes.

Erickson: And so when I say that you have worked with amazing competence, I mean it. Even though **you don't really know just what it was that you did, nor how you did it.** You don't realize what you meant or what you said when you declared that you had lost the war single-handedly. That isn't entirely a wisecrack. It was meant to be, but I think in the back of your mind you realize that it wasn't. You had lost the war. Do you know what it was? Are there two other letters in the word war? Answer with your hand. [*Subject writes, yes.*] Do you know what they are? [*Subject writes, yes, and then the letters* t-e.] When you lost the war, what did it mean? It's a distressing, agonizing thing, isn't it? You lost a distressing thing, and that's something nice to get rid of, isn't it? Now you are beginning to see why I am not concerned about your trip. Do you see? Isn't that delightful? [*Subject laughs.*] Now one other thing. I want you to know that I thank you for your generosity, your kindness, in permitting me to do things in my way. I appreciate it tremendously. It was very kind of you to permit me to do things my way, and in return I'll try to do a lot of things your way. Is that fair enough?

Subject: Yes.

Rossi: You express your characteristic appreciation for the work the patient does and you add your views about *not knowing* "what it was that you did, nor how you did it." You are thereby giving primacy and potency to her unconscious, even though you helped her attain as much conscious understanding as possible.

Erickson: How did she lose her fear of water? She adds the *t*-e to *war* to lose *water.*

Rossi: I don't get it.

Erickson: I told her she was going to lose something. She loses two letters from *water* to make *war.*

Rossi: Your explanations do stretch one's credulity; she has only lost some letters! I wondered if there was some symbolic connection between the words *war* and *water,* but I could not find it. [*Rossi now summarizes the entire case to date, using Table 1 as an outline.*] By the end of that session [Section 2.15], most insight-oriented therapists might have terminated the case, assuming that since Jane's understanding and working through was complete, her symptoms would disappear accordingly. But instead of encouraging her to go swimming, you do the opposite and actually prescribe the symptom [Section 2.22]. After all that insight, why did you feel she was not ready to swim?

Erickson: You're only assuming about her childhood situation. You really don't know, even after all your theorizing. In prescribing the symptom, I place *my* inhibition on her swimming.

Rossi: So now it becomes your inhibition of swimming, not hers. That's the important thing about prescribing the symptom: you can change your inhibition later.

Erickson: Yes, I can change mine!

Rossi: She's finding it much harder to change hers. So that's the important switch that takes place in symptom prescription: *you displace her inhibition of swimming from her mind to yours!*

Erickson: Yeah. [*Erickson tells the case in which he helped a couple consummate their marriage on* Thursday *by insisting that they do it on* Friday.* The point is that the young bride was "offended" by Erickson's "presumption to name the day," and so did it a day earlier "because she wanted her choice of day"!*]

Rossi: So in that case you were prescribing the symptom

---

*See "Patient H" in "Special Techniques of Brief Hypnotherapy" in Erickson, 1954b/1980.

by telling them not to consummate the marriage until a certain date. You thereby provoked the wife into asserting her choice by doing it a day earlier than you permitted!

2.24   Awakening from Trance: Carrying Out a Minor Posthypnotic Suggestion; Giving the Subject an Opportunity to Discharge and Displace Hostility onto the Therapist

Erickson: And if you want to feel mad at me, go right to it. A psychiatrist is somebody you can get mad at and who won't take it personally. Go to sleep now, and wake up. Close your eyes and sleep deeply. Did you have something you wanted to say? Close your eyes and sleep deeply. All right, now. Take it easy, and awaken, and feel refreshed and zestful, even though a bit tired. But really enjoy being awake.

Subject: Hello everybody. [*Reaches for a cigarette*]. May I have one of yours [the Lucky Strikes]? You wouldn't like a Phillip Morris?

Erickson: That was beautifully said. I wouldn't like one.

Subject: If Sister Louisa could see me now! I didn't tell you about this, but the priest who gave us a lecture on psycho-analysis—I want you to realize this—I'm playing with the devil. You, too!

Erickson: Well, I think I'll be able to throw him for a loop. The devil, I mean.

Fink: Is there something in the second shelf of the bookcase you'd like to ask about?

Subject: Mr. Estabrooks? That reminds me. You know Mr. Esta-brooks, a friend of yours. **He says nasty things about you**—not real nasty—but he says you don't believe that in hypnotism a person would kill someone else. He says it's all a matter of operator attitude—that if you really thought they would do it, they would do it. He says some pretty nasty things about you [*referring to Erickson*].

Mr. Beatty: He must be a pretty good sport, at that.

Erickson: You see, I **took his book apart** in a most unkind fashion.

Mr. Beatty: I wonder, has he sold many copies of his book (Estabrooks, 1943)?

Subject: Frankly, the copy in the library is **very worn.**

Fink: Recently?

Subject: Ann and I have been doing some reading. Father Patrick had just finished lecturing us on psychoanalysis and keeping away from Freud's books. So we went to the library and got one of his books. We have to hide it because every once in a while they come and look over our rooms to see what books we are reading.

Erickson: The priest evidently did an excellent job of interesting you in Freud. Do you feel a bit tired?

Subject: A little—well, not particularly. I just came out of three scrubs with Dr. Roberts, in which nothing was right—as usual.

Erickson: Any questions you want to ask me?

Subject: No, not that I can think of. I'll probably think about them after I go home.

Erickson: Would you like to think about them while you are here?

Subject: No—no.

Rossi: In this final section of the session, she carries out the posthypnotic preference for Lucky Strike cigarettes that you suggested in the previous section: "**Now, after you awaken, I want you to prefer a Lucky Strike cigarette.**" Why did you do that? Were you just demonstrating a posthypnotic suggestion, or was it a marker to help you assess her ability to carry out posthypnotic suggestions?

Erickson: [Nods indiscriminately.]

Rossi: You end this session by giving her an opportunity to ventilate some hostility toward you. You believe that this is important and inevitable, because in some concrete fashion, patients resent having their symptoms taken away. So you give them an opportunity to recognize, discharge, and displace their hostility in some direct manner, lest they express it by hanging on to the symptom.

The subject apparently does not pick up on your suggestion to ventilate hostility in any obvious way, but gives vicarious veiled expression to it by relating how Dr. Estabrooks **"says nasty things about you."** Then a moment later she takes another "dig" by noting that Estabrook's book is **"very worn"** (meaning *well read*), even though you **"took his book apart"** when you read it.

Evoking and Utilizing Psychodynamic Processes

3.0 *Assessing and Reiterating Previous Hypnotic Work; Source of Headache as Aftereffect of Hypnotherapy*

Erickson: Well, Jane, what's on the books for tonight?

Subject: Ever since I've been here I've been trying to remember my shorthand.... I'm supposed to go out from here tonight not being afraid of swimming or of water. Is that right?

Erickson: With some better understanding. Do you recall how it has to be done?

Subject: No. I remember some things. Dr. Fink, do you remember? I told you about "this damn war," and then adding *t-e* [to *war* to make *water*]; and then there was a long word but I still don't know what that is.

Erickson: Anything else?

Subject: Oh, yes. I sincerely hated my mother and my father and my little sister. Let's see. I could say, too, that it shouldn't be the water I should be afraid of. That was more or less of a cover-up. I was pretty mad at my mother and father, and instead of staying mad at them, I hated water. My own deductions.... There was something else.... You said something about suppressed emotions. You seemed to think that I think it's a sign of weakness to cry and do foolish things, but I don't think I do.

Present in 1945 *for Session* III: Dr. Milton H. Erickson, Dr. Jerome Fink, the subject (who is also referred to as "Miss S" and "Jane"), and the subject's friend, "Ann Dey." *Present for the* 1979 *commentaries*: Dr. Milton H. Erickson and Dr. Ernest L. Rossi.

Erickson: What do you think?

Subject: No, I don't think I do. Anyway I don't think I think I do. When I see other people crying and going through things like that, I never think they are weak.

Erickson: But you think it's weakness on your part.

Subject: It all depends on why I was crying.

Erickson: Anything else?

Subject: Yes. I know there's something I've forgotten.

Erickson: How did you feel after that session?

Subject: **I had a rip-roaring headache.** Otherwise it was quite enlightening. I mean, I never imagined I could absolutely want to strangle my mother and father, and Helen too.

Erickson: How do you feel about discovering these things?

Subject: It's very interesting. It probably would be useful, too, if I just knew how to use those things, now that I've got them. It's like having a car and not knowing how to drive it.

Erickson: That's something one learns.

Subject: Yes.

Rossi: This session takes place at the end of June, about three weeks after the previous session in which she experienced a great deal of psychodynamic insight. At the end of that session you suggested that she not try to swim yet. You begin this session with your typical assessment of the previous work. When you ask her how she felt after the work, she reports, "**I had a rip-roaring head-ache.**" Do you have any idea why she experienced that headache? We know from her previous remarks that she also experienced headaches after her hypnotic sessions with Dr. Fink.

Erickson: Yes, she uncovered all her memories last session, but here she has amnesia again. She's lost all perspective. She recalls only a small part of it.

Rossi: Is that because she still has conflict about it?

Erickson: No, she hates Helen. Why? Because Helen was heavy and held onto the tub, so the accident was not Jane's fault. Her mother misunderstood, her father misunderstood, all the things she mentioned [see review in Table 1, Section 2.15]. You see, it was a large picture with many elements.

Rossi: And it's crucial to understand those individual elements of the situation.

Erickson: And she's having a headache trying to sort them out in her mind.

Rossi: So her hard work, the difficult mental effort, is causing the headache.

3.1 *Trance Induction with Motivating Questions the Conscious Mind Cannot Answer; Apparent Resistance to Trance Induction as a Bid for Quid Pro Quo; Resistance and Laughter as Emotional Balance and Release in the Transference*

Erickson: Have you thought much about swimming?
Subject: I almost went last week.
Erickson: Why didn't you?
Subject: I decided I hadn't better.
Erickson: Why?
Subject: I think you told me not to. So I decided better I hadn't.
Erickson: How do you feel about deciding not to go?
Subject: Not particularly bad. I really didn't want to go, anyway. I used to go when it was something I couldn't get out of.
Erickson: How much trouble did you have getting out of it?
Subject: No trouble at all. I just told her flatly I couldn't go.
Erickson: How did you feel about that?
Subject: Not particularly bad. I don't know why. She asked me, and I said no, although I shouldn't tell her I'm just not going.
Erickson: Did you apologize to yourself afterwards?
Subject: No.
Erickson: What would you have done last May?
Subject: Well, I probably would have gone. She is quite an insistent person, and her feelings are hurt if you look at her cross-eyed.

Erickson: How else would you have felt last May?

Subject: Let me see. I probably would have made a million and one excuses, but I wouldn't have told her I just didn't want to go. Then I would have been very angry at myself, or if I couldn't have gotten out of it, I would have gone and hated every minute of it.

Erickson: And you didn't do that this time?

Subject: No.

Erickson: Do you think you could ever do that again?

Subject: Probably not.

Erickson: Was it a frightening invitation this time, the way it would have frightened you last May?

Subject: No, I don't think I was frightened. I just didn't want to go.

Erickson: Last May would it have been a frightening invitation?

Subject: Well, of course, when they asked me I could always think of a good excuse why I shouldn't.

Erickson: This time you could say either yes or no?

Subject: Uh-huh.

Erickson: Do you think it was fair for me to ask you to give me that promise?

Subject: Certainly. I mean, you wouldn't have asked me if it hadn't been fair.

Erickson: Sometimes we feel things like that are unfair.

Subject: If I had been dying to go swimming—but I was glad to have an excuse not to go.

Erickson: When do you go on this summer trip?

Subject: July fifteenth, isn't it, Ann?

Erickson: And is there anything special you are doing to get ready for it?

Subject: I'm going to spend a lot of money between now and the seventh of July.

Erickson: For what?

Subject: I know what you want me to say. You want me to say I should be buying a swimming suit. I suppose I'll have to.

Erickson: Why?

Subject: Because you can't go swimming without one.

Erickson: Why a new one?

Subject: I'm celebrating. After all, you should celebrate once in a while.

Erickson: Anything else you want to mention?

Subject: Oh, yes. I found an error in what I told you before. I told you the time I tipped Helen out of the high-chair, I was pulling her to the door. I asked Mother about that, and she said she didn't think so. She said she thought I was trying to take her back into the dining room where Dad was. At last, it seemed so from the way the chair was, the way Helen was, and the way I was, that that must have been it.

Erickson: Actually, of course, the essential thing is the way you remembered it. Does that really alter the story any?

Subject: No. I just wondered how come the error. Theoretically, things like that don't happen, do they?

Erickson: Suppose you remember something about that red book in the bookcase. And then you go to the bookcase and find it's not a red book after all—it's really a blue book. It's the sort of error you can make. It's your own attitude toward the book. Still anything more?

Subject: Let's see. No, I don't think there is.

Erickson: Do you know what your real feelings are now?

Subject: About what?

Erickson: Swimming.

Subject: Well, I think I can try it now. I mean, there's absolutely no logical reason why I should be afraid. Of course, there wasn't before, either. I don't know whether I would be afraid. I don't think I would.

Erickson: Would you really like to find out what your feelings are?

Subject: Certainly.

Erickson: How would you go about doing that?

Subject: Just go swimming and see what happens.

Erickson: Is there any other way?

Subject: I don't think so.

Erickson: **Would you like to find out if there is another way?**

Subject: What is the other way?

Erickson: **Would you like to find out?**

Subject:	He just doesn't answer any questions. Certainly.
Erickson:	**Suppose you go to sleep now.**
Subject:	I'm not going to go to sleep. I'm going to see whether Mr. Estabrooks is right or not.
Erickson:	You are?
Subject:	Uh-huh.
Erickson:	Would you like to know if I'm right?
Subject:	Certainly. Why not? [*Erickson checks reprints.*] He is going through his whole library.
Erickson:	You see, I have published the same thing Estabrooks has.
Subject:	That's too bad.
Erickson:	So I agree with Estabrooks. There are some correct things in his book. That is one place where I agree with him.
Subject:	One of the few?
Erickson:	Yes. For how long do you want to find out if Estabrooks is right?
Subject:	If you say so, I think I'll believe you. What about hypnotism while someone is asleep? He says if you go to a sleeping person and start to talk to them, you don't get consent or you don't get disapproval.
Erickson:	I can't remember the pages where Estabrooks says that hypnosis and sleep are entirely different things. Also he says that one can be transformed into the other. Then he says that they are identical. He doesn't make up his mind.
Subject:	So where does that leave the truth?
Erickson:	The truth is that if you want to hypnotize a sleeping person, you have to rouse them from the sleeping state.
Subject:	I'll have to write that down. "Dr. Erickson says...."
Erickson:	Suppose you go to sleep.
Subject:	Do you think I ought to?

Rossi: This is one of your favorite approaches to facilitating trance induction: *You ask a series of motivating questions that the conscious mind cannot answer.* The only way the patient can get an answer is by turning inward and reflecting for a few moments. This inward turning can easily be deepened into trance by labeling it as "sleep" and by implying that the patient is going into hypnosis so that the unconscious can reveal the answer. Many of your questions that her conscious mind cannot answer, of course, are actually mobilizing her mental sets that will facilitate the experience of age progression* that will soon take place. An example is your question, "**Would you like to find out if there is another way?**"

The subject certainly manifests resistance to trance induction when she does not respond to your questions about her emotions and to your suggestion, "**Suppose you go to sleep now.**" You are implying that she needs to go into trance to find out about her emotions. However, you then apparently realize that it might be best to go along with her questions about Mr. Estabrooks, which we know from the last session is her indirect way of expressing hostility toward you. Why is she so resistant at this time?

Erickson: In ordinary life, if you want someone to do something for you, the best way is to do a lot of things for them first. So I let her pick an argument with me.

Rossi: So you are giving her control?

Erickson: At that time.

Rossi: So later she will give control to you *quid pro quo*?

Erickson: Uh-hum.

Rossi: And since she has taken an awful lot from you, she also has to dish some out for you?

Erickson: That's right.

Rossi: This is a regular aspect of your work in which you help people discharge their hostility and resentment for

---

*See Section IV in Volume II of Erickson, 1980, for extensive discussions of the phenomenon and therapeutic application of time distortion.

whatever they have to take from you. Most therapists don't do that. It may be that a lot of resistance is actually a way of balancing that emotional checkbook between therapist and patient.

Erickson: Did you notice the tremendous laughter? [*Here Erickson is referring to another recent case observed by Dr. Moore and me in which the patient's laughter betrayed the release of much pent-up hostility and resistance.*]

3.2   Trance Induction Utilizing Patient's Motivation and Behavior with a Contingent Suggestion: Reframing Resistance into Cooperation

Erickson: Suppose you go to sleep.
Subject: All right, I will. May I continue smoking my cigarette?
Erickson: After you are asleep, yes. Go to sleep now. Go to sleep. Go sound asleep. And **as soon as you are sound asleep, I want you to start smoking.** As soon as you are asleep, sound asleep, I want you to take a drag of your cigarette. And sleep deeply and soundly. Deeply and soundly. Go way deep asleep. Sleep comfortably and easily. Go deeply, soundly asleep. Go sound asleep. Go sound asleep. Take a drag of that cigarette as soon as you are asleep. [*Subject takes drag of cigarette.*] Sleep sounder than you have ever slept before. And enjoy that cigarette. And you will, will you not? And you will keep sleeping soundly. Sound and contented sleep. And you are sleeping, are you not? And you will keep on sleeping, will you not? Will you not? And enjoy your cigarette. Keep smoking. [*To observers*] Note transformation of a resistance object into one of cooperation [*Back to subject*] And are you sleeping soundly now? [*Subject nods*] Are you remembering and understanding the things that happened to you before? Are you comfortable about them? Depressed by them?
Subject: No.
Erickson: Are you glad to have an understanding of them?
Subject: Yes.

Erickson: Do you feel confident about what will happen tonight?
Subject: Yes.
Erickson: Do you think there is any other way to find out how you will feel about going swimming than just trying to go swimming?
Subject: There probably is.
Erickson: Can you think of what it might be? I want you to just keep on sleeping, sounder all the time. Do you like smoking cigarettes? Would you like to quit smoking? Take another puff and enjoy it. Sleeping sounder all the time. Sleeping soundly and comfortably. Do you want another puff? Take another. [*Subject puts out cigarette.*] I'm going to write a question for you here. Let your hand write the answer. Yes or no. Answer yes or no.
Rossi: You utilize her own wish to smoke as a means of facilitating hypnotic induction by using a contingent suggestion that "**As soon as you are sound asleep, I want you to start smoking.**" This is a clear example of your Utilization Approach. You encourage any behavior the subject is motivated for and simply hitchhike your hypnotic suggestions onto it. Thus even behaviors that appear as resistance can be reframed into the process of therapy.
Erickson: Yes, and that sets up the situation of having her hand write the answer yes or no.
Rossi: I notice, by the way, that when you did this work back in 1945 you seemed to repeat yourself a lot more in the traditional authoritarian hypnotic style.
Erickson: That's because it was an experimental case and we were focusing on psychodynamics.

3.3   Pseudo-Orientation into Future Time: Implied Directive with a Behavioral Signal for Somnambulism

Erickson: Sleep soundly. Keep sleeping deeply. And now I want you to recall some of those things that happened. I want you to recall that time has changed very quickly. And it did happen, did it not? And now I want you to understand, listen carefully and understand, that time is going to change again. And it is now June, 1945. And I'm going to change time again. I want you to forget June, 1945. Forget June, 1945, and yet be able to listen to me and understand me. And time is going to change and you won't know what day it is or what month it is, and you won't even care. You will just be comfortable sleeping deeply and soundly. You won't even care what day it is. All you want is to sleep. And now time is changing, and I want you to realize that time has changed very quickly. Still you don't know the day and you don't care. Soon it is going to be August, 1945. August, 1945. And it is really going to be August, 1945, and before it will be August, 1945, many things must happen to you. Many different things. And slowly I want those things to happen to you. I want them to go through your mind—every day in July and every day in the first week of August. I want these days to be clear in your mind until slowly you begin to recall even the last week in June, 1945. And now sleep and let time go by until it is August, 1945. Just keep sleeping as time goes by, as things happen to you— many things happen. And in August, 1945, you are going to come to see me. You are, are you not? **When it is August, 1945, I want you to sleep with your eyes open, and talk to me, and tell me those things that happened the last week in June, and in the weeks of July and the first week of August. And you've got to tell me about swimming, what you did about it, and how you did it.** [*Subject opens eyes.*] Hello. [*Subject smiles.*] Same old people again.

Rossi: Your sentence, **"When it is August, 1945, I want you to sleep with your eyes open . . . and how you did it,"** is a clear illustration of how you use the implied directive* for her to give a behavioral signal when she is

---

*See "Indirect Forms of Suggestion" in Erickson & Rossi, 1980.

in a somnambulistic state (in deep trance with eyes open and acting as if she were awake) and ready to reorient herself into future time. You know that she will have an opportunity to swim when she goes on vacation in July. You therefore pseudo-orient her into time future to August, when she will have a session with you after her vacation. Here she is to tell you about how she "did it"—presumably, how she went swimming. You do not tell her directly that she will swim during her vacation. Direct suggestion might arouse too much resistance, even though she is in trance. Instead your suggestions bypass all the resistance she has amassed against effort or suggestions about swimming. Pseudo-orientation into time future allows you both to assume she has succeeded in swimming and now need only tell you how she did it.*

Erickson: Yes.

3.4   Personality Integrity in Somnambulistic Trance

Subject: The wicked five! [*The subject is referring to the five members present in this session.*] Any volunteers for the skull on the desk?
Erickson: What skull?
Subject: The skull that should be there.
Erickson: Why?
Subject: Don't you think there should be one there?
Erickson: I have two skulls in my possession. In fact, I carry one of them with me.
Subject: "Grin, thou hollow skull."
Fink: Does that bear any relation to the skeleton in the closet?
Subject: What do you mean, the skeleton in the closet?
Erickson: I don't want you to tell me anything about how you got here tonight. But you have got quite a story to tell me, haven't you? When was the last time you saw me?
Subject: June.

---

*See also, "Pseudo-Orientation in Time as a Hypnotherapeutic Procedure" (Erickson, 1954a/1980).

Erickson: Yes, I'm still wearing my best suit. [*Subject examines clothing of people in room.*] Never mind that. I arranged the whole thing.

Subject: I won't worry about it.

Rossi: You have often insisted that patients retain their personalities in trance, and the subject's sardonic humor in this section is an illustration of your point. Dr. Fink tries to respond with a pun about a skeleton in the closet in hopes of getting some psychodynamic material flowing, but Miss S will have none of it. She acts as if she were awake, but she is actually in a somnambulistic trance.

Erickson: Yes, she thinks she is awake.

3.5   Confusion in Time Orientation: Implication and Questions to Sustain and Extend Time Future; No Lies, But Implies!

Erickson: You don't need to. It's up to you to do some talking. What about the last week in June?

Subject: You know how it is. You sort of die to go on vacation. You watch everyone else get ready and then you hate them. Then they are gone and the place is absolutely deserted.

Erickson: Were you at _____ this week?

Subject: This week? I go routinely, every Saturday or Monday.

Erickson: What day of the week is this?

Subject: I can't see that calendar.

Erickson: I wouldn't trust that calendar anyway.

Subject: Is it written in Greek?

Erickson: What day of the week is it?

Subject: Let's see.

Erickson: You really don't know, do you?

Subject: No. That's silly. I very seldom forget what day of the week it is.

Erickson: You have more important things to think about.

Subject: But I should remember the day of the week. Now, do we have to go through that process to find out what day it is?

Erickson: **What has happened to you? I saw you in June, didn't I?**

Rossi: It is interesting to see how she rationalizes not being able to see a calendar that is apparently in full view. She then uses confusion to avoid knowing the date. All this is so she can be consistent with your suggestions orienting her into the future. You reinforce this pseudo-orientation by continuing to press for information about what happened since you saw her last June. You continue to act as if it is August 1945 (time future), and press her about "**What has happened to you? I saw you in June, didn't I?**" You do not actually *lie* but you do *imply* that you are in the future. So even if she was not pseudo-oriented into the future when she opened her eyes, you continue to press that implication, thus giving her unconscious more time to learn how to reorient and role-play the future.

3.6 Confusion and Amnesia in Pseudo-Orientation to Future Time: "Irrelevant" Asides Always Relevant

Subject: Yes. You have a remarkable memory for all the people who come and go that you see. It's amazing.

Erickson: Go on.

Subject: Let me see. You told me I would tell you what I did. I'll tell you something—I don't remember.

Erickson: Was it a good summer?

Subject: Most summers are pretty good.

Erickson: But was this summer a good summer?

Subject: Yes.

Erickson: What did you see me about in June?

Subject: About swimming.

Erickson: That's a good place to start.

Subject: Swimming?

Erickson: Yes. Where did you go?

Subject: I went to Ann's on her second week of vacation.

Erickson: How long a vacation did you have?

Subject: I had two weeks, but we didn't get our vacations at the same time.

Erickson: The second week of your vacation was the same time
            hers was?
Subject: No. I tried to get a week off then, but they did give me
            Sunday off instead of Saturday. Or did I? I don't know
            what I did. You have me all confused.
Erickson: Well, I want to know about it. Tell me about swimming.
Subject: Well, let me see. We drove down with Paul on Saturday.
            And I did buy that new swimming suit.
Erickson: You did? What color?
Subject: It was down at Demery's store. I think it was Demery's
            store. No, it wasn't either. It was another little store near
            Demery's. I can't think of the name. It was a yellow
            two-piece—real sharp looking.
Erickson: Did it make the moths shout, "Here comes another
            shortage?"
Subject: Yes.
Erickson: Go on.
Subject: I don't remember. I had to come back Sunday night. We
            must have gone swimming. It's right on the lake.
Erickson: Yes, go on.
Subject: I'm suffering from an amnesia. When did we go swimming?
Miss Dey: You ought to know.
Subject: But I don't.
Erickson: Did you enjoy it?
Subject: Certainly. It was wonderful. But I don't remember when I
            went. The next time I'll keep a diary.
Erickson: Was it really wonderful?
Subject: Oh, yes. The water was cool!
Erickson: What did you think about as you were swimming?
Subject: Just how nice it was, and about how to get Ann wetter
            than she was!
Erickson: Did you remember how you had been scared of swim-
            ming before?
Subject: Yes.
Erickson: How did that affect you?
Subject: It was funny. I mean, it was really funny.
Erickson: Did you really enjoy the swimming?

Subject: Uh-huh.

Erickson: How many times did you go in swimming?

Subject: I don't know. I'm dumb tonight. I can't remember anything. I have a very good memory.

Erickson: Why do you keep looking out the window?

Subject: It looks so cool out, and I know it isn't. It reminds me of Lisa's—my sister's—place, with all the trees and everything. They have a river cutting through their place, like these Wild West affairs when the hero goes dashing down across the river on a horse. It's absolutely beautiful.

Erickson: Have you ever thought about that river being beautiful before?

Subject: Oh, yes. It's very nice. But I never wanted to get wet in it before. I'll probably come down with some horrible disease. There must be something you get from contaminated river water. I presume it's contaminated, though there aren't any signs up.

Erickson: How many times did you go in swimming there?

Subject: Just once.

Erickson: When was that?

Subject: The last of July. I had a dental appointment. **You really should get more sleep, Dr. Fink.**

Rossi: Should I eliminate some of these irrelevant asides when we publish this? For instance, her last remark to Dr. Fink?

Erickson: No, they are relevant! I attend upon the immediacy |of her imaginary experience|—on what could have been unpleasant. She gets away from that by telling Dr. Fink he **"should get more sleep."**

Rossi: That's how she gets away from her unpleasant dental appointment?

Erickson: Yes.

Rossi: She is struggling between confusion and amnesia in this section, perhaps because her unconscious just doesn't know yet how to respond to your future orientation suggestions.

3.7   Persisting Questions to Facilitate Pseudo Memories of Successful
      Coping with the Swimming Phobia: Utilizing the Apposition of
      Opposites to Motivate Hypnotic Work

Erickson: Tell me about this swimming.
Subject: My vacation started the 28th. I went out on Friday and
            came back on the 30th. Dr. McNally called.
Erickson: Started the 28th of what?
Subject: July.
Erickson: 28th of July?
Subject: Yes.
Erickson: And when did you go swimming at Miss Dey's?
Subject: She had her vacation before I did, you know.
Erickson: It was a weekend?
Subject: I had to get someone to work for me. They wouldn't give
            me a week off. I should get someone to work for me
            every day. Ann, for instance. She could come back and
            work for me.
Erickson: Did you have trouble breathing in the water?
Subject: Did you ever get your mouth and ears and nose full of
            water?
Erickson: Yes.
Subject: You have a little trouble breathing.
Erickson: Did you have to persuade yourself to go swimming?
Subject: No.
Erickson: Can't you tell me a bit more about the whole month of
            July than that? How did you happen to go to Lisa's?
Subject: How did I happen to go? It's the accepted thing. And I
            had a lot of fun. I like to go there.
Erickson: What took you swimming in the river?
Subject: I was just out walking. I was walking along the river. And it
            was so nice.
Erickson: And you had your swimming suit on?
Subject: No.
Erickson: Where did you change?
Subject: I went back to the house. Lisa didn't like the idea too
            well. Contaminated river water! She looks so cute when
            she gets all flustered.

Erickson: Does she know how you used to be afraid of swimming?

Subject: No. I never tell her anything except the things that make me laugh, and that might make her laugh.

Erickson: Tell me, do you remember last June better than you remember July?

Subject: Oh, yes. We had classes and got summer privileges. All sorts of things happened in June. Now if you ask me about June . . .

Erickson: Tell me, how much worrying did you do in June about swimming?

Subject: I don't think I worried about it.

Erickson: How did you look forward to swimming in June?

Subject: I was really anxious. I was really going to look at myself objectively and see if I was really afraid of it or if I wasn't.

Erickson: When you went swimming in July, did you think about the time you had spent with me?

Subject: Oh, yes. And I thanked you a hundred million times.

Erickson: You did?

Subject: Uh-huh.

Erickson: **Tell me, do you smoke Luckies all the time?**

Subject: No.

Erickson: You don't?

Subject: I was just wondering how you get them.

Erickson: Do you like Luckies?

Subject: A cigarette is a cigarette. Unless they are Philip Morris.

Erickson: Then what are they?

Subject: There must be a name for them. And for Chelseas and Raleighs, too.

Erickson: Do you still dislike Chelseas?

Subject: Did you ever smoke one?

Erickson: Yes, I have.

Subject: Look at Dr. Fink.

Fink: I'll be glad when this week is over with.

Subject: Of course, when you're a resident you don't have to keep running all the time, do you? You do?

Erickson: Is that all you're going to tell me about your summer?

Subject: I went to my Grandma's for a week. I didn't go swimming there. She always thinks of the silliest details—such as you might get pneumonia and a million other things. And she worries when you leave the house: "I wonder if they really went where they said they were going." It's so much easier on her not to go swimming.

Erickson: How did you feel about it?

Subject: About not going? I would have liked going, it was so hot. But it makes Grandma happy not to go, so we just don't go.

Erickson: Remember the evening with me the last of June?

Subject: Yes.

Erickson: How did you feel about swimming then? How did you think you might feel about going swimming? Remember how you felt last June?

Subject: I wondered whether I would still be afraid and pretend I wasn't, or whether I just wouldn't be afraid.

Erickson: What do you think about those ideas now?

Subject: Now I know.

Erickson: Anything more you want to tell me about swimming?

Rossi: She initially shows a great deal of resistance to her pseudo-orientation into time future when she is to have a successful swimming experience. She evidences confusion, inconsistency, amnesia, and escapist fantasy (being cool at her sister's place). Your approach is to persist by continuing your orienting questions that can only be answered by her making up a pseudo memory of a successful swimming experience. Right?

Erickson: Yes.

Rossi: All your questions and remarks are prompts and cues that imply she has already had the experience and need only tell you about it. Would you say that this sort of continuous prompting is a key ingredient to your successful utilization of pseudo-orientation in time?

Erickson: If you lie often enough, people believe it.

Rossi: Perhaps that's why I've not been successful with it. I haven't pursued patients with the orienting questions that continually imply they are in the future—until they themselves catch on and join the game, so to speak.

Erickson: [*Erickson now gives examples of how prompts and cues are necessary in any time reorientation procedure.*]

Rossi: Why did you ask her about smoking *Luckies* in the middle of this section (**"Tell me, do you smoke Luckies all the time?"**)? Were you checking up on the persistence of your posthypnotic suggestion that she would prefer a *Lucky Strike* upon awakening [Section 2.23]?

Erickson: Apparently something must have been omitted [in the transcript]. I was questioning her about her choice.

3.8 Facilitating Human Potentials by Inner Rehearsal and Cognitive-Behavioral Integration: The Apposition of Opposites

Subject: It was terribly hot in the operating room. Just roasting. And all the doctors get ice collars. And I wished I were a doctor so I could have an ice collar. . . . When Ann wasn't there at the end of June—not that I missed you!—but it was rather lonesome.

Miss Dey: Thanks.

Subject: No one to talk to until one o'clock in the morning, and no one to come in and wake me up at one and talk until two.

Erickson: **Was the water cooling when you went swimming?**

Subject: Yes, very much. It moves back and forth and you hold your breath until it hits you again.

Erickson: Is there anything else you can tell me?

Subject: I know it must have been a busy summer, because summers always are. But I don't know what I did with all that time.

Erickson: Did you accomplish a reasonable amount?

Subject: Yes.

Erickson: To your entire satisfaction?

Subject: No. I never do as much as I want to. The days aren't long enough; the weeks aren't long enough; and there aren't enough nights in one night.

Erickson: When are you going swimming again?
Subject: I can go anytime. The places are crowded, though. Webster
            Hall is only a little way from the hospital.
Erickson: You say that very easily, don't you?
Subject: It is.
Erickson: But you say that very easily. Now last May you wouldn't
            have said it that way, would you?
Subject: No.
Erickson: When are you going swimming again?
Subject: I can always go. Mother likes to go out to Crystal beach.
            I don't see why she is partial to that place.

Rossi: She begins this section with an apparent non
sequitur by complaining about the hot operating room
in an aside to Miss Dey. She apparently is resisting your
inquiries about the details of her pseudomemories of
swimming. You ingeniously utilize her remark about the
discomfort of the hot operating room, however, to return
her to the task at hand by asking, **"Was the water cooling when you went swimming?"** This is an example of
your penchant for the *apposition of opposites**: you utilize
the discomfort of heat to motivate her to explore the
comfort of cooling as a positive association for swimming.
You are using as many motivating, emotional and
sensory-oriented questions as you can to deepen her
construction of as vivid and successful swimming experience as possible in her imagination. But more than
imagination is involved; you are encouraging the inner
rehearsal of an integration of as many of the positive
cognitive-sensory-emotional-behavioral components of
swimming as possible in order to facilitate her actual
swimming potentials.

---

*See Erickson & Rossi, 1980. The general significance of "the opposites" for a theory of mental
functioning has been discussed by Jung (1960). A more recent neurological discussion of the
organization of cerebral processes as opponent systems is presented by Kinsbourne and
Smith (1974).

3.9   *Maturity as a Criterion for Valid Hypnotherapeutic Work; Indirect
Social Reinforcement of Psychological Growth and Maturity*

Erickson: You found out something else about swimming, didn't
you?
Subject: Something else?
Erickson: Yes. Why did you used to be afraid of swimming?
Subject: It was probably a carryover from all those crazy things I
did when I was a little kid. I probably had to be afraid of
something, and I wouldn't be afraid of people.
Erickson: **Do you feel older now than you did last May?**
Subject: Not particularly.
Erickson: Do you feel more comfortable?
Subject: Yes.
Erickson: In all relationships?
Subject: Yes.

Rossi: I believe you use a subjective sense of greater
maturity within the patient as a criterion for the validity
of hypnotherapeutic work. Does the fact that she does
not feel older at this time indicate that more exploratory
or psychodynamic work needs to be done?

Erickson: No. [*To Dr. Sandra Sylvester, who has joined us*] Do
you feel older since you ate Christmas dinner? [*It is now
March.*]

Dr. Sylvester: No, but I feel older since I learned how to
frame a picture [*laughs delightedly because "framing a picture" was a key to some of her own maturing hypnotherapeutic
work with Erickson recently*].

Erickson: I gave Miss S that question, **"Do you feel older
now than you did last May?"** to get her away from her
experience. "Framing a picture" was a summary of an
experience for Sandy that enabled her to feel more
maturity.

Rossi: When you are able to objectively summarize a past
experience, you feel older and more mature.

Erickson: Yes.

Dr. Sylvester: [She smiles and beams happily, and Erickson exchanges a knowing glance with me. I realize that Erickson is now taking this opportunity to indirectly reinforce Dr. Sylvester's recent maturing experiences by having her confirm them publicly with me. That is, under the guise of asking her a question to help clarify the case material, Erickson is actually indirectly asking her to talk about her own recent hypnotherapeutic growth experiences in the presence of another professional (myself). This is a way of publicly confirming and reinforcing her maturity and growth in the interpersonal dimension (see Section 2.20).]

3.10   *Allowing Patients to Win Battles That Will Benefit Them*

Erickson: Do you remember last June when you wanted to see if Estabrooks was right, or if I was right?

Subject: I wanted to see your reaction.

Erickson: What was it?

Subject: Absolutely calm. Just as though it could be expected. Disgusting!

Erickson: Did I distress you?

Subject: I hoped it might be something else.

Erickson: What?

Subject: I hoped you would look very disgusted, but there was no reaction whatsoever.

Rossi: In this short section you are indirectly integrating her hostility toward you. Are you now using Estabrooks as a vehicle for displacing and discharging hostility whenever you sense it building up in the current therapy session to the point where it may disrupt your work?

Erickson: No. I am proving to her that Estabrooks should agree with me. It is my success. She tried to bring a barrier between Estabrooks and me and I point out there was none.

Rossi: So you do not allow her to get you upset. Why didn't you let her win that battle and show some disgust as she wanted?

Erickson: You only let the battle be won by the patient when it is of value to the patient. There was no advantage for her here.

3.11 Setting up a Posthypnotic Suggestion; Building an Associative Network: "How About Luckies?"

Erickson: Remember how you lit your cigarette and stalled for time?

Subject: I'm afraid I was stalling for time.

Erickson: Do you remember what I did about that cigarette?

Subject: Oh, yes. You just said, "Just keep right on smoking now—it doesn't make any difference," or words to that effect.

Erickson: What effect did it have?

Subject: None. It tasted good.

Erickson: Remember you went into a trance smoking [Section 3.2]?

Subject: Oh, yes. You asked me if I liked smoking, or if I wanted to give it up, and I said no because if I had wanted to give it up, I would give it up.

Erickson: Well, do you suppose I ought to give you a package of cigarettes to reward you for swimming?

Subject: No, I don't need any reward. I had mine.

Erickson: How long does a package of cigarettes keep?

Subject: How long?

Erickson: Yes.

Subject: Opened or unopened?

Erickson: Unopened.

Subject: Let's see. Of course, I never had them around long enough to know if they got stale very soon or not. Camels are a pack to go around the world, so they probably never get dry.

Erickson: How about Luckies?

Subject: I doubt if they age much. They have cellophane around them.
Erickson: This package doesn't.
Subject: How unusual. I thought they all had cellophane on them.
Erickson: Not during summer months.
Subject: Why not?
Erickson: They haven't put any cellophane on them since around last June.
Subject: Then I don't imagine they would keep very well.

Rossi: To the uninitiated, this section might seem as if it were just so much small talk about cigarettes. Actually you are building an associative network with *Luckies, time, going into a trance smoking, last June*, and *keeping cigarettes fresh* that will come together in an important posthypnotic suggestion about swimming you will soon give her. Right?

Erickson: Yes.

3.12 A "*Trance in a Trance*"?: *Structuring Amnesia and Compounding Confusion to Further Depotentiate Mental Sets and Learned Limitations*

Erickson: Tell me, do you think you could go into a trance tonight?
Subject: Probably. But I don't know why I should.
Erickson: Do you want to go into a trance? Can you actually give me the day of the month?
Subject: I was thinking August 20th, but it isn't August 20th.
Erickson: That's right, it isn't.
Subject: Doesn't anybody know what day it is?
Erickson: Yes, I know. But you don't.
Subject: Why don't you tell me?
Erickson: I left that as a reason for you to go into a trance.
Subject: You mean you don't think I could find out unless I went into a trance? I think I could. I'm sure I could. When I wake up in the morning I don't run over to Dr. Erickson

and tell him to put me in a trance so I can tell what day it is. I ask somebody. Ann usually tells me. But now she won't tell me.

Miss Dey: Don't ask Dr. Fink—he's asleep.
Erickson: How about going into a trance?
Subject: Why should I?
Erickson: I would like to have you go.
Subject: You should have a purpose in going into a trance. I haven't any purpose.

Rossi: When this section begins she is already in a somnambulistic trance in which she is speaking with her eyes open and acting as if she were awake. [See Section 3.3 in which this somnambulistic process was initiated.] Now you apparently structure an amnesia by reorienting her to the beginning of this session with your opening remark about whether she thinks she can go into trance tonight.

Erickson: Yes.

Rossi: She puts up a resistance to the idea, even though she is already in trance. Then in an utterly flabbergasting way, you give her a reason for entering trance by making her realize through your question that she doesn't know what the date is. But what sense does it make to motivate her to go into trance when she is already in a somnambulistic trance? What are you trying to do? Are you trying to achieve a "trance in a trance"? Or is this simply a way of deepening trance?

Erickson: I'm increasing her disorientation.

Rossi: Is there really such a state as a "trance in a trance," or is that just a way of talking?

Erickson: Just a way of talking.

Rossi: She is already in a trance, but you pretend that she isn't and that you want her to go into one. You are really just scrambling up her mental sets. This is a way of increasing confusion and depotentiating her conscious sets and learned limitations.

Erickson: [*Nods yes.*]

3.13   Evoking and Utilizing Psychodynamic Processes; Multiple Levels of Remembering and Forgetting in the Apposition of Opposites; Not Knowing, Confusion, Wonder, and Surprise

Erickson: But I have a purpose.

Subject: Besides finding out the day or the date?

Erickson: Remember last June how you wanted to see if I could put you in a trance?

Subject: Yes.

Erickson: Didn't you really get that question answered then?

Subject: In a roundabout sort of way, yes. I asked you another question and you never did answer it. I believe you laughed. What was it—operator attitude? I thought about it after I went home and I told Ann about it.

Erickson: That is one of Estabrooks's terms.

Subject: Related to you, I believe.

Erickson: It's a term that he invented to explain why I could accomplish certain things with subjects and he couldn't.

Subject: Now that isn't nice.

Erickson: I think it leaves us in the same situation that Estabrooks is in. It's a nice term, but no good use to be made of it. Go to sleep. Go to sleep. Way, deep, sound asleep. Way, deep, sound asleep. Way, deep, sound asleep. Way, deep, sound asleep. Way, deep, sound asleep. Way, deep, sound asleep. Go very sound asleep. Still deeper and sounder asleep. Go deeply asleep. And keep sleeping deeply and soundly and continuously.

And as you sleep deeply and soundly and continuously, I want you slowly, gradually to achieve an understanding of the present situation. I want you to be aware that you are deeply asleep. I want you to be aware that I changed time for you. I want you to be aware of those things you told me and to believe those things. I want you to view all those things seriously and earnestly. And I want you to understand that they constitute a demonstration of what real thinking exists in your own mind. I want you to know that this is June and not August. I want you to realize that you seemed to have spent your vacation, and to recall in full everything you said to me, so that you can really know how you, in June, really deep within yourself, anticipated spending your vacation. Do you understand what I mean? And you didn't have to go swimming to find out what your attitude would be, did you? You know it deep within yourself what it is. Isn't that a fact? Not only swimming in the lake, but in anticipation swimming in the river. Did you not? And you found yourself looking forward to swimming in Webster Hall. You found out **what your real attitude toward swimming was.**

Now this is knowledge that you possessed when you came into this room, but didn't know you had. Isn't that right? I want you to keep that knowledge in your unconscious. Do you understand? I want you to keep this knowledge in your unconscious and not to discover it until later this summer. Do you understand? Just as you repressed and forgot painful things in the past, I want you to repress this knowledge until the right time comes for it to burst out into your understanding, so that you can actually have the experience of finding yourself going down into the water, and going into the water, and really enjoying it. Do you understand? And I want it to be a tremendously pleasing surprise to you. So that even when you walk down to the lake, **wondering** how you will feel, and then walking out into the water, you will still be **wondering** and then getting deeper into the water and still **wondering.** And then **all of a sudden discover that you really do enjoy it—to have it come as a surprise to you.** Do you think my suggestion is a good one? And will you cooperate with me? Completely? So that you really won't know anything about it until it happens? Is that right? And that means that you have got to have an amnesia for what happened here tonight. And you won't mind that. A complete amnesia for what has happened here tonight. Of course, you can think about Estabrooks and any bit of unrelated information.

Erickson: I'm tying her up completely!

Rossi: You are depotentiating her conscious sets. It is confusing! At first you say she will understand and remember, and then you say she won't. In setting up your important posthypnotic suggestion about swimming, you carefully juxtapose *remembering* and *forgetting* in a way that would seem to satisfy two levels of need: on one level there is her personality need to *know* what is going on, and on another level there is a need for a *conscious amnesia* so that her unconscious can be free to facilitate the actual swimming experience in its own way. This is a clear example of how you use the opposition of opponent mental processes to facilitate hypnotic experience.

Erickson: [Nods yes].

Rossi: You depotentiate conscious mental sets with your emphasis on her *not knowing* how it is to be done. She can *wonder,* and thus build her *expectancy.* Right?

Erickson: Yes.

Rossi: As is typical when the unconscious makes a dramatic, developmental jump, you remark that she can later "**all of a sudden discover that you really enjoy it—to have it come as a surprise to you.**" These suggestions all form an associative network, which build up a certain level of expectancy and tension that can only be discharged by the actual swimming experience. You have allowed her to find and experience "**what your real attitude toward swimming was**" via pseudo-orientation in future time, and how you are structuring a posthypnotic suggestion that will allow her to bypass the conscious resistances that may still be present.

Erickson: Given that she dreaded swimming—she knew that she ought to learn and therefore that she would dread to learn. Now I set her up with **wondering**. And you **wonder** about pleasant things.

Rossi: **Wonder** is associated with pleasant things. You changed dread into **wonder** as a step toward a positive development. This is a radically different approach from the simple, direct posthypnotic suggestion to change behavior. You are continually aligning her inner psychodynamics so that the desired behavior is the natural result of the tensions you set in motion. *You are evoking and utilizing psychodynamic processes rather than simply analyzing them or commenting on them.* Would you say this is a fair description of your approach?

Erickson: Yes.

Rossi: You utilize and actualize a patient's own psychodynamic processes rather than simply analyzing them. You illustrated how you evoked and utilized isolated mental mechanisms and psychopathology in two early papers in 1939 (Erickson, 1939a&b/1980). But it wasn't until you wrote that paper in 1948 on "Hypnotic Psychotherapy" (Erickson, 1948/1980) that you first described and illustrated how you utilize a subject's own psychodynamics in hypnotherapy. Was this an original approach of yours?

Erickson: It was, as far as I know.

3.14 *Posthypnotic Suggestions for Swimming with a Reward to Reinforce Therapeutic Gains: Smoking "Just Afterwards"*

Erickson: And now there is something more that I want you to do, and I want it to be a surprise for you. [*Erickson writes on a package of cigarettes.*] Open your eyes and look at this. It says, "**Just afterwards.**" I'm going to give you this package of cigarettes. I want you to unconsciously protect this package of cigarettes. And just be curious about them, but not to smoke them. Then after you go in swimming, and while you are enjoying the swimming, I want you to recall this package of cigarettes as something that you can smoke just after you get out of the water. Do you understand?

Rossi: Apparently the transcript is missing your full instructions to her at this point. You are beginning to present the posthypnotic suggestion that you began setting up back in Section 3.11.

Erickson: I had her swim out to a raft on a lake. She was to sit on the raft, look out at the water, and discover a secret waterproof pocket in her suit—

Rossi: —in which she carries the cigarettes you gave her marked "**Just afterwards**"—

Erickson: —and matches! She is to enjoy her smoking fully. She can enjoy smoking after swimming.

Rossi: So the enjoyment of smoking is made contingent upon the swimming, and is a reward as well as a cue when she sees the words, "**Just afterwards.**"

Erickson: That cue comes to consolidate her therapeutic gains in swimming.

Rossi: How did you know that she would have the opportunity to swim out to a float (raft) on her vacation?

Erickson: Her friend, Ann, had told me about it ahead of time when she told me about their proposed vacation together.

3.15   *A Posthypnotic Associative Network Utilizing Wonder, Amnesia, and Not Knowing (Secrets) to Map Out and Actively Evoke Therapeutic Responses; Nonverbal Right-Hemispheric Directives to Hide Suggestions from Consciousness*

Erickson: And you are sure that you will do this, and that during the rest of this month and during July, until after you go swimming, you will continue to keep this package of cigarettes and wonder very vaguely why you keep them.

And you will take good care of this package? You are sure of that? I am going to put it in your purse. And you won't let any harm come to that package of cigarettes, will you? And if anything happens, if you lose that package of cigarettes, you will have an answer for it that keeps you from thinking and keeps you from remembering. Now, are you perfectly clear in your own thinking about this? Do you want to put this other arm down? [*Erickson lowers subject's arm*] Is there anything you would like to say to me? While you are deeply asleep, you can recognize how you are looking forward to the summer. But you won't be able to know until you are awake, and you won't know when you are awake. That is keeping your secret from yourself, in other words, isn't it? And this is one time you can really keep a **secret** from yourself, isn't it? Just think these things over until you are very, very clear in your mind. **And map out in your mind how you are going to put away that package of cigarettes, and protect it**, and yet be sure to take it with you. And if by any chance you lost it, what would you do?

Subject: I wouldn't lose it.

Erickson: No. But I can tell you something you could do in case lightning destroyed it. You could get another package of cigarettes and wonder why you wrote "**Just afterwards**" on it. You could just wonder why. But no matter what happens, you could still have a package of cigarettes. Isn't that right? And since you are still deep asleep, you have lost a surprising amount of fear of water, haven't you? It is a very comfortable thing, isn't it? Can you tell me what day it is now?

Subject: June.

Erickson: Yes, June. Can you tell me what day?

Subject: The 27th.

Erickson: And tomorrow will be the 28th, will it not? Are you perfectly comfortable in your unconscious about things now? And remember, you have a date with me in August. Isn't that right? Or sooner, if you get eager to tell me how smoothly things work out. And if Miss Dey ever opens her mouth to make you aware consciously, get her train of thought changed around for her, won't you?

Subject: [To Miss Dey] I'll strangle you!

Erickson: I'm looking forward with tremendous interest to your accomplishment of this entire complicated pattern. Aren't you? Is there anything further you wish to discuss now?

Subject: I don't think so.

Erickson: You remember what we talked about while we were alone? And I want you to take that general attitude. You will, will you not? That's right. And now shortly I am going to awaken you, and you can leave here wondering what the purpose of this visit was; but **that will be a secret that will belong to your unconscious.** Are you ready to awaken?

Subject: Yes.

Erickson: All right. Awaken comfortably and easily. **What happened tonight is a secret to you.** . . . Now, what would be a good inscription for this book?

Rossi: You now set in motion the associative network you began setting up in Section 3.11. The package of Lucky cigarettes on which you wrote "**Just afterwards**" becomes a cue that continually reinforces the posthypnotic suggestion: she will enjoy the cigarettes after she enjoys the swimming. Smoking the cigarette becomes contingent upon enjoying swimming. The positive feelings associated with smoking become tied to the desired behavior of swimming. You give her many suggestions about how she will "**map out in your mind how you are going to put away that package of cigarettes and protect it . . .**" You are thereby evoking an active unconscious process by which she is continually working on something that will terminate in carrying out the implied posthypnotic suggestion to swim successfully. Since it is a secret from her conscious mind ("**That will be a secret that will belong to your unconscious.** . . . **What happened to-**

night is a secret to you."), this active unconscious therapeutic work is protected from her learned limitations and criticisms.

This is highly characteristic of your approach to posthypnotic suggestion.* You do not assume that just because she is in trance she will carry out your posthypnotic suggestions. Rather, you build up an associative network that utilizes her own motivational process; you suggest a whole chain of behaviors that will lead with step-by-step inevitability to the final desired therapeutic outcome. Do you agree with that?

Erickson: Yes. Where the transcript says I lowered her arm, I was actually putting the package of cigarettes in her hand and then directing her hand to wrap them in the folds of her skirt. That was a nonverbal cue as to how she would later wrap the package of cigarettes into her bathing suit and keep it a secret from herself.

Rossi: You expected her to generalize that nonverbal suggestion from her skirt to her bathing suit? Why didn't you just tell her directly to do that?

Erickson: To keep it from her conscious mind and save it for her unconscious.

Rossi: So when you do something nonverbally, it tends to be assimilated in the right hemisphere and thus kept secret from the conscious mind.

Erickson: When you are having a special dinner with music in the background, you do not pay much attention to the music, do you?

---

*See Chapter 4, "Posthypnotic Suggestion," in Erickson and Rossi, 1979.

SESSION IV*

Active Therapeutic Trancework

4.0 *Assessing Previous Hypnotherapeutic Work: Questions Evoking
Uncertainty, Doubt, Wonder, Curiosity, Expectancy*

Fink: Speaking of interesting conflicts, the elderly psychiatrist at the hospital was discussing philosophy with me this morning, and he was telling me the most unusual circumstance. He thinks he can partly account for his conflicts in religious matters. His mother has been dead for 44 years, and when his father died, by the terms of his father's will, they had to exhume the body and rebury it in the grave next to his father's. And he was there when they removed the remains and transferred them to a different receptacle. Imagine! His own mother!

Subject: Why did he have to go?

Fink: He didn't say. It went through Probate Court and had to be signed by the Department of Health. There was a terrific amount of red tape before they could even touch it. It was most amazing.

Erickson: Where did you go on your vacation?

Subject: Oh, roamed around. Went to my sister's and stayed with her for a while. That's all. Of course my folks wouldn't want a trip while I was on vacation, and of course V-J Day wouldn't come while I was on vacation.

Erickson: When did you get back?

---

*Present in 1945 for Session IV: Dr. Milton H. Erickson, Dr. Jerome Fink, the subject (who is also referred to as "Miss S" and "Jane"), and the subject's friend, "Ann Dey." Present for the 1979 commentaries: Dr. Milton H. Erickson, Dr. Ernest L. Rossi, Dr. Sandra Sylvester.

Subject: The 18th. I came back the night of the 17th.

Erickson: **Remember what you said to me over the phone?**

Subject: Yes.

Erickson: What was it?

Subject: Let me see. I told you I had a wonderful time. I would like to go back and have it all over again. In fact, I was ready to go back the day afterwards.... Oh, I asked you why you never took a vacation.

Erickson: Yes. Anything else?

Subject: You tell me what I said. Is it important?

Erickson: Yes.

Subject: It couldn't have been. I remember important things. You said hello, and I said hello.

Erickson: You're sure of that?

Subject: I identified myself, and you asked me if I had had a nice vacation. I said it was wonderful, and why don't you take one? You said you didn't take them, and I said you should. Then you said you don't take vacations—you just wait for people to tell you about their vacations. I said that's very nice, but I think you should take one. I think you asked me where I had been—no, you didn't either— yes, you did! And I told you. I believe I asked when I could see you. You said your brother was here and you would be busy last week. You said that Dr. Fink would be in Detroit tonight, and be able to pick us up. I said that would be fine. And we agreed that everything was settled. Then we said goodbye. Have I missed anything?

Erickson: No, you really haven't. You just worded it so.

Subject: **Don't look so wise, you three. You, too!**

Erickson: You felt sorry for me.

Subject: Oh, yes. I said I felt sorry for you because you never had a vacation.

Erickson: No, that wasn't what you said.

Subject: I felt sorry for you about something else?

Erickson: Yes.

Subject: Why should I feel sorry for you?

Erickson: Because I had to sit and listen to what wonderful times other people had on their vacations. Remember that?

Subject: Yes. Because you really don't get a kick out of hearing about other people's vacations. You know how it is—in the nurses' home, all the girls would come back from their vacations. You ask them where they had been and they tell you and you just sit and say, "Wasn't that nice?" You're just asking them, that's all.

Erickson: Do you think that's true here?

Subject: No, not with you, maybe, but with the ordinary run of people.

Erickson: Is there any change in you right now from the last time you were here?

Subject: No. . . . I have changed. . . . My best friends won't tell me. . . . Dr. Fink, are you getting sick?

Fink: No.

Miss Dey: That's a pity.

Subject: No, I don't think I have changed. Not any more than anyone else does in that length of time. . . . I'm not nosey. I'm just curious.

Fink: Is it all right if I give this [a note] to Dr. Erickson?

Subject: Yes. As if I could stop you. You realize I can stand anything except an unsatisfied curiosity.

Fink: Is that right?

Subject: Na-a-a. You're just trying to get me mad.

Erickson: How much of a tan did you get?

Subject: I had a bit, but it faded right out. I did get just a small one, though, but the next day it had died.

Miss Dey: Me, too.

Erickson: How did you feel about coming out here?

Subject: Willing to come. Anxious to come.

Erickson: Why?

Subject: Curiosity.

Erickson: Why are you curious?

Subject: Most people are intrigued by things they don't know anything about. I'm one of the ten thousand.

Erickson: What don't you know about?
Subject: You. That's right. People who think intrigue me. You think. Therefore you intrigue me.

Rossi: You begin this session with a typical series of questions ostensibly oriented to reviewing and assessing previous hypnotic work. But right from the beginning when you ask her, "**Remember what you said to me on the phone?**", you are actually *fixing her attention* with questions and *evoking uncertainty and doubt.* You question her in such a way that she tried to give you all the details, yet it is inevitable that she forget some. She tries to protest this to the members of the group when she then says, "**Don't look so wise, you three.**" This means that she already feels put into a position of uncertainty and doubt. *Her usual conscious sets are already being depotentiated so that she must make desperate inner searches looking for what will satisfy you and the group.* That is, while carrying out an apparently normal conversation, she is actually being shunted into the first three stages of your trance induction: you are (1) fixing her attention, (2) depotentiating her habitual forms of reference, and (3) initiating unconscious searches. Do you agree that is what you are doing by asking these questions? You are essentially initiating an exploratory set?

Erickson: Yes.

Rossi: A natural consequence of this approach is that her sense of curiosity and expectancy are aroused. Correct?

Erickson: Yes.

Rossi: This is exacerbated by the evident collusion between the other members of the group and you, as manifested by Dr. Fink passing you a note. Are you purposely evoking this sense of curiosity, wonder, and expectancy as a part of the therapeutic process? Do you make a conscious effort to intrigue your patient?

> *Erickson:* Yes. [*Erickson exchanges knowing glances with Dr. Sandra Sylvester, who has experienced this being intrigued by Erickson's hypnotherapeutic work.*]
>
> *Dr. Sylvester:* This is like a *déja vu* experience [*recalling aspects of her own recent work with Erickson.*]

4.1 Symptom Resolution: End of the Swimming Phobia and Related Water Fears; The "Domino Theory" of Psychological Problems; Objectivity Comes with Maturational Jumps; A Double-Binding Question

Erickson: Well, now. Shall I continue questioning you while you are awake, or shall I put you in a trance?

Subject: I think I can answer you while I am awake.

Erickson: Go ahead.

Subject: But there's nothing to tell.

Erickson: Nothing to tell?

Subject: I remembered everything.

Erickson: Yes.

Subject: I remembered everything that happened here that night. And that projection into the future—if anyone had asked me about six weeks ago if that were possible, I would have said no! Absolutely and utterly no!

Erickson: What projection into the future?

Subject: When you asked me if I had been swimming on my vacation. And I hadn't! I hadn't been on my vacation. I told you about going to Ann's, but I hadn't been there yet. Oh, and I remembered about the cigarettes. That was something out of this world.

Erickson: Tell me about it.

Subject: I got there about eight o'clock at night. We had a boat, so we rowed about the lake. Ann kept looking at me, expecting me to do something. Nothing happened, so we went home. The next morning we went swimming over by the public beach. We swam around, and then we were on the float, and I thought suddenly—the cigarettes! Just like a bolt from the blue. That was quite remarkable.

Erickson: I still want to know more about it.

Subject: About my vacation?

Erickson: About the swimming and the cigarettes.

Subject: The cigarettes were marvelous.

Erickson: How much trouble did you have keeping that package of cigarettes?

Subject: None. I hid them from myself—out of temptation's way. I put them away from myself under the towels in the dresser drawer in the cigarette case.

Erickson: How much trouble did you experience in keeping them hidden?

Subject: Not very much. I think they would have been safe on top of the dresser, except someone else might have come in and said, "Ah, cigarettes?" It wasn't hard to keep them.

Erickson: How did you react when you discovered those cigarettes?

Subject: [To Miss Dey] I was in the car, wasn't I? First, I didn't know where I got them. I thought I must have bought some Luckies that I didn't see. Imagine buying things you don't see. But I thought, "Well, I got them somewhere," and that's important. And then "**Just afterwards**" was written on them, and I knew it was your writing because I had seen your writing before. Then I questioned that creature [indicating Miss Dey] about it. She said, "I don't know where you got them. Don't ask me where you get your goods." So I knew they were from you and there must be a purpose. So I thought, "Someday I'll know, although I may be an old woman with spectacles!" So I just put them away to wait.

Erickson: So you rowed around in a boat, and the next day you went swimming, and you were on the float at the time you recalled the cigarettes. What did you do?

Subject: Then I was anxious to go home.

Erickson: How did you get back?

Subject: We rowed back. And she told me my muscles wouldn't be sore. They weren't that day, or the next day.
Miss Dey: I didn't make any promises. Mine weren't sore.
Erickson: How many times did you swim after that?
Subject: We swam in the morning—most of the time that morning—and then once again just before I came back.
Erickson: Did you enjoy swimming?
Subject: Very much.
Erickson: Why?
Subject: I wasn't afraid anymore. I was telling Ann, it isn't as though I went and jumped off a 20-foot board. I'm still not that brave. **But when I used to drive over a bridge, I would be anxious to get to the other side. But now there is nothing to it.** Still I don't like to get my face wet. But that will come with practice.
Erickson: You actually enjoy it?
Subject: Yes, very much.
Erickson: Remember how you used to feel about it?
Subject: Yes. I worried about it. I wondered if I had to go and if I couldn't find a plausible excuse to get out of it.

Rossi: I guess you threaten her a bit with your initial double-binding question ("**Shall I continue questioning you while you are awake, or shall I put you in a trance?**") that focuses her into a therapeutic direction: she had a choice of being questioned while awake, or she will go into trance—but whichever choice she makes, she will be moving in a therapeutic direction. She then goes blithely on to tell about an amazing fulfillment of your posthypnotic suggestion that led her to enjoy swimming and an apparent resolution of her swimming phobia. You would think she would be overjoyed and shouting about this marvelous cure! Yet she seems curiously bland about it. Indeed you have to pull it from her. Why is that?

Erickson: It's now so much a part of her.

Rossi: Having resolved the swimming phobia is already so much a part of her that she is blasé about it?

Erickson: Yes. She knows it is something I gave her that is now a part of her.

Rossi: It's already a part of her ordinary identity? If she jumped and shouted about it, that would indicate it was still a new and precarious development with which to impress you. This is similar to what we discussed in the last section: we are able to be objective and matter-of-fact about past emotional issues when we have made a genuine, growth-maturing jump beyond them.

By the way, I notice that she also indicates the resolution of another related fear of water when she says: "**But when I used to drive over a bridge, I would get anxious to get to the other side. But now there is nothing to it.**" This indicates the spontaneous resolution of another of her important, early, traumatic experiences when she was carried over the water on a cable by Larry (see Table 1). This illustrates your "domino theory" of psychological problems and growth: When you deal with one issue successfully, other related problems tend to fall in line and cure themselves.

4.2   Therapeutic Hypnosis as an Active Process of Inner Work

Erickson: What did you think about the projection into the future?

Subject: That was amusing. I told you I wanted a yellow bathing suit. I saw a girl from the nurses' home try on a yellow bathing suit and I thought it was stunning. Then I told you I went swimming in the river. I don't know why I told you that. I don't think I would do that on a bet. It looks very muddy and it isn't deep enough. It's just not the thing you go swimming in.

Erickson: Go on.

Subject: Let's see. I don't know why I ever told you that. A projection would be your plans for the future. It would depict the future as you thought it was going to be.

Erickson: No.
Subject: No? Okay, let's hear about it.
Erickson: Your projection into the future was **a statement of your past wishes, hopes, desires, fears, anxieties, all re-stated in the corrected form.** Now you don't want to go wading in that river. And you gave the proper and the hoped-for reason. Remember what you said?
Subject: You mean what I said last time about the river?
Erickson: Why didn't you go wading in it?
Subject: Because it was contaminated? You mean because it wasn't very deep?
Erickson: Yes.

Rossi: You are very careful and insistent here about what you mean by a mental projection into the future. It is not to depict the future as she thought it was going to be; rather it is "**a statement of your past wishes, hopes, desires, fears, anxieties, all restated in a corrected form.**" That is, in her pseudo-orientation into time future, Miss S was not simply passively relating a fantasy of what she hoped for. She was more actively engaged in an inner process of changing and correcting past images, expectancies, and programs of behavior. Is that your point here? Your therapeutic approach involves an active inner process of changing one's mental dynamics rather than the passive expression of a simple hope or fantasy. Is that right?

Erickson: [Nods yes]

Rossi: In your original paper on pseudo-orientation in time as a hypnotherapeutic procedure (Erickson, 1954a/1980), you report how the patient evidences many signs of strain, excitement and hard work during trance work and exhaustion after a period of pseudo-orientation into time future. In the last session, Miss S showed a great deal of resistance, confusion and difficulty during the active phase of her pseudo-orientation when you had to question her persistently to orient her to her therapeutic task. A happy, idealistic fantasy about the future will not do. A patient has to do hard, active work in trance, is that right?

Erickson: Yes.

Rossi: So, this is very different from, for example, T. X. Barber, who feels that in hypnosis you are just "thinking and imagining along with" the therapist (Barber, 1972, 1978, 1984). You talk about this as an active inner engagement rather than just a passive experiencing of wishes. That's what a patient really is to do in pseudo-orientation in time future, and I think perhaps that's why I failed with it in the past. I had my patients talk passively about what would be nice. When you do trance work, it's not a sleep-like trance but an active process that is going on in the person.

Erickson: [*Erickson describes an analogous situation when demonstrating to a "city girl" how to milk a cow. As she watches the demonstration, she may make active though perhaps only semiconscious minimal movements of her dominant hand and fingers as she imitates and rehearses how she will actually move them when she tries to milk the cow.*]

Rossi: Um-mmm. So she learns step by step, with active inner rehearsals before she actually does it. In a similar manner, hypnosis does not involve passive fantasy but an active grappling and changing of one's inner experience to activate one's potentials.

4.3   Rejecting Inappropriate Therapeutic Hypotheses

Subject: Now what was written on that little slip of paper that Dr. Fink gave you?

Erickson: One of Jerome's ideas. [*Gives paper to Miss S.*]

Subject: That's an ad for "Life Buoy" soap. A buoy in the water.

Fink: Were you interested in boys in the water?

Subject: That is beside the question and highly irrelevant.

Rossi: Miss S certainly has no problem putting down what she feels is an erroneous therapeutic hypothesis:

her swimming phobia is somehow related to her fear of boys, and therefore she cannot life-buoy in water. She rejects the *buoy-boy* homonym as having any real psychodynamic significance for her. What is your view?

Erickson: I think that part of her fear might be associated with boys [but there is more to it].

Rossi: So this was a nice example of a patient rejecting an erroneous or too one-sided therapeutic hypothesis. You can't just make up anything and have a patient accept it.

4.4 Accessing Therapeutic Change: The Spread of Phobic Fears

Erickson: Approximately how many times did you go swimming?

Subject: You mean at Ann's? About four times.

Miss Dey: Three times.

Erickson: The last time was just before your bus left?

Subject: Yes, we caught the bus on the fly.

Erickson: Have you been swimming since?

Subject: Yes, I went out to Rouge.

Erickson: And how did your cigarette taste when you smoked it?

Subject: Oh, very good. I have been very fond of Luckies ever since.

Erickson: Now, what is the change in you? Are you changed from the last time I saw you?

Subject: Not very much. I don't think I'm afraid very much any more.

Erickson: What other fears have you lost? Crossing bridges—you lost that one.

Subject: Yes.

Erickson: You never told me about that one. Why?

Subject: It just never occurred to me.

Erickson: What other fears have you lost?

Subject: I didn't realize I had any other fears. What have I been hiding?

Erickson: Well, how long have you realized you had that bridge-crossing fear?

Subject: I don't know. It's been a long time.

Erickson: Haven't you more or less blanketed that under your water fear?

Subject: Probably.

Erickson: Was there anything else that you have discovered?

Subject: Look how he has chewed up his cigar so he wouldn't have to smoke it up [referring to Dr. Fink].

Erickson: What habits of yours have you changed?

Subject: Oh, now I'm changing habits.

Erickson: Miss Dey, do you know of any?

Miss Dey: I think I'm noticing one right now.

Subject: Right now?

Miss Dey: She said she always smoked cigarettes with her left hand. She just took that one with her right hand.

Subject: I have noticed that, too. But I don't think that has any bearing.

Erickson: Shall we find out if it has any bearing?

Subject: Let's think about it. Maybe I was a leftist.

Erickson: Anything else?

Subject: Help, please! Coaching, please!

Erickson: Coaching from the audience is permissible.

Subject: Now I need help. After all, the audience always seems to know more than I do.

Fink: Do you recall any change in attitude with respect to marriage?

Subject: Marriage? I didn't know I had any attitude toward marriage. One of the necessary evils. Let's see—change in attitude with respect toward marriage.

Rossi: All this change taking place, and yet she doesn't want to admit anything.

Erickson: Remember how you used to resent taking a bath?

Rossi: Me? Resent taking baths? Yeh, maybe. [Laughter]

Erickson: Just "maybe"? Why are you so bland about it now?

Rossi: Oh, I see. It's a long-solved difficulty. I still feel funny when people comment how much better my hair looks now that it's styled. I feel, "Gee, was it really that bad before?" I haven't solved that problem so I'm not bland about it yet. So you're saying being bland means it's really resolved.

Dr. Sylvester: Another thing is, it's part of who you are.

Rossi: That's right. It's so well settled.

4.5 Questions that Set Up Automatic Ideomotor Responses from the Unconscious

Erickson: Shall we find out if you lost any other phobias?

Subject: I didn't think I had any.

Erickson: Shall we find out if you have lost some others?

Subject: Sure. But you can't lose anything you don't have.

Erickson: I'll tell you. These gloves are lying with their fingers that way. Okay, if you change them around, it will mean that you have lost some other phobias.

Subject: That's highly improbable, don't you think?

Erickson: Well, watch it because you've got a free right hand.

Subject: That's the power of suggestion. It's like telling me that I would be more comfortable in that chair than I am in this one. Whether I would be or not, I would get up and go over there.

Erickson: All right. If the gloves get reversed, you will name the phobia.

Subject: I guess I better think of a phobia quickly.

Erickson: But the phobia won't come to you until the glove changes— unless there is no phobia.

Subject: But there probably is. And I won't be able to think of it until I turn the glove?

Erickson: No.

Subject: I might as well turn the glove. I inherited that.

Miss Dey: Quit shifting the blame.

Subject: What am I afraid of? Remember, coaching is legal. Look at these eager-eyed people. All right. If I turn the glove, I'll think of something I have been afraid of. [Turns glove.]

Erickson: We'll find out.

Subject: My splurges into religion?

Erickson: Have you changed any of your habits? Nobody here knows what I am driving at.

Subject: Do I?

Erickson: I'm trying to get it from you.

Subject: I smoke more.

Erickson: Do you mind if I take Miss Dey out in the hall and get some information?

Subject: No, go ahead. Ann, remember you might want to borrow some money from me sometime. This is all so fascinating.

Rossi: Now you and Miss Dey have a private conversation in the hallway. Is that what happened?

Erickson: [Nods yes.]

Rossi: What's your purpose in setting up this automatic questioning of the unconscious at this point?

Erickson: To find out if there was something I had overlooked.

Rossi: Why don't you trust her conscious mind? You trusted that her unconscious mind might have something that her conscious mind still doesn't have?

Erickson: [Nods yes.]

4.6 The Dynamics and Resolution of a Hidden Tub-Filling Phobia

Erickson: How long were you away on vacation?

Subject: Three weeks.

Erickson: And where were you these three weeks?

Subject: At _____.

Erickson: And where did you enjoy your bath most?

Subject: In a tub. What's wrong with that?

Erickson: Why not a shower?

Subject: Well, I like to sit in the tub with a magazine and a cigarette—sit there for hours while everyone outside the door clamors, "Let me in!" [And I say,] "Sorry, taking a bath."

Erickson: Previous to last January, how did you like tub baths?

Subject: I have always liked to take a tub bath except that I don't like to wait for the tub to fill up. If you could just push a button and it would just be filled up, it would be all right.
Erickson: What is your attitude toward that now?
Subject: Now I don't mind. Probably that's from not being afraid of water anymore, although I have never been afraid of a bathtub full of water.
Erickson: And you don't mind doing that now?
Subject: No. I can always smoke a cigarette while I wait.
Erickson: That's another phobia you have lost—this fear of the tub filling up.
Subject: That's silly. I haven't been afraid. I was always anxious for it to fill up. But if it were a fear, why wouldn't I be content to have it take a long time?
Erickson: That would force you to repress your fears at an unconscious level. The information I wanted from Miss Dey was what arrangements you have for bathing in the nurses' home. That is what I was talking to her about.
Subject: It's amazing.

Rossi: I'm not altogether convinced about your review of her phobia about the tub filling up. You may be correct, but it seems unprovable with the information at hand. If she avoided filling a tub and preferred a shower, you would certainly take it as evidence of a tub-filling phobia. But you take the reverse: being anxious for it to fill up as proving the same thing. Classic psychoanalytic theory would rationalize this by saying she has a reaction formation to her tub-filling phobia that makes her anxious for it to fill up. It's a kind of double bind that is unfortunately built into the structure of psychoanalytic theory that can spuriously prove its own hypotheses regardless of what the patient does. This sort of thing makes a mess of science, but it can be useful as a therapeutic paradox.

Erickson: Each time we fill up the tub and wash something, the water decreases.

Rossi: That's right. The water level decreases.

Erickson: But when her little sister fell backward into the water, it increased.

Rossi: Right. So she would therefore have a fear of water increasing. I see. So this is what you were thinking of when you assumed she had a tub-filling phobia. And, in fact, she was anxious about the tub filling with water, and she lost that fear without realizing that she had lost it until you commented on it here. You were really thinking about those things! You assumed that since Miss S's sister fell back into the water, the water went up and therefore Miss S would have fear of water coming up in the tub. Okay, you convinced me. I read this case so carefully, yet I forgot about that early tub incident. I couldn't imagine why or where you had pulled this out of the air. Now it makes sense.

4.7   The Panphobic Nature of Most Phobias; Personality Maturation; Resolving the Transference Relationship

Erickson: You know where I got my tip on that, don't you?

Subject: No. Oh! Now what changes have come over you, Dr. Fink? Well, he smokes a cigar.

Erickson: The way you said that word—*lifebuoy*—and broke it up.

Fink: Well, it was broken up.

Subject: Yes, it was. After all, what's so peculiar about that? If you say two words, you don't put them together. Oh, well, it's a great life.

Erickson: Well, I'm very glad you enjoy swimming now. And you did keep your implied promise to me over the phone, didn't you?

Subject: What was that?

Erickson: Sleep, now. And you will sleep, will you not? Will you not, Jane? Go deeply, soundly asleep. And are you sleeping deeply and soundly? [*Subject nods yes*] And you did give me an accurate account of your vacation. And you really did go swimming. And you really lost the major part of that anxiety, and you are no longer afraid of bridges. And you no longer have that anxiety about the tub filling up. And it pleases you very much. You have actually lost a lot of worries that you would rather not discuss now, and it is a pleasing thing to lose those other anxieties. And you have lost them, have you not? There is a common sense way of handling things, and it is a common sense thing to lose anxieties without distorting one's life, and you really know that. It won't be necessary for you to let anxiety overcome you anymore, isn't that right? Now, is there anything more I can do for you? [*Subject shakes head, no*] Will you feel free to call on me at any time? And may I have the privilege of calling on you some time for help? [*Subject apparently nods her head, yes.*] Are you sure of that? One never knows when one may need help, and a time might arise where I would need the benefit of your assistance, and I would like to have the privilege of calling you. And now as you look back at things, you are only half a dozen months older than when you first met me. But in actual experience and understanding, you are much older—more than six months older. That is one of the changes that is apparent to look at you. Now, is there anything further we should discuss tonight? Anything you want to say to me privately?

Subject: [*Long pause*] I really have a better brand of cigarettes. The business at hand has been concluded. The business at hand is finished.

Rossi: Did you awaken her before she said that?

Erickson: There is a pause there.

Rossi: What happened during that pause?

Erickson: She just awakened and made some awakening remarks.

Rossi: Your firm conviction regarding the actual panphobic nature of most so-called simple phobias is very important. Is it characteristic of your approach that you always seek out related phobias and work toward resolving them along with the patient's main, presenting phobic problem?

Erickson: Yes. We don't live in an isolated world.

Rossi: The presenting phobia happens to be only one of many things. You realize there are many other things so you try to resolve the whole thing. There's no such thing as a simple phobia. There is always a panphobic response to many things.

Erickson: A person with a cat phobia visits someone with a cat and finds that he didn't like the furniture, he didn't like the cooking, he didn't like anything about the person or the place. Now why shouldn't he like those people?

Rossi: I don't know, why?

Erickson: Have you heard of horsehair upholstery and furniture?

Rossi: Oh, yeah. I've heard of that.

Erickson: And cats have fur.

Rossi: I see, so it generalized that way. So most phobias and fears do generalize in ways the person doesn't even realize.

Erickson: Yes.

Dr. Sylvester: I have another question. Why did you question her so closely about all the things she might be afraid of? Was that another way of therapeutically integrating the experience? It's like the left hand doesn't know what the right hand is doing, and so you're letting the left hand know what the right hand is doing—so that it's a fully integrated experience?

Erickson: Yes. And saying it out loud helps the conscious mind accept what the unconscious already knows.

Rossi: [In 1987] Erickson resolves the transference in a way that was typical of his demonstration work. Since this was a demonstration case rather than a typical clinical situation in which the patient seeks out a therapist and pays for therapy, Erickson felt there was a need for a careful, open-ended resolution of transference issues. He had an unusual but very comfortable and practical way resolving the transference in these situations. He would leave open the possibility that the subject could call on him any time in the future for further help if it was needed. At the same time, he would ask if he could "have the privilege of calling on you sometime for help?"

What Erickson usually meant by this type of comment was that he might ask the subject to participate at some time in the future in a research project or professional demonstration. Erickson felt that this was often a fair *quid pro quo*: "I helped you by giving you therapy; now you help me in my scientific and professional work." The unresolved transference and sense of obligation that the free therapy might have engendered is thus "paid for" by donating equal time to help others.

References

Barber, T. X. (1972). Suggested ("hypnotic") behavior: The trance paradigm versus an alternate paradigm. In E. Fromm & R. Shor (Eds.), *Hypnosis: Research Development and Perspectives* (pp. 115-182). New York: Aldine-Atherton.

Barber, T. X. (1978). Hypnosis, suggestions, and psychosomatic phenomena: A new look from the standpoint of recent experimental studies. *American Journal of Clinical Hypnosis, 21*(1), 13-27.

Barber, T. X. (1984). Changing unchangeable bodily processes by (hypnotic) suggestions: A new look at hypnosis, cognitions, imagining, and the mind-body problem. *Advances, 1*(2), 7-40.

Bateson, G. (1979). *Steps to an Ecology of Mind.* New York: Ballantine Books.

Bateson, G., Jackson, D., Haley, J., & Weakland, J. (1956). Toward a theory of schizophrenia. *Behavioral Science, 1,* 251-264.

Erickson, M. (1935/1980). A study of an experimental neurosis hypnotically induced in a case of ejaculatio praecox. In E. Rossi (Ed.), *The Collected Papers of Milton H. Erickson on Hypnosis. Vol. III. Hypnotic Investigation of Psychodynamic Processes* (pp. 320-335). New York: Irvington.

Erickson, M. (1939a/1980). Demonstration of mental mechanisms by hypnosis. In E. Rossi (Ed.), *The Collected Papers of Milton H. Erickson on Hypnosis. Vol. III. Hypnotic Investigation of Psychodynamic Processes* (pp. 203-206). New York: Irvington.

Erickson, M. (1939b/1980). Experimental demonstrations of the psychopathology of everyday life. In E. Rossi (Ed.), *The Collected Papers of Milton H. Erickson on Hypnosis. Vol. III. Hypnotic Investigation of Psychodynamic Processes* (pp. 190-202). New York: Irvington.

Erickson, M. (1948/1980). Hypnotic psychotherapy. In E. Rossi (Ed.), *The Collected Papers of Milton H. Erickson on Hypnosis. I. The Nature of Hypnosis and Suggestion* (pp. 35-48). New York: Irvington.

Erickson, M. (1954a/1980). Pseudo-orientation in time as a hypnotherapeutic procedure. In E. Rossi (Ed.), *The Collected Papers of Milton H. Erickson on Hypnosis. Vol. IV. Innovative Hypnotherapy* (pp. 397-423). New York: Irvington.

Erickson, M. (1954b/1980). Special techniques of brief hypnotherapy. In E. Rossi (Ed.), *The Collected Papers of Milton H. Erickson on Hypnosis. Vol. IV. Innovative Hypnotherapy* (pp. 149-173). New York: Irvington.

Erickson, M. (1964/1980). The "surprise" and "my-friend-John" techniques of hypnosis: Minimal cues and natural field experimentation. In E. Rossi (Ed.), *The Collected*

Papers of Milton H. Erickson on Hypnosis. Vol. I. The Nature of Hypnosis and Suggestion (pp. 340-377). New York: Irvington.

Erickson, M. (1980). *The Collected Papers of Milton H. Erickson on Hypnosis* (4 Vols.). E. Rossi (Ed). New York: Irvington.
Volume I: *The Nature of Hypnosis and Suggestion*
Volume II: *Hypnotic Alteration of Sensory, Perceptual, and Psychophysical Processes*
Volume III: *Hypnotic Investigation of Psychodynamic Processes*
Volume IV: *Innovative Hypnotherapy*

Erickson, M., & Rossi, E. (1974/1980). Varieties of hypnotic amnesia. In E. Rossi (Ed.), *The Collected Papers of Milton H. Erickson on Hypnosis. Vol. III. Hypnotic Investigation of Psychodynamic Processes* (pp. 71-90). New York: Irvington.

Erickson, M., & Rossi, E. (1975/1980). Varieties of double bind. In E. Rossi (Ed.), *The Collected Papers of Milton H. Erickson on Hypnosis. Vol. I. The Nature of Hypnosis and Suggestion* (pp. 412-429). New York: Irvington.

Erickson, M., & Rossi, E. (1976/1980). Two-level communication and the microdynamics of trance. In E. Rossi (Ed.), *The Collected Papers of Milton H. Erickson on Hypnosis. I. The Nature of Hypnosis and Suggestion* (pp. 430-451). New York: Irvington.

Erickson, M., & Rossi, E. (1977/1980). Autohypnotic experiences of Milton H. Erickson. In E. Rossi (Ed.), *The Collected Papers of Milton H. Erickson on Hypnosis. Vol. I. The Nature of Hypnosis and Suggestion* (pp. 108-132). New York: Irvington.

Erickson, M., & Rossi, E. (1979). *Hypnotherapy: An Exploratory Casebook.* New York: Irvington.

Erickson, M., & Rossi, E. (1980). The indirect forms of suggestion. In E. Rossi (Ed.), *The Collected Papers of Milton H. Erickson on Hypnosis. I. The Nature of Hypnosis and Suggestion* (pp. 452-477). New York: Irvington.

Erickson, M., & Rossi, E. (1981). *Experiencing Hypnosis: Therapeutic Approaches to Altered States.* New York: Irvington.

Erickson, M., Rossi, E., & Rossi, S. (1976). *Hypnotic Realities.* New York: Irvington.

Estabrooks, G. (1943). *Hypnotism.* New York: Dutton.

Gazzaniga, M. (1985). *The Social Brain: Discovering the Networks of the Mind.* New York: Basic Books.

Haley, J. (1963). *Strategies of Psychotherapy.* New York: Grune & Stratton.

Haley, J. (1973). *Uncommon Therapy.* New York: W. W. Norton.

Haley, J. (1985). *Conversations with Milton H. Erickson.* (3 vols.). New York: Triangle Press.

Hilgard, E., & Hilgard, J. (1975). *Hypnosis in the Relief of Pain.* Los Altos, CA: Kaufman.

Huston, P., Shakow, D., & Erickson, M. (1934/1980). A study of hypnotically induced complexes by means of the Luria Technique. In E. Rossi (Ed.), *The Collected Papers of Milton H. Erickson on Hypnosis. Vol. III. Hypnotic Investigation of Psychodynamic Processes* (pp. 292-319). New York: Irvington.

Jung, C. (1960). *The Structure and Dynamics of the Psyche. Vol. III. The Collected Works of Carl G. Jung.* (R.F.C. Hull, Trans.). Bollingen Series XX. Princeton: Princeton University Press.

Kinsbourne, M., & Smith, W. (Eds.) (1974). *Hemispheric Disconnection and Cerebral Function.* Springfield, IL: Charles C Thomas.

Mead, M. (1977). The originality of Milton Erickson. *American Journal of Clinical Hypnosis, 20*(1), 4-5.

Pribram, K. (1971). *Languages of the Brain: Experimental Paradoxes and Principles in Neuropsychology* (3rd Ed.). New York: Brandon House.

Rossi, E. (1967). Game and growth: Two dimensions of our psychotherapeutic Zeitgeist. *Journal of Humanistic Psychology, 8,* 139-154.

Rossi, E. (1968). The breakout heuristic: A phenomenology of growth therapy with college students. *Journal of Humanistic Psychology, 8,* 16-28.

Rossi, E. (1971). Growth, change and transformation in dreams. *Journal of Humanistic Psychology, 11,* 147-169.

Rossi, E. (1972a/1985). *Dreams and the Growth of Personality* (2nd Ed.). New York: Brunner/Mazel.

Rossi, E. (1972b). Dreams in the creation of personality. *Psychological Perspectives, 2,* 122-134.

Rossi, E. (1972c). Self-reflection in dreams. *Psychotherapy: Theory, Research, Practice, 9,* 290-298.

Rossi, E. (1973a). Psychological shocks and creative moments in psychotherapy. *American Journal of Clinical Hypnosis, 16,* 9-22.

Rossi, E. (1973b). Psychosynthesis and the new biology of dreams and psychotherapy. *The American Journal of Psychotherapy, 27,* 34-41.

Rossi, E. (1973c). The dream protein hypothesis. *The American Journal of Psychiatry, 130,* 1094-1097.

Rossi, E. (1977). The cerebral hemispheres in analytical psychology. *The Journal of Analytical Psychology, 22,* 32-51.

Rossi, E. (1979). Davina's recent dream. *Sundance Community Dream Journal, 3,* 110-113.

Rossi, E. (1980). As above, so below: The holographic mind. *Psychological Perspectives, 11,* 155-169.

Rossi, E. (1986a). Altered states of consciousness in everyday life: The ultradian rhythms. In B. Wolman (Ed.), *Handbook of Altered States of Consciousness* (pp. 97-132). New York: Van Nostrand.

Rossi, E. (1986b). *The Psychobiology of Mind-Body Healing: New Concepts in Therapeutic Hypnosis.* New York: W. W. Norton.

Rossi, E., & Cheek, D. (1988). *Mind-Body Therapy: Ideodynamic Healing in Hypnosis.* New York: W. W. Norton.

Rossi, E., & Ryan, M. (Eds.) (1985). *Life Reframing in Hypnosis. Vol. II. The Seminars, Workshops, and Lectures of Milton H. Erickson.* New York: Irvington.

Rossi, E., & Ryan, M. (1986). *Mind-Body Communication in Hypnosis. Vol. 3. The Seminars, Workshops and Lectures of Milton H. Erickson.* New York: Irvington.

Rossi, E., Ryan, M., & Sharp, F. (Eds.) (1984). *Healing in Hypnosis. Vol. I. The Seminars, Workshops, and Lectures of Milton H. Erickson.* New York: Irvington.

Sperry, R. (1968). Hemispheric disconnections and unity in conscious awareness. *American Psychologist, 23,* 723-733.

Watkins, J. (1949). *Hypnotherapy of War Neuroses.* New York: Ronald Publishing.

Woodworth, R., & Schlosberg, H. (1954). *Experimental Psychology.* New York: Holt and Company.

Index